I am 23 years old and I have a fatal disease. According to everything that I have been able to read about this disease gives me ~~every~~ reason to believe that I will die within the next two years. I surpose that I should be filled c̄ fear at the very thought of dying, but I am not afraid. I do not believe ~~that~~ this disease will be the cause of my death. ~~and~~ I cannot give up hope because I believe and trust in my God and Jesus Christ.

Since the very beginning I have been confident that God has his reasons for my ~~suffering~~ illness. In some ways this has been a wonderful blessing because I feel that I am a better person, because through this I have found Jesus Christ, my Lord.

Billie

A Love that Couldn't Die

by
Ed Beck

**BRISTOL
BOOKS**®

BILLIE
A Love that Couldn't Die
© 1989 by Ed Beck
Published by Bristol Books

An earlier version of this book was published by Here's Life Publishers, Inc., 1983, as *A Love to Live By*
Revised Edition, November 1989

Library of Congress Card Number: 89-62541
ISBN: 0-917851-37-4

BRISTOL BOOKS
An Imprint of Good News, a Forum for Scriptural Christianity, Inc.
308 East Main Street • Wilmore, KY 40390

Dedicated to Adolph Rupp, Harry Lancaster, Norman Faircloth,
three coaches without peer

Contents

Billie Ray Beck as she appeared in her nurse's uniform.

The 1958 NCAA championship University of Kentucky team coached by Adolph Rupp (left) and Harry Lancaster (right). Ed Beck is number 34.

Ed Beck hands Kentucky Governor A.B. 'Happy' Chandler funds raised by the 1958 NCAA championship team to fight cancer.

Ed grabs a rebound in the 1958 NCAA championship game played in Louisville, Kentucky. The contest, which began when Ed squared off against Seattle University star Elgin Baylor for the jump ball, ended with the Kentucky underdogs trouncing Seattle, 84-72.

Ed Beck and Billie Justine Ray on their wedding day, September 11, 1955.

Ed and Billie outside their apartment in Lexington, Kentucky, in the spring of 1956. Billie's illness left her weak and exhausted, but she was determined to fight.

1

Daybreak

I leaned forward in my chair toward the hospital bed. The slight form which had been so restless was now beginning to relax. I glanced out the window where the rosy blush of a Georgia dawn silhouetted the magnolia trees.

Daybreak. The hour my young wife, Billie, loved best. Despite heavy medication to blunt the terrible gnawing of cancer, she had writhed and moaned all night. But now, as the room slowly lightened, she visibly relaxed. A bright shaft of sun warmed my arm, moved to the bed, rested on her wasted body and illuminated her still lovely face. She murmured softly, and her labored breathing seemed to become easier.

For 46 agonizing days and nights Billie had lain in this bed. It was now early morning of the 47th. The hospital room was as sterile and bland as it had been since I first rushed to Billie's side. Nothing much had changed except Billie—whose only choice was to lie there, gasping through pain and discomfort between hours of restless hypo-induced sleep.

Stretching back in my chair I glanced at the morning sports page that had slipped down my lap. Headlined was the championship game in the Nation College Athletic Association (NCAA) tourney between the University of North Carolina and Michigan State. Down at the side of the page a smaller article wrung my heart: BILLIE BECK NEAR DEATH.

I glanced over at my wife; she was somewhat calm now. She suffered most in the afternoons, and despite the drugs was restless through the night. But early dawning always seemed to bring that uneasy peace and calm.

There was a step at the door. I looked up. It was Billie's older sister, Helen Newby.

"How is she?" she whispered. "Did she have a good night? Has she suffered much? Did she eat anything?" These were the usual questions we mechanically asked when we arrived to spell each other.

I slowly shook my head.

Helen leaned over the bed and whispered to Billie who did not open her eyes. I leaned back in my chair and looked at her gratefully. For 46 agonizing days and nights she had been helping to watch over Billie. I stood up, rubbing my burning eyes, stretched and yawned.

Helen looked up at me. "Ed, why don't you take a break, go home, shower and get something to eat?"

I mumbled a protest.

"But you've been here three nights and two days without rest. Go ahead, I'll be with Billie."

"All right," I sighed, "but if there's any change, anything, you will. . . ?"

"Of course." She waved me to the door. "I'll call you."

It was only a 15 minute drive to Helen's small house on the outskirts of Macon. On that Saturday morning, in the early spring of 1957, I drove it mechanically as I had done for the past several weeks. The house was empty when I walked in, for which I was grateful—no need to talk. The rooms reflected the haphazard living of the past eight weeks while the family's thoughts were in that hospital room I had just left.

The hot shower drumming on my chest was soothing, though it couldn't wash away the deep-down ache within me. After the shower I found myself reaching for my razor. For a moment I looked at it questioningly. *Shave now?* I wondered. *Why not when I get up from my nap?* But a strange inner compulsion seemed to urge me to be ready to move at a moment's notice. So I quickly shaved, dressed and stepped into the kitchen where I made some toast and coffee. I was so tired I could hardly chew. When finished, I glanced at the clock, almost noon. I fell back on the bed and just lay there, staring at the ceiling, wanting to sleep but baffled by the odd feeling that something of vital importance was about to happen.

What was it? I knew that the NCAA basketball play-off between Michigan State and North Carolina was coming up in two hours. My team would have been one of those in the play-off if we had won the last round a week ago. But basketball was another world, another time.

My only concern right now was a little southern belle in that hospital room eight miles away. While breathing a prayer for her, I fell into a deep trance-like sleep.

Suddenly it seemed as if someone shook me awake. I sat bolt upright and looked around the room. No one was there. The clock showed 12:43 p.m.; I had slept less than a hour. But now my heart pounded, and my stomach had tightened as it did just before a big game.

Only I wasn't facing a game. What *was* this strong sense of preparation I was feeling? I perched on the edge of the bed, my mind racing. There had been no phone call from Helen. But the inner message was clearer than a call: *I had to get to the hospital immediately.*

Slipping on my shoes I ran to the kitchen door where my car waited outside in the carport. I hesitated at the door, seeing my dirty lunch dishes on the table. I was about to put them in the sink when the thought came: *Why deal with mundane things when the meaning of your life is calling?* I was opening the door when the telephone shrilled. I stepped back and grabbed it.

"Ed," It was Helen. "The nurse is here. I don't think there is anything to worry about but Billie's pulse is a little weak, and the nurse says it's skipping."

"I'll be right there!" I shouted, starting to hang up the phone.

"Now don't worry," soothed Helen. "I'm sure she's all right, but I did want to let you know."

I stood for a moment in the kitchen breathing hard, sweat beading my forehead. Now I knew, despite what Helen said, my wife was dying and I had to get there immediately.

I jumped into the car, backed out of the driveway and accelerated down the street. *Watch for children,* I kept telling myself. It was a beautiful, spring Saturday afternoon and they'd be out. At the same time my urgency intensified. I had to get to the hospital as soon as possible! I had promised Billie I would be with her when she died, and it was a promise I had to keep.

Should I begin speeding so a police cruiser would see me and give escort? No, I reasoned, the explanation would take too much time. So I drove on, my mind spinning like a computer, selecting the fastest route. The last six months had taught me how important even a minute can be.

My hands gripped the wheel as an unmistakable certainty gripped me that I was going to be too late. *No, no,* I cried silently. *I will get there on time. I will!*

Billie and I had so often talked about this dreaded moment.

"It will be all right, honey," she had sighed, "as long as you're with me holding my hand." I had locked her in my arms, promising that I would be with her. I had buried my head in her bosom, my tears moistening her dress as I promised that I would be with her.

But now I was still three miles from the hospital and totally helpless. I was not going to be with Billie; I was going to be too late!

Why had I napped? I berated myself. *I could have slept in the chair at the hospital. Why had I left?*

With pounding heart, I swerved the car into the doctor's parking lot entrance where I had been given permission to park. Ahead loomed the familiar silhouette of the hospital. Hospitals. I've always had a love/hate relationship with them, and this one was no different. Its staff had done so much for Billie; yet they were unable to accomplish the one thing that we had hoped and prayed for—her healing.

As I slowed to a stop in the lot, a cold desolation suddenly filled my heart. Was I too late?

2

The Blue Cyclone

I wasn't late for the basketball game one memorable Saturday night my freshman year in high school. Working all day on my feet in a local grocery store seemed to be the worst thing I could do the day of a game. It could wear you out. But I discovered such work tired me just enough to relax me, and I always played better when I was relaxed. Besides, as a freshman I was already a first string varsity player, and we were undefeated.

This particular night we were playing Byron, a small school just nine miles up the road. It was a game we did not take lightly, but we knew we could win if we just played average. I knew if I played great I could pour in the points, pull off the rebounds and see my name in the paper. For a 14-year-old, 6' 7", 192-pound rising star, I was out to make a name for myself in the basketball world.

As I walked into the Fort Valley, Georgia, gym it was beginning to fill to its 1,700 capacity. A ripple of applause greeted me as I walked down the side of the court during a time out of the girls game in progress. I loved it! As I headed to the dressing room my eyes focused intently upon a young woman sitting behind the team bench. I had seen her previously, but now she seemed even more beautiful. I sat a couple of rows above her pretending to watch the game, but it was my view of her that seared into my mind.

When I reluctantly entered the dressing room, I asked one of my teammates, "Who was that lovely creature in the second row?"

"That's Billie Ray—you know the Ray family that lives over in Crawford County," Eddie said. "She goes to Roberta High School and dates James Bozeman."

My heart sank. To date a girl like that you had to be older, have a car and possess more guts than I. Still, over the next few years when I would see Billie Ray by chance, my thoughts were refreshed and refocused.

I was overjoyed when I made the Green Waves, our basketball team, for the consuming passion of everyone in Fort Valley was its high school athletic teams. Perhaps it was because nothing much else happened in a town of 7,000 people located in mid-Georgia and surrounded by peach orchards.

More likely it stemmed from the arrival of a young athletic coach named Norman Faircloth. He was an unusual kind of coach with the aptitude for instilling a quest for excellence into a group of boys. As a result Fort Valley always seemed to excel in regional and state tournaments.

Coach Faircloth had no assistants and was our football, basketball and track coach. Thus the 30 boys that went out for teams became his extended family. I was one of those boys.

I had never seen a college or professional game. But every sports magazine was digested and every technique rehearsed constantly. My big dream was to play one day on a team that would win the coveted NCAA championship. I was even more enthused when Coach Faircloth said I could probably make a college team if I was willing to pay the price. In fact, when my stepfather was transferred to Jacksonville, Florida, basketball had become such a part of my life at Fort Valley that I pleaded to remain there, and did, living with the William Khoury family.

By the time I was a sophomore and had begun playing center, the Green Waves had won the coveted state championship. Even though we just missed winning it the following year, I had been an all-state selection for three years and college coaches and scouts were already contacting me. My dream seemed to be approaching reality. But despite the constant letters and phone calls from other schools, there was only one on which I had set my sights: Duke University.

The main reason was that Duke had a good theological seminary. By the time I reached my senior year in high school, I had set my heart on becoming a minister. Perhaps it was because our church and the many loving people I had met there had always been a regular part of my life.

"Whatever you do in life, Edward," said Mrs. Jeanette Wheaton, my petite but indomitable Sunday school teacher, "make sure it's big enough for you."

What would my calling be? I wondered. Earlier, as a junior in high school, I had decided to give full-time service to the Lord. For a while I thought I'd be an engineer who would go overseas and build hospitals and bridges for needy people.

Then, an older man I respected highly, A. L. Luce, Sr., of the Blue Bird company, a local firm that built school buses, gave me something to think about.

"Anything you do for God will be all right, Ed," he said, as I sat in his office one day. "But the real issue is, What can you give him that will be your total best?"

He didn't say anything as he studied his desk for a moment. Then he looked up at me. "My own feeling is you'd make a mighty fine preacher."

I was impressed, not only because I respected this man highly, but because deep down inside I had been sensing the same calling.

By the time I was a high school senior I had a "license to preach" from the Methodist Church and was already addressing youth groups and local meetings as a lay speaker.

But basketball was my consuming interest in the spring of 1954 as our high school team raced toward another undefeated season. The state championship tournament was less than a week away in the big auditorium in Macon. Now in my final high school year we were geared for our second championship. Fort Valley was already tasting victory.

Then the ceiling seemed to fall in on me; I became violently ill with pneumonia. All my dreams for my final year in high school were heading down the drain. Gloom hung over the school as Coach

Faircloth conferred with doctors who ordered me into the hospital. In the middle of that sad refrain I came face to face once again with the girl of my dreams, Billie Ray.

I *had* imagined all kinds of conversations, envisioned technicolor dreams of cool summer evenings in a romantic setting. But naturally my imagination worked a lot better than my mouth as she entered my hospital room. I was so shocked I could not even mumble a greeting worth remembering.

Billie had graduated from high school a few years before and had been away in nurses training. I heard that she planned to attend medical school, but returned to the valley to work as an R.N. to save some money for tuition.

Here was my chance to transform dreams into delightful realities, and all I could do was mumble. *Oh God, I hope she thinks that fever has gotten my tongue, that I'm drowsy from medication. I hope she does not realize that I'm greater in imagination than in reality.*

She was all business, and she did not treat me with the deference the rest of the hospital staff used on what they felt was part of the basketball hope of their town.

She acted as if she did not have the time or inclination to get caught up in the anticipatory thrill of making Fort Valley's star well in time for the state tournament.

After that first lost opportunity, I prepared better for following encounters. I found myself anticipating her visits. I had learned her hours and had even been able to hear her arrival down the hall by the special swish of her white uniform and the unmistakable sound of her walk on the linoleum in those hospital corridors.

What is it about another person that first captivates one's attention? Is it true that each of us has a composite in our brains and that somehow we have taken the best from all the people we have ever met or read about and created the perfect female, or the perfect male? Are we constantly on the search for that *one* that will come closest to this ideal? Call the phenomenon whatever you want, when Billie swished into my room and smiled all the bells rang and I heard the inner voice yell *Bingo*.

There was no mistake that Billie fulfilled my picture of a "perfect woman." I watched her as she prepared to administer a penicillin shot. She was 5 1/2 feet tall, slender with long shapely legs. Her skin had a bronze tint as if she had just arrived from vacation on a Florida beach. Delicate high cheekbones were overwhelmed by eyes as dark as midnight; yet, in them was that distinctive sparkle of the first star on the horizon. Her chestnut hair hung softly to her shoulders, and I wanted to run my fingers lightly through it.

My daydream came to an abrupt end when she approached me with the hypodermic syringe. There seemed to be a distinct gleam in those jet black eyes and a faint smile on her nicely shaped lips as she said, "Roll over, it's time for your shot."

Her hands, however delicately shaped as they were, were exemplarily professional. As the needle entered my derriere I winced, more from fearful anticipation than from actual pain; Billie was not only a skilled nurse, she had a rare gentleness and compassion.

Some evenings she would come into my room to talk. Sometimes we'd laugh when she talked about "Miss Bigfoot and her ingrown toenails," and sometimes we'd speak in hushed tones of "Mrs. Pain and her losing battle with the Big C."

As we talked, I came to see within Billie an exceptional and very warm person. Maybe it was her maturity compared to my sheltered life, maybe it was her white uniform and status as my nurse. Whatever it was, I soon realized I had very positive feelings for this attractive young lady.

As we talked we shared hopes and ambitions. I told Billie about my dreams of college basketball and she told me about her plans to become a medical doctor. "It just isn't happening when I thought it would," she confided.

"Money," she gave a quick smile in answer to my questioning look. "That's why I temporarily dropped out of medical school to resume nursing work. In a few years I hope to have enough money to continue."

We talked of many other things during those quiet evenings. I told her about losing my father as a little boy, and she told me about her Indian great-grandmother whom I assumed to be the reason for Billie's delicate bronze tint.

Then, everything became more serious as the state basketball tournament neared. With our first game only a few days away, I followed a ritual in which I left the hospital only for daily practice at the high school gym and then returned straight to my bed for medication and therapy.

The hospital staff hovered over me while townspeople visited with small gifts, pep talks and prayers that I would be completely well very soon. I had the good sense to know it wasn't really me but the state championship that everyone was concerned about. It now hung in the balance, and our team with its limited number of players could not afford my absence.

Again, the only one who didn't seem to worship the championship was Billie. I still felt she had an eager gleam in her eye when she administered my penicillin shots, but I did begin to feel better by the weekend. With the tournament beginning on the next Tuesday, I figured I'd be released from the hospital to return to classes and practice. But my doctor had other ideas. I would remain a patient and be released only temporarily for the entire tournament! That meant I would make the 30-mile drive to Macon for the game and then be rushed right back to the hospital room which I was now beginning to hate.

And who was going to be my chauffeur and medical attendant?

Nurse Billie Ray. I was certain that all the nurses had drawn straws for the chore and she was the loser. But later I learned that she had volunteered.

On Monday we went to our local gym and practice session. Billie in her white uniform, carrying a little black medical bag, was at my side constantly except in the dressing room and on the court.

My teammates made a few good-natured remarks about my being a prima donna until they saw Billie take out her formidable-looking hypodermic syringe. Wide-eyed and humbled, they almost became compassionate when I faked a blood-curdling moan as the needle punctured my skin.

Our first game at the tournament was scheduled for 3 o'clock Tuesday afternoon. That morning the hospital staff visited me one by one to "wish me luck" and "good shooting." The kitchen staff prepared a special meal under the supervision of my "medical observer," and Billie even brought it to me.

As I hurriedly ate, she cautioned me to take it easy: "Don't wash your food down, Ed," and other such choice tidbits. She reminded me of Marine Corps drill sergeants I had seen in movies until I suddenly sensed that she was more worried about my well-being during the coming game than I was.

A few minutes before departure time Billie returned. I was amazed. No white starched uniform now but a soft-looking brown suit that fitted her slim curves beautifully. She had put on some make-up, and as she stood in the doorway saying that we must leave soon, she looked totally lovely.

The only hint of her profession was the distinctive black bag she carried. I carried my green and gold Fort Valley high school athletic bag as I followed her out of the room and down the corridor toward the hospital exit. I had checked it twice to make sure my jersey with its "Number 3" was there. Somehow I always worried about forgetting my jersey. My shoes and supporter never bothered me but that jersey was my fetish.

In the hospital parking lot we walked to Billie's car, a 1951 black four-door Mercury.

"Where did you get this tank?" I asked as we got in. "Well, if that is the way you feel about my car you can just go on the school bus with the rest of the team," she sniffed as she pulled out of the lot. I may have been a dumb jock, but I knew quickly that I made no points at all by poking fun at her car.

A year earlier she had begged her brother Bobby, who was always buying and selling cars, to find her the perfect car. Following strict instructions and specifications, Bobby had finally found the car. Completely renovated and souped up, its black paint job made the car almost equal in hue to Billie's eyes.

As we purred down the highway, past the peach orchards on our way to Macon, I could see that the car was an extension of her personality—sleek and beautiful with a deceptive grace about its lines. Yes, this was Billie mechanized. As our relationship grew I would continue to call her car the *Tank*, but only when I wanted an emotional response.

As we drove on with the windows down, Billie's chestnut hair whipped around her neck and chin. Occasionally she would gently run her hands through her hair and once I got my nerve up and did it for her. She looked in my direction, smiled and said, "Thank you, now get your mind on the game."

In Macon, after we parked and began the two-block walk to the arena, people in passing cars honked and waved, shouting, "Go, go, go Green Waves!" Since I was wearing my state championship letter jacket, I felt they knew who I was. I could feel my stomach beginning to churn and my hands began to sweat. Always a sign that I was getting pumped up.

As we entered the arena, a wave of applause and shouts swelled from the stands where the Fort Valley fans were gathered. After all, their star athlete had gotten out of a hospital bed to play the opening game of the state tournament. I was walking with head down, the gait of the humble athlete, but I was glorying in the recognition and adulation, and I was so proud that lovely Billie was right by my side overhearing every positive comment. The applause was enough to keep the adrenalin flowing and the palms sweating. I was getting ready to play, and Billie was going to see me do what I did best. I did not believe that anything else at that moment was better.

The excitement of preparing for battle mounted within me as we went through warm-ups. The game began right on time. The whistle blew, the centers leaped for the ball, and the court became a maelstrom of shouting, swerving, sweating combatants.

As the tallest prep basketball player in the state that year I got the tip, as I had all year. We always did the same thing—test out the defense to see if it was zone or man-for-man. Our opponents, making a critical mistake that afternoon, played a straight man-for-man defense. With only one 6' 3" player on the other side I was going to have a field day.

In the first 12 minutes of the game I dominated the defensive board and sank four hook shots, along with three tip-ins and one free-throw which rounded out a three-point play. I had 15 points and 12 rebounds and was heading toward a top performance game. Then it hit. I felt as if someone had opened the faucet and drained out every drop of my blood. I was exhausted. The days in the hospital had taken their toll.

Billie sat right behind our bench line-up and at times I caught a glimpse of her watching me. During one brief lull she mouthed the words: "How are you feeling?" I answered with a weary nod, for I had become tired more rapidly than usual.

I felt as if I were dying, but too proud to give up and ask my coach for a rest. Exhausted, I did unusual things on defense. Instead of moving my feet to stop drives, I reached in and committed three stupid, lazy fouls, my normal two-game total.

The half time buzzer sounded, and all I could do was lay my weary body on the dressing room floor. But when my coach asked how I was, I lied, "Oh, I'm fine—ready to go." I was the last one out of the dressing room. Billie remarked that I looked "awfully pale and you're sweaty hot." Even though I felt light-headed I told her I was fine.

The second half of the game no sooner started when I committed my fourth foul and was taken out of the game. Groans mounted from Fort Valley fans even though we had a 17-point lead.

However, as I anxiously watched the battle continue, our lead dwindled alarmingly, and I kept glancing at Coach Faircloth who ignored me. There were some fine clutch plays by several of our substitute players and finally, with four minutes left in the game, Faircloth nodded at me and I ran on to the floor. I simply controlled the boards and scored two more goals. We won by 12.

Earlier Billie had instructed me not to shower after the game but to immediately dress warmly and meet her for a quick drive back to the hospital. However, I lingered amid the dressing room victory celebration until the team manager came up to me. "Ed, you're wanted outside, and she's got fire in her eyes."

I quickly dressed, thinking of an angrily placed hypodermic needle to come, and met Billie who hustled me into the car and drove back to the hospital.

By the time I reached my room I was totally exhausted. I quickly showered and retired after a quiet meal alone in the room with Billie. I learned later she had posted a NO VISITORS sign on my door—her desire, not the doctor's.

The rest of tournament week would follow the same routine. Though we did not play on Wednesday we had to play the following Thursday, Friday and Saturday.

Since I felt my fatigue during the first game might have stemmed from being bed-ridden so long, I decided to have two workouts at the gym instead of just the regular afternoon practice. My doctor approved, and Billie again accompanied me making sure I was well-insulated from the early March cold winds.

As Billie drove me to the game Thursday evening, she gave me a run-down on all the telephone calls that had come to the hospital for me—as the doctor had instructed that all calls be held. Many were from coaching and scouting staffs who said they would be at the games Friday and Saturday nights.

"Well," I chuckled, "if we get beat tonight they'll have to watch somebody else."

However, their confidence was not in vain. We continued our roll Thursday and Friday night. As we drove back to Fort Valley Friday night, Billie was quiet. I didn't have much to say either. It would be the last night she accompanied me because my doctor felt I had progressed to where I could travel with the team Saturday night.

I had to admit to myself that I would miss her. And yet, I also had to realize that she had gone with me strictly in a professional capacity. After all, she was three years older than me, was planning on a medical career and had more important things on her mind than a high-school basketball player.

Back in the hospital she saw me to my room and stood in the doorway as I hung up my coat. Over my shoulder I said, "Sure has been nice traveling with you," and then added, grinning, "I'll miss the Black Tank."

"O.K., smarty," she pretended to pout.

Now that we were saying goodbye for the last time, I suddenly felt awkward.

"Say," I said, "how about letting me take you out for a steak dinner sometime?"

She smiled. "Sure, just say the word." She started to turn and leave. "Well, Ed, I've enjoyed being with you," she said. "Take care of yourself, you hear?"

"What, no shot?" I asked.

"No," she laughed, "the doctor feels you're well on your way and I'm glad. I wouldn't want *that* to be the last thing about me you remembered."

"Well," I said, suddenly not wanting her to leave. "Thanks for all your help."

She smiled, quickly waved. "Goodnight, Ed, and good luck tomorrow!"

I had planned for this moment even though I did not want it to come. I intended to walk over to her, take her in my arms and give her a goodbye kiss. Instead I stood across the room, and before I could move toward her she turned and walked down the hall. I could not believe that I had failed. I stood there for a long moment, hearing her high heels click down the hospital corridor until all was quiet. I walked toward the bed and suddenly realized how empty my room seemed.

On Saturday morning I was released from the hospital. That night, as the state's only undefeated team, we would play Blackshear for the state championship. A town in southeast Georgia that several years earlier had dominated basketball in its area, Blackshear was out to topple us from our throne.

I rode in the bus with the team to Macon that night. I missed Billie. *Would she be at the game?* I wondered. She had not been at the hospital when I checked out. But then, why should she have been? *Better concentrate on basketball,* I told myself.

The Macon arena was packed to the rafters. Standing room only and the largest contingency came from the Valley just 33 miles away. My mother and step-father were right in the middle of the partisan crowd sitting next to coach Hal Bradley of Duke University. I was gracious to the other coaches and scouts that night, but there was only one coach who would have the seat of honor next to my parents. I had no doubt that Hal Bradley would be my mentor for the next four years while I attended Duke University, and I wanted my mother's opinion of him.

In the previous three games of the state tournament we had dominated the game from the opening tip. Though some were a little closer than others, we'd had all of the games well in hand by the last quarter. The Blackshear game was different. They were not intimated by our undefeated streak. For years Blackshear had dominated the state, they had the same coach, and the team was made up of the younger brothers of players from undefeated teams. So from the opening moments of the game they were aggressive.

Red hot, they scored during the first six possessions. We called our first time out just half way through the first quarter with Blackshear leading 12-3. If they continued at the same pace they would score nearly 100 points in a 32-minute game.

We'd hoped to put the fear of God into *them,* now they had done a number on *us*. Hesitant and unsure of ourselves, we made some foolish floor mistakes. I could not believe that we would be humiliated in the biggest game of the year with all the coaches and scouts and Hal Bradley watching. Now I was grateful for the called time out and the challenging words from my coach.

Give Blackshear their due. They had taken away my pivot game, especially on the right side of the foul line. All the other teams had let me slide down into the key, where my forwards had fed me the ball with ease, and I had taken jump hook shots near the base line. But Blackshear had placed a man right in front of me when I went deep into the key. My forwards could not get me the ball, and their long shots were not falling. We were in trouble.

Coach Faircloth gave us our instructions! We were behind by nine, but the game was young. We had to stop their torrid 100 percentage, and we had to begin dominating them offensively rather than allowing them to dominate us defensively. And that is exactly what we did.

I did not slide down into the key but played the high post near or on the foul line. They did not post a man in front of me—that was their first mistake. The next four times I came down the court I started from the low post and came to the high post. Every time my guards hit me on a dead run, and I shot four long, arching hook shots from the foul line that hit nothing but net. There was bedlam at the Macon Arena! The long arching hook shots had become my trademark throughout my high school career, and I was tired enough to be relaxed enough to be red hot. Blackshear called time out just before the end of the first quarter. We were only one point behind, but the Fort Valley locomotive was gaining steam. Our only thought was championship trophy.

In the second quarter Blackshear put two men on me wherever I went. They paid dearly for that decision. I stayed on the high post, and my forwards and guards ran the other three defensive men ragged. At the half we had a comfortable 10-point lead and felt as if Blackshear would play us straight up man-to-man the second half. They did, and they began employing another tactic.

Some of the Blackshear players directed a psychological word game toward me. For the first time in my high school playing career as a preacher-to-be I was constantly cursed. As we lined up for a free throw, one of my opponents would lean over or walk by and whisper "Hey, Beck, I hear you're going to be a blankety-blank preacher boy," or "Is it true that you're a son-of-a-bitching preacher?" It continued through the game. The only problem for Blackshear was that as the obscenities became stronger I was inspired to play better. I guess if you call a person a demon you had better be willing to take the consequences of playing against someone possessed, and I was. One dream, one thought, one obsession, another state championship trophy and jacket would soon be mine.

We won the game by 14. The Fort Valley crowd was exploding in cheers and congratulatory shouts. A Blackshear boy who had guarded me most of the game but had never joined in the hazing, walked over and stuck out his hand. "I'm sorry about those guys saying all those things," he said, "They really didn't mean it. They just thought it would help us win."

I smiled and shook his hand. "I know."

"God bless you and your future," he added. "I know you will have a great one."

"Thanks, friend," I said, and then went out with my team to receive the trophy as the 1954 basketball champions of the State of Georgia.

Afterward, as I was buttoning my shirt in the dressing room, a man pushed through the door and introduced himself. "I'm Buddy Parker from the University of Kentucky and Coach Adolph Rupp asked me to see you play. You're good, you know."

He apologized for breaking in but said he had to catch a plane back to Lexington. Then he came right out with his mission. "Beck," he said, "we want you to play at the best basketball school in the world!"

I thanked him for his compliments and offer but said I was going to Duke University. "Coach Hal Bradley sat with my folks tonight," I added, "and that's the school where I want to play."

He wiped his brow with his handkerchief. "Well, think it over, Beck. We'll stay in touch with you."

As we walked out of the dressing room I glanced up and saw Billie. My heart leaped and, saying a quick goodbye to Buddy Parker, I rushed over to greet her. For the first time she was not carrying that little black bag. And instead of just a smile she embraced me with a congratulatory hug.

I was elated, "Gosh, it was so good of you to come to the game," I said enthusiastically. Then I found myself telling her that I missed her.

Embarrassed at this admission, I stared at the floor for a moment; then, attempting to recover, I looked up and said, "Hey, how about that big steak dinner we talked about?"

"I haven't forgotten," she laughed.

"When?" I pressed.

"Give me a call at the hospital," she said. Then, looking over my shoulder, she laughed, "I've got to go; I think there are a million other people who want to see you."

"Take care," I said, watching her slip through the crowd, passing my parents and Coach Bradley who were coming toward me. Dad, Mom, Coach Bradley and I went to a restaurant and talked long into the night about Duke and my future with the school. We set a date for me to visit Durham within a month. Then my folks and I drove back to Fort Valley where I climbed wearily into bed. It was 2:00 a.m. and church would come much too early. As I slipped into oblivion I wondered if just once I could sleep late.

I found myself struggling up through a thick fog of deep sleep. What was that noise? At first it seemed faint, but then a pounding at the front door broke through my stupor. Accompanying it was the insistent ringing of the doorbell. I glanced at my watch: 6:30 a.m.

The family I lived with—the Khoury's—were Roman Catholic, and I knew they had already left for early mass. But there it was again, the ringing doorbell and constant pounding on the front door. Finally I got out of bed, slipped on my pants and made my way to the door looking for signs of smoke or fire. As I peered through the window I could hardly believe my eyes. It was the man who had broken into the dressing room last night.

Still in a sleep-drugged state, I opened the door to be greeted with, "Hi! Buddy Parker again. Sorry to wake you but I just had to see you. Got to the airport last night and just couldn't get on that plane. I said to myself, 'Buddy, you need to see Ed Beck again and save him from making the biggest mistake of his life! There's only one school for him, the University of Kentucky!'"

I tried to speak, but the beefy, enthusiastic man rattled on like a machine gun. "C'mon, get dressed. We're going out for breakfast because I need to talk to you. That was a great game you played last night—the way you shot hooks and rebounds. You could be a great one at the University of Kentucky. You would get to play with the greatest coach in the world."

He stopped, took a quick breath and raced on. "I played there. I wasn't good but I wore the Big Blue and I'll never forget it; changed my life. I played with the greatest players of the game. We won national titles and we'll win 'em again."

I stepped backwards and he followed me. "The state championship you won last night and the one you won two years ago were really wonderful, Ed, but they're nothing compared to the NCAA championship. Duke will never win one of those titles. Only Kentucky will win, and you need to play on a team like that. You made all-state for three years and that's great, congratulations. But that's nothing compared to making All-American, and, Ed, you can do it!"

He took another breath.

"But you won't do it at Duke, my friend. The nation and all the sports writers will be watching you at the University of Kentucky. That crowd last night was great, yeah. How many there? Four or five thousand? That's wonderful. At Duke you'll play before three, four thousand a game maybe. But at the University of Kentucky you'll play before standing room crowds every night, 12 or 13,000 people at the greatest basketball arena in the world, the University of Kentucky Memorial Coliseum!"

Parker stared at my bare feet.

"Ed, why aren't you getting dressed? We need to go and eat, and you need to hear about the school where you are going to spend the next four years of your life!"

In a trance, I made my way to my room to dress; Buddy never left my side nor did he stop selling UK. The Blue Cyclone had landed.

3

Do Clothes
Make the
Man?

As explosive as Buddy Parker's sales pitch was, its power was soon lost in the whirlwind of activities and travel which swept me up. Besieged by more than 70 inquiries—phone calls, letters, telegrams, personal visits—from different colleges and universities, I tried to respond to all, but after a few days just gave up.

And despite Buddy Parker's glowing portrayal of the University of Kentucky and its famous coach, Adolph Rupp, I was still positive about Duke University. However, Coach Faircloth advised me not to burn any bridges behind me. "You never know, Ed, what might happen," he said.

After reflecting on his words, I began to see the merit of his advice. With this attitude, I began visiting college and university campuses to see their facilities and examine their programs. I soon discovered that most schools did not know what to do with a pre-ministerial student.

Engineers? Georgia Tech was all geared up for them. Teachers? University of Georgia was the place to go. Would-be lawyers and doctors? Most colleges had programs designed for them. But prospective clergy was a different breed. Facilities for these seemed an after-thought in many of the schools, and usually I was sent over to the ancient language department consisting of a few offices in the oldest building on campus.

The exceptions were universities that had full-fledged theological seminaries, such as Duke and Vanderbilt. Bob Polk, then head basketball coach of Vandy, did an excellent selling job of the theological seminary on the campus in Nashville. So sound was his presentation via letters and phone calls that I promised before I decided on any school I would visit Vandy and view its program. Little did I realize that that promise would be the catalyst for my final decision.

My positive attitude concerning Duke University had convinced most of my Fort Valley supporters that it was the school I would be attending. I'm sure Coach Hal Bradley felt the same for he kept in telephone touch weekly until we finalized the date for my trip to Durham.

I was excited, not only because of visiting Duke, but also because I had never flown before. I was driven to Macon for the flight to Atlanta where I would change planes for Durham. As I boarded that small DC-3, my stomach had more butterflies in it than at any game I had ever played. I did not know what to expect but was too proud to admit my ignorance. Any 6'7" all-state basketball player certainly should not be afraid of a small airplane journey. I was terrified.

A friend had told me that the safest place in the plane was the very last row of seats. So that is where I headed, and I sat with my face glued to the window. Before the plane even taxied to the runway, I was wishing I had never boarded it. But by the time the trip was over I had fallen in love with flying. I wasn't afraid of it again—until the return trip two days later.

As the DC-3 droned over Georgia farmland, I found myself thinking of Billie. I had begun to miss her. I felt sure that she had already forgotten about me. After all, she was out making a living on her own in a demanding profession. Why would she be interested in someone just graduating from high school?

Duke University was as beautiful as I had been told. As our car wound through the campus, I was overwhelmed by the school's massive size and its lovely, peaceful gardens. I was more certain than ever that this is where I'd spend my next four years. I had yet to learn that what we plan and what actually happens may be two different things.

I started my first night on campus with the annual basketball banquet for the University team. Another new boy, Bobby Joe Harris (later a star player for Duke), and I were to be guests at the banquet, and we would be introduced to the audience and media.

As I unpacked my little suitcase that afternoon I began to suspect that I had a problem. I had never owned a white shirt and tie, sports coat or full suit of clothes. The only garments I ever wore were casual jeans or khaki pants with sports shirts and sweaters. It wasn't because I didn't care about my appearance. It was just that there were no clothes available in the stores in our area that would fit me. And local townspeople accepted me just as I was.

When Bobby Joe stepped out of his room dressed in a handsome suit, white shirt, attractive tie and well-polished shoes, I knew I was in trouble. I was certain the entire Duke team would be similarly attired.

There I stood in khaki pants, a short-sleeved print shirt and tennis shoes.

Coach Bradley came by to pick up Bobby Joe and me since we were to sit next to him at the head table. When he arrived I could tell he was taken aback by my appearance, even though he didn't say anything.

I immediately apologized for failing to bring anything suitable for a banquet. I was too ashamed to tell him that the best clothes I owned were the ones I was wearing.

Coach Bradley was not only gracious about it but immediately set about remedying the situation. "No problem," he said. Then he called a number of the basketball team members down to our dormitory room and wrote down a list of sizes. Within fifteen minutes he had a whole set of clothes from about six different team members. Some of the items did not fit too well, such as a size 13-D shoe on a 14-B foot, but as my mother always said, "Beggars cannot be choosers."

We all went to the banquet and everything was fine.

However, even though I appreciated the efforts of Coach Bradley and the team to make me feel comfortable, the whole episode made me feel very uneasy and out of place. Certainly it was my undue reaction to a very innocent situation. But I began to feel that this school was only for the rich and the party set. This was a totally incorrect evaluation, but a seed of doubt had been planted—a doubt about my fitting into Duke University's social life. But I still loved the school and felt it was for me.

After a day on campus and interviews with professors and department heads, I sat down with Coach Bradley for a visit before catching my flight home. My respect for him had not diminished one bit. However, as we talked about my future with Duke, I felt very subdued as he handed me a grant-in-aid document to sign which would formalize my commitment to Duke.

I took it and read it carefully, not as much to learn what it entailed but to give me time to think about the conflicting thoughts whirling in my mind.

Finally, I handed it back. "I'm sorry, Coach Bradley," I apologized, "but I just can't sign this right now."

He sat back in stunned surprise, which I could well understand as I was the one who had told the world that Duke was my positive choice.

"What's wrong?" he asked.

"Nothing, really," I said, "but I promised Bob Polk of Vanderbilt that I wouldn't sign anything until I visited his campus." I added that I had also promised the University of Kentucky the same. Though the latter wasn't exactly the truth, I suddenly felt myself in a corner and was trying to fight my way out of it.

"Well," he said slowly, "you have to remember, Ed, that we only have a few scholarships to offer, and there are other boys waiting if you don't want to join us."

Then he leaned forward. "But remember, Ed, we really want *you* on our team. In fact, I can guarantee you that you'll play first-string at Duke for at least three years." (Freshmen were ineligible to play varsity at that time.)

"How can you guarantee me that with all the other players you have?" I asked.

"Because I've seen you play, and there's no doubt in my mind."

Once again he urged me to sign, and again I brought up Vanderbilt. I explained that I wouldn't be going there for two weeks and the University of Kentucky after that.

"Well, Ed," he said, "we can hold your scholarship for 10 days only. You've got to make up your mind on Duke before then."

As one of the Duke people drove me out to the airport I sat in the car feeling confused. All of my high hopes for this trip had tumbled down around me. My clothing problem had embarrassed me more than it should have, but my real quandary was the time deadline I faced. Until now, I had been led to believe that these trips to various campuses would be fun and exciting, not just for the educational experience but for seeing distant parts of the country unknown to a small-town boy from central Georgia.

To add to my stress, turbulent weather struck my Atlanta-bound plane, tossing it around like a cockleshell on a rough sea. Tornado warnings were posted for Atlanta, and we circled the city for 40 minutes. I clutched my seat and prayed through clenched teeth. Nausea overwhelmed me, and then I remembered a friend saying that eating something was the best cure for air sickness. So I accepted the food tray offered by the stewardess. At that moment the plane lurched like a bucking bronco and food trays literally flew into the air. People were covered with peas, meat and gravy. We were told to throw our trays into the aisle.

Because of the continuing bad weather, I was forced to spend the night in Atlanta, but when I phoned Coach Faircloth he said not to worry, that he'd have me picked up the following morning at Macon and bring me home to Fort Valley where he had a surprise waiting for me.

"What about Duke?" he asked.

"I'll tell you about it tomorrow," I sighed.

The flight the next day was smooth, and I soon found myself in love with flying again. The sun was warm and bright as we landed, and a car from the school was waiting outside the terminal.

It was a relaxing ride back through the Georgia countryside, and as we pulled up to the school I saw two men standing near the east wall of the red brick auditorium. One of them was Coach Faircloth who waved me over to him. The other man looked familiar but I knew I had never met him before. He stood at least 6'3" with a silver mane of hair, and he studied me intently. As I approached them Coach Faircloth shook my hand with a hearty "Welcome back!" and then began to introduce me to his companion. Before he could finish, the stranger broke in and said in a distinct midwestern accent: "Do you know who I am?"

I studied him for a moment and said, "No sir, I'm very sorry but I do not know your name."

"Well, son," he drawled, "that's too bad because when I tell you, you'll never forget it. It's going to become a very important name in your life."

He took my hand in a vice-like grip, riveting me with his piercing gray eyes. Coach Faircloth was chuckling as I stood transfixed.

Finally I blurted, "Sir, who are you?"

"Adolph Rupp," he boomed. "Adolph Rupp of the University of Kentucky. The number one basketball team in the country this year. And don't you forget it!" I never did.

4

An Unforgettable Evening

It wasn't long before I found myself making another airplane trip, only this time in another direction—to Lexington, Kentucky, where I would look over the university.

However, before I made any decision I had something far more important on my mind than basketball. It was seeing Billie again. So I decided to take advantage of my promise to take Billie out for that steak dinner we had talked about during my hospital stay. It was my one excuse, I felt, for contacting her again, and I wasn't about to let it go by.

I had trouble right from the start. First, every time I called Billie she seemed to be working the evening shift. And when she wasn't slated to work nights she was called in to work double shifts.

Then, just when I was about to quietly back off, figuring this was Billie's polite way of letting me know she wasn't interested, lo and behold she accepted my invitation!

Now I faced an even bigger problem. Billie lived some seven miles out in the country on her family's farm, and I had no way to get there. However, a friend owned a car and after definite promises that I would treat it as my own, I set out for the date which I had been looking forward to for months.

My plan was to take Billie to Macon—not only because that was where the better restaurants were, but the drive would give us an opportunity to relive all the trips she and I had made a couple of months before during the state tournament. I was to pick her up around seven, and that would give us a leisurely hour to follow the back roads to Macon.

I enjoyed the beautiful spring evening as the main highway took me past the Blue Bird Bus Manufacturing Company with its row upon row of yellow school buses awaiting delivery and on past the hospital where I first met Billie. A half mile further I turned onto a narrow country road for the six-mile drive to the Ray farm.

There was something special about the evening as the road wound through rolling farmland under a crystal clear sky with a three-quarter moon glowing on the horizon. Nostalgia filled me as the car rumbled over the bridge crossing Taylor's Mill Creek, and I quickly glanced to the left to see the old swimming hole where we boys used to skinny-dip on hot summer days. Such days as these, I sensed, would not come again.

As I thought about the girl I would soon meet my heart quickened, and then I remembered to watch "the curve." Just a mile from the turn-off to Billie's house was a very sharp curve to the left. Billie had warned me about it, though I had often driven it with bravado in the company of fellows and girls.

Now, I carefully slowed for it, and as I prepared to turn into her lane I began to feel those butterflies in my stomach. In fact they had begun fluttering early in the day. I couldn't understand why. After all, I told myself, I was just fulfilling a dinner promise. I *did* look forward to telling her of my meeting with the famed Adolph Rupp, even though I suspected she didn't really know who he was. When I had called Billie about four o'clock that afternoon to confirm our date, she remarked how much she was looking forward to it. "And please watch that last curve, Ed," she added.

Now my heart was thumping as I turned onto the red clay lane that led to the big white house with its barns and corrals. I shrank from the thought of going through family introductions. Billie was one of seven children. And though the three older ones were no longer home, her three younger brothers, Bobby, Danny and Jimmy would probably be there, along with her mother and father. As it was nearing harvest time, I hoped, except for Billie, that they all would be out in the peach orchards.

I was relieved when my tires crunched on their drive to note that only Billie's 1951 Mercury was there.

Getting out of the car, I brushed off my new sports coat and matching pants and straightened my tie. I certainly wanted to make a good impression on Billie. I also made sure the passenger door was unlocked so I could usher her in with aplomb.

As I walked slowly toward the front steps leading to the big, wide porch, I heard a screen door slam at the back of the house. Billie's Black Tank was parked back there. As I glanced over in that direction, the car lights blazed on, and its mighty engine burst into a roar. Tires spewed gravel and the Tank lurched down the driveway toward me. Brakes squalled and Billie, the only person around who drove like that, dramatically waved to me to open the passenger door.

If I had known what was coming, I would never have done it. But I was in a state of euphoria at seeing her, and I started to climb into the car, ready with my well-rehearsed greeting of "how lovely you look."

Instead, a grim-faced Billie snapped, "Hurry and get in. I need your help. We're late!"

Late—late for what? I was 10 minutes early. The Mercury catapulted out of the driveway in a cloud of dust and gravel. Pressed back into the seat by the acceleration, I stared wide-eyed at my date and then noticed the little black bag on the seat between us.

I was afraid to ask what was going on. The speedometer climbed past 60 m.p.h., and I froze as I saw the narrow, dark, dirt road hurtling toward us at unbelievable speed.

Too frightened to speak at all, I heard a tiny whimper from the back seat. Curiosity overcame terror, and I turned around to see the whitest eyes in the blackest face I ever saw. It was a boy of about nine. He was gripping the front seat with all his might, and he seemed paralyzed with fear. I empathized with him.

"It's his mother's time," said Billie nonchalantly, as she swerved the big Mercury to avoid a pothole.

"Her time?" I stammered.

"Yes, she's going to have another baby, and we need to help her."

"We?"

"Yes, *we*," said Billie. "Tyrone has already done his job by running three miles to tell me his momma needed me."

"Now, when we get there, Ed," continued Billie, matter-of-factly, "make sure you get everyone out of the house. The children and men will just be in the way. Probably one of the neighbor ladies will be there and she can stay."

"If there's no water on the stove, get one of the men to get some from the well and make sure a fire's burning to heat that water." She glanced at me to make sure I was listening.

I nodded, gulping as the Black Tank slowed around a curve.

"There are cloths and towels in my trunk; get them out and stand by the bed to help me deliver the baby."

"Deliver the baby!" My insides turned to water. My fear of speeding on this narrow, country road was wiped out by the unbelievable prospect facing me. At the age of 17 the only thing I knew about childbirth was from an educational film titled "Mom and Dad" at the local movie house, that had shown the birth of a child. All the kids went, including me, but I had closed my eyes during most of it. Now, here was Billie telling me I was going to *help*? She must be crazy! Why I had never even seen a naked woman in my life. Oh, I had seen some pictures passed around school, but this would be a live woman!

Help a birth? *Oh God, help me,* I prayed. *Why was I 10 minutes early tonight? If I had been a few minutes later Billie would have been gone, and I would have missed all this.*

I hung onto the seat as the Mercury slued around a sharp turn and roared toward a row of small cabins. Kerosene lanterns bobbed in the distance. The boy behind me began crying. Was he frightened by Billie's driving or worried about his mother?

"Why don't we take her to the hospital?" I asked Billie.

She shot me an incredulous look.

"They can't afford it! Don't worry, Ed. I deliver most of the babies on the little farms around here. More kids are named after me than I can count."

The Black Tank skidded to a halt. As Billie opened the door, a chorus of excited voices greeted her.

"Oh Miss Billie, Georgia Mae is fine but she sure needs you, honey."

Billie dashed for the cabin, and I took off my jacket and tie and placed them in the back seat. Blood stains, I remembered, were hard to remove. With a churning stomach, I opened the trunk and pulled out the towels and cloths stacked there. As I straightened up with an armload, a huge, black man took it from me. "I'll tote it," he rumbled.

I followed him into the cabin which was dimly lit with lamps and heavy with the odor of kerosene and cooking grease. The walls were covered with all kinds of paper and cloth. Among them were several pictures of Jesus carrying children and lambs, plus two pictures of Franklin Delano Roosevelt.

As my eyes adjusted to the dim light I saw a bed in one corner with a writhing woman on it. As she moaned, two women next to the bed assured her that everything would be all right. One of the women was Billie. She said not to worry, and I thought, *that's right, because I'm doing enough worrying for all of us!*

I asked the big man to put the towels on the table and then get everyone out of the house because Billie needed room to work.

"Yes, Mr. Ed," he said, "we know what to do. Miss Billie has been here before."

I was surprised. "You know my name?"

"Oh sure," he replied. "We know who *you* is." And his face gleamed with a big smile.

My heart leaped. I *had* been on Billie's mind after all. After the man left I could hear him tell everyone to go next door because "as soon as something happens, Mr. Ed will call us." Would I be able to walk, much less talk, when it *did* happen? I wondered.

"How's the water doing, Ed?" barked Billie. I had completely forgotten about it, but thankfully someone already had it on the stove.

She threw a sheet at me. "Hang it from the wall down the side of the bed so Georgia Mae can have some privacy." I did the best I could making certain I stayed on the *outside* of the sheet. I told myself it was because I did not want to embarrass the woman in the bed, but I really did not want to be embarrassed myself. I finally got the sheet in place, and I walked over to the big cast-iron cook stove. Water was bubbling in a black metal pot.

"The water's hot," I called.

"Good," said Billie, looking back at me from the bed. A faint compassionate smile crossed her face. "You all right?"

"Sure," I lied. "What do you want me to do now?"

"Nothing yet," she said, "it will be a little while. Her contractions are still two minutes apart."

What does that mean? I wondered, but I was too embarrassed to ask.

I headed for the door. "Call me when you need me."

"Come back and help me with the water," she ordered. Together we poured some into metal basins and filled the black pot to its brim and placed it back on the stove; then I threw some pieces of oak into its blazing maw.

The woman on the bed continued to moan softly while the neighbor kept applying a wet cloth to her forehead murmuring, "That's fine, Georgia Mae, you is doing just fine."

I felt I needed the cloth more than Georgia Mae—my new white shirt was soaked with nervous perspiration. And then came the moment I was dreading.

"All right, Ed, we need you now." It was Billie, her voice was terse and authoritative. "Hold Georgia Mae's hands and tell her to push when the contractions come. I think the baby's coming."

Suddenly I forgot my embarrassment, my clumsiness. I had become part of a wondrous event. I took the mother's hands and began urging her to "Push, Georgia Mae, push!" Just as I had urged my teammates at the state tournament, I urged her on. Georgia Mae gripped my hands and arm so hard I winced, and then I saw one of the most wonderful things I have ever seen in my life.

"It's here," breathed Billie, as I watched her delicate hands clasp a newborn head and firmly, yet tenderly, guide the red, wizened little human into a release from its womb.

"Georgia, it's a little girl!"

The joyful smile on the mother's face was like the sun coming up. Billie held the little girl up even before the cord was cut to show her to Georgia Mae.

"Oh, Miss Billie, I is so proud; we are going to name her Billie Ray!"

Two hours later I sat with Billie in her own kitchen eating a hot roast beef sandwich with potatoes and gravy.

"Well," I smiled, "it isn't a steak, but I think it's the best meal I ever ate."

Billie smiled quietly, and I looked at her for a long time across the table. In her company I had just witnessed a miracle, and I saw Billie helping to perform it in her own loving way.

I wasn't sure if my feelings for her were admiration or love. But I did know this delicate lady was a very special person.

It was nearly 11 o'clock when we walked out onto her front porch and said goodnight. Looking at her in the pale blue moonlight with the aroma of magnolia blossoms filling the air, I was overwhelmed by her loveliness.

"Well, we'll have that steak dinner in Macon soon," she smiled.

I nodded, too choked up to say anything. Then she hugged me, reached up and kissed me on the cheek.

I was so taken aback I could only stand there like a dumb athlete.

"Thank you for a lovely evening, Ed," she said softly. I almost laughed.

The next Monday morning my teammates besieged me. "What did you do on your date with Billie Friday night?" "Did you go to Macon?" "Did you see a movie?" "Hey, Ed, did you get to kiss her goodnight?"

I could just hear myself answering, "Oh, we had a great time. We delivered a baby together. It was the best date I ever had." Suppressing a laugh, I said, "Oh nothing much. Nothing much really."

5

Are You
Good Enough?

There was no fanfare that Saturday morning in mid-May when I signed my name to a grant-in-aid scholarship at the University of Kentucky. I sealed that commitment to UK alone in my bedroom.

Two months earlier, when I visited Lexington for the first time, I still had misgivings about UK being the school for me. Perhaps it was Buddy Parker's persistent early-morning promotional pitch, perhaps I was feeling more and more positive about Vanderbilt. Yet, I had to admit that the Blue Cyclone had intrigued me; besides, I had never seen the famous bluegrass area and with the university paying my plane fare, what could I lose?

Harry Lancaster, their assistant basketball coach, with whom I had talked on the phone several times, greeted me at the airport. A massive man with a ruddy complexion and shoulders that looked four feet wide, he welcomed me with a solid handshake and a smile as warm as the sun. I liked him instinctively.

There was a spring snowfall flying and he said, "You've got to be crazy to want to come to this country to play basketball when you could play where it's warm and dry!"

I was soon to discover that Harry, like Adolph, was a master psychologist. As we headed toward the city, we passed the world-famous Calumet Farms with its white board fences, trademark of the race-horse country. I simply nodded as they told of famous horses from that farm; horse racing had never interested me.

However, when we arrived at the University's dormitories where some of the athletes lived, I found myself taking notice. It wasn't the facilities as such for they were actually old buildings on a quadrangle built in the early 1930s. What did impress me was the fact that the athletes were mixed in with non-athletic students. On the other campuses I had visited, except Vandy, it always seemed as if the teams were isolated from the rest of the student body.

Coach Lancaster introduced me to Billy Evans who became captain of the 1955 varsity team. A gracious, good-humored fellow, he took me on a quick tour of the campus. I first noticed its size; the student population numbered some 7,000 and I thought, *that's as many as there are in my home town*. We strolled through the red brick buildings and at the end of the two-hour tour, as if totally unplanned, we arrived at the Memorial Coliseum, the spectacular home of UK's fighting Wildcats.

We walked inside the huge building and onto the glistening boards of its playing court. Although there was no one in the arena except Billy and me, I could feel and hear the 12,000 screaming fans singing, "On, On, U of K, we will fight for the right. . . ." Not even the Blue Cyclone, Buddy Parker, had overstated its magnificence; I had never seen anything like it. I almost wanted to ask Billy, "Where do I sign?" but I played the "total control" game.

Billy then walked me by the trophy cases representing some of the greatest college basketball teams in history. I gaped at the photos of the "Fabulous Five" of NCAA and 1948 Olympic fame. I spotted a photo of Bill Spivey, a boy I had seen play at Warner Robbin's High School in Georgia when I was in junior high. At that time he played barefoot because they couldn't find shoes large enough for his feet. Besides that, he couldn't even catch the ball, much less throw it! Now, here was his picture with "All-American" printed under it. I knew there were two men responsible for that—Adolph Rupp and Harry Lancaster.

"By the way," I asked Billy, "where is Coach Rupp?"

"He's in Florida watching the New York Yankees' spring

baseball workouts," Billy replied. He explained that he and Casey Stengel were close friends and almost every year Coach Rupp tried to make it down to the spring training schedule. Then he added that Coach Rupp had suffered a slight heart attack during the past season and had gone south to rest and recuperate.

We passed through the dressing-room area where facilities I hadn't even dreamed existed. "Every player receives clean, dry uniforms each day," Billy told me. I could hardly believe it. In high school we wore the same things over and over until hardly anyone could stand the odor; we just didn't have the washing and drying facilities.

Finally we walked down the corridor lined with the coaching and athletic offices. It was the Blue Corridor of honor, its walls covered with photos of all the All-Conference and All-American players of legend. I had read about most of them as a young boy. Would it be *my* destiny to wear the same blue and white of these all-time greats?

Billy stopped and pointed out Coach Rupp's office. "Well, here's where I leave you, Ed," he said. Coach Lancaster was waiting for me in the "inner sanctum." More psychology was on the way.

I knocked on the door.

"Come on in, the door's open."

As I opened it, I noticed that it was not a regular 6'8" door which I, at 6'7", could walk through without lowering my head. It seemed at least an inch lower, so when I ducked to enter, Coach Lancaster shouted with glee.

"You'll do, Ed. Anyone who has to duck to enter this office is big enough to play here. We believe you are good enough, but," he leaned back in his chair and surveyed me, "that remains to be seen."

That was like a gauntlet thrown at my feet. I didn't realize then that UK's intensive research on me had uncovered the fact that I always seemed to excel under challenges.

Sitting next to the coach was another massive man who was introduced to me as Bernie Shively, the UK Athletic Director. Over the next four years I found him to be a sensitive, caring man, but on that day, the only thing I could think of was how *big* those guys were. Bernie excused himself saying he hoped I'd be coming to the University. After he left I settled in a chair and Coach Lancaster was silent as I examined the walls covered with pictures of famous people in both the athletic and entertainment world. There were also photos of the Hereford cattle which were Adolph Rupp's pride and joy, and even *they* posed next to basketball players. I wasn't sure whether The Baron was prouder of the bulls or the brawn, but I knew both were U.S. Choice.

Coach Lancaster apologized again for Coach Rupp's absence and then noticed that the huge trophies lining his desk had captured my attention.

When I asked him about them it was obvious he had been waiting for this moment. He outlined the history of the national titles that each trophy symbolized, including the most recent, the HELMS award for the United States' most outstanding team. I stared at it in awe, and Harry went for the psychological clincher.

"Ed, the other schools you've visited just talk about these trophies. But we have them. And we'll win more. We get the best high school athletes in the country because this is where they want to come. We've asked you to come here to look us over to see if you like us and. . ." he was silent for a moment, "and for us to see if we like you."

I looked at him quizzically.

"Now, Buddy Parker says you're good enough," he continued. "We really don't know whether you are or not. We hope you are, but remember, if you come here you may not be able to make the team."

Suddenly I wondered if I was hearing clearly. For the first time in my college visits I was hearing a man tell me I'd have to prove myself.

Harry continued. "Now we want you to look over our campus, talk to our professors and staff. We hope you'll like us, Ed, but we also want you to know that if you decide to go somewhere else, we'll sincerely wish you well." Then he leaned across his desk and smiled. "But I also want you to know that when and if we ever play you, we'll beat you."

So far no mention had been made of a scholarship. I now had the feeling that the next 24 hours would make the difference whether they liked me enough to give me one.

By now it was late afternoon and I was checked into a nice downtown hotel. I had dinner that night with some Kentucky alumni and friends, followed by a parade of visitors who came to my room to tell me how much they loved UK. I was flabbergasted by such fan loyalty.

One loyal fan who came that night was Mr. C. A. Kenny, chief operator of Stoner Creek Stud Farm of Paris, Kentucky. He was a gentle, soft-spoken man, and as I watched him move around my room I could envision him with horses, very much in control but so gentle in his handling of them. He was an avid UK admirer, not just athletically but academically, and that impressed me. In coming years I was to learn just how wonderful a person he was.

I fell into bed exhausted, my head whirling.

The following morning I visited the various professors. Yes, the Ancient Language Department was in the oldest building on campus. And even though most of the professors were older men, I was very impressed with their enthusiasm toward me as a potential student athlete.

I realized that athletes interested in the ministry were quite rare at that time, and I was a kind of novelty to them. But, I enjoyed talking with men who, though deeply engrossed in Greek, Latin, philosophy, history and sociology, were also avid fans of Big Blue athletics. They let me know that they believed academics and athletics not only could go hand in hand but also actually complemented each other.

So, by the time I finished visiting with the professors who would be involved in my real reason for university study, preparation for seminary, I had been swept off my feet.

After lunch in the Student Union with Dean Kirwin of the history department, who was also on the NCAA governing committee, I walked over to Memorial Coliseum again. I stood there alone in the cavernous building sensing the strong spirit in the air. I found myself drawn to this school and believed that I'd like it even more as time passed. And of course, that dream was always in the back of my mind—someday I wanted to help win an NCAA championship title. At UK, it just might be possible. However, I began to wonder if they would offer a scholarship. Tuition aid was a necessity for me since I had no other support, and, of course, if the school offered me anything beyond a scholarship, I would have to report it to the NCAA governing committee.

I walked back to the Athletic Building and found Coach Lancaster in his office. His shelves were laden with working documents and books about all phases of basketball. I was to learn that Harry Lancaster was probably the most astute student of the game in America. For though already a great coach, he still continued to study every nuance of the game.

"Any more questions you need answered, Ed?" he asked, looking up with a smile.

"No, not really," I answered, reluctant to mention my question about tuition.

When he again asked me how I liked UK, I told him how well impressed I was but as we talked I noticed that he seemed much more business-like. *Had he uncovered some unfavorable reports about me*? I wondered. To add to my uneasiness he did not mention anything about a scholarship. Frankly, I'd expected him to pull a document out of his desk drawer and say, "Sign on the dotted line."

Instead, he slipped on his jacket, jingled his car keys and said, "Come on, I'll take you to the airport. We're a little early so it will give us a chance to stop at my house on the way. I'd like you to meet my wife if she's home."

We drove leisurely several miles from campus and pulled down a street past some very ordinary looking houses. I was convinced both he and Coach Rupp lived in palatial mansions. Instead, I discovered that Coaches Lancaster and Rupp lived in modest homes much like the one in which I had grown up.

Mrs. Lancaster was lovely and gracious and informed me their daughter, Toni, would be attending UK shortly. It seemed that every conversation I'd had in Lexington centered on the university.

Then the coach and I drove on to the airport, making small talk about the weather and the lovely bluegrass area. We finally pulled up to the airport terminal, but still he had not mentioned a scholarship. As I opened the door to get out he thanked me for coming. After I expressed my appreciation for his hospitality, I couldn't stand the suspense any longer.

"Coach," I blurted, "have you offered me a scholarship to come to UK?"

"Why, sure we have," he grinned. "We wouldn't have had you come here if we hadn't planned on that."

"Well," I stammered, "don't I have to sign something?"

"Oh, it's back in my office," he said. "I'll send it to you in a couple of weeks or so."

Conscious of deadlines pressed on me by other schools, I asked about the time limit.

"What do you mean?" he asked.

"Uh, well, how long do I have before signing the grant-in-aid?"

"How long?" he mused. "Oh, our classes begin next fall around September 15th, so any time before then will be fine."

As I picked up my suitcase, he smiled and waved. "No hurry, Ed. Hope to see you in September. And, hey, I'll tell Coach Rupp hello for you."

Somewhat in a daze I walked to the ticket counter. I couldn't believe the lack of pressure. The ticket agent read my name, smiled and said, "I hope you liked your visit to UK. We look forward to seeing you play here next year." Pressure can be subtle.

A week later I received a letter from Harry Lancaster thanking me for my visit and enclosing a grant-in-aid form.

"Sign and return any time," read the post-script.

Weeks later I signed it and went to the Fort Valley post office where I bought a three-cent stamp to return it. UK was the only school that did not enclose a stamped, self-addressed envelope with their grant-in-aid forms.

But as it turned out, it cost me a lot to go to the University of Kentucky, and that three-cent stamp was just the beginning.

6

Moonlight Confessions

It was a most poignant spring. Soon I would leave for my summer work in northern New York State where I had worked on a construction crew for several previous summers, resurfacing a dam on the Hudson River near Saratoga Springs. But instead of returning to Fort Valley in the fall, I would be going to Kentucky.

Billie Ray and I would be separated by a thousand miles, and I found that fact most difficult to accept. We still never had a real date, and I ached to know this lovely girl better.

I tried to forget it in preparing for the coming high school graduation exercises scheduled for the end of May. Also, I was scheduled to speak at the Sunday night worship service at the First Methodist Church. I had spoken there before, but this was going to be my farewell to the congregation of which I had been a part for seven years.

As I worked at my desk on my message, memories floated back over the years, and I remembered how this congregation had become like a family to me. When my step-father's work took my family to Florida, I pleaded to stay in Fort Valley where I had already found real fulfillment and companionship playing basketball. Coach Norman Faircloth, already my confidant, became my local guardian, and a local family, the William Khourys, graciously let me have a room in the back of their home.

Though all of these friends were extremely helpful and supportive, the people of the First Methodist Church became my extended family in a unique way. I had originally been reared a strict Lutheran in the inner city of Milwaukee where I had spent the first 10 years of my life. After we moved to Georgia, my English-born Mother settled upon the Methodist Church which she in her own way felt was "closest to Lutheran polity and theology." None of us challenged Mother, as we couldn't admit we didn't know what "polity" meant.

The church was near downtown, and our home was about a mile away. Many evenings I would walk downtown to see what was going on under the bright lights. There never was much activity there, and I'd soon begin my return trip.

On my way home I'd pass our Methodist Church, a small brick structure built around the turn of the century with an illuminated board announcing Sunday services. A side door was always left open for anyone who wanted to enter for prayer or meditation.

I would usually stop in the late evening hours, and I'd settle in a pew in the quiet sanctuary. There for a few minutes I would talk with God about my life, my goals and how I was progressing.

I felt very much at home looking at the beautifully curved altar surrounded by ornate Christian symbols of carved walnut and polished brass candelabra. Sometimes a small light was left burning in the choir loft which provided an eerie, mystical, yet comforting atmosphere for a young boy with questions. The Khoury's house was only a block from the church, so I went there quite often, especially in the evening. It had become a retreat for me where I could dream dreams and just be myself—with the Presence I always sensed there.

Though the regular youth programs and activities usually bored me, I found myself intrigued with the revival meetings held twice a year and lasting anywhere from eight to 15 evenings. I attended every one. As with all youngsters, my theological understandings were in a state of flux. They were churned even more by the

persuasive power of the visiting speakers. I was appalled by some
things I heard from a few of them.

They said things that seemed to divide rather than unite people.
One night a snowy-haired preacher from North Carolina spoke
forcefully and descriptively about the reward of a Christian life—an
eternity in heaven with closeness to God and converted loved ones.
Then he turned from that beautiful thought to outline the different
groups of people he said would never get there—Roman Catholics,
Jews, Masons. The list went on and on. How a person could share
one moment the thought of the love of God in all of its beauty, and
then summarily send huge percentages of the human race to an
eternity without the love of God seemed incongruous to me.

There, too, seemed to be no compassion, no brokenness, no
remorse. I saw very few men or women in those years who preached
with an attitude of contriteness. Some were hypnotic in their
cadence, some were elevating in their elocution, but there were only
one or two that were compassionately sensitive to a teenage boy.

One was a preacher from Virginia. John Huston was a boring
speaker in contrast with many of the others, but he went out of his
way to converse with me. He wanted to hear my life story and future
hope. He was extremely encouraging, and I went to every service
he preached.

During this series of services when I was 16 I went forward at
an end of the service to kneel at my favorite spot at the chancel rail.

This time the person kneeling across from me was my Sunday
school teacher, Jeanette Wheaton. Instead of asking the usual
questions which I could not answer, all she said was: "Ed, I'm so
happy that you came tonight. We'll talk later, but let's just pray
now."

As we prayed, all I could remember was a feeling of acceptance
and deep concern for my spiritual well-being.

That night when the church was dark, I made my way back to
that same spot at the altar and continued to search my soul. There,
overpowering all the human words of encouragement from the past,
I heard the growing intensity of a small inner voice which I now
believed was leading me. In that quiet moment it seemed so
clear—not as it had been in the meeting with singing, praying and
preaching, stimulating as those things were, but in this time of

peaceful reflection in that dark sanctuary—I was overwhelmed by the mystery of my God and the majesty of my Christ.

Jeanette Wheaton was true to her word about "talking later." One Sunday afternoon in our empty classroom, she reached out to touch my struggling young soul. As she let me know she understood my anxieties concerning the emotionalism and methodologies of revival meetings, she simply said, "Remember, Ed, it takes all kinds and all ways to win people to Jesus Christ. I know that for some the emotional experience is the only way they will find him; for there are those who look more for the 'signs of the experience' than the experience itself.

"But the danger is," she continued, looking pointedly at me, "that sometimes people get so turned off by the outward expressions they see, they miss the inward experience."

She reached forward and took my hand, the sun streaming through the window forming a halo behind her slightly gray hair. "Always remember, Ed, that Jesus just wants to be your closest friend. He wants intimacy in your life. He wants to know you and he wants you to know him better than you will ever know anyone.

"That is why he talked about our loving him more than members of our earthly family," she continued. "And this is a challenge we all face. For you have the capabilities to perform great things for him. Finding his purpose for you is not something that will happen quickly, or only at an altar, though that will be helpful. It is a commitment that you must keep and constantly care for."

My teacher smiled and sighed softly. "Just live for Jesus, Ed, because he lived and died for you."

From then on there was one objective from which I would never turn—the friendship between my Lord and myself. Thanks in great part to Jeanette Wheaton, I had come to know that if we are truly created by God as unique and gifted human beings, then it stands to reason that God will deal with each of us differently through varied perceptions, experiences and feelings.

I also came to believe that some of us, like myself, may come to know our Savior by self-interrogation; we doubt, we question, we search until we find ourselves surrounded by the God who wants to know us more than we ever wanted to know him.

And so it was that I was found by the One who, as Jeanette

Wheaton said, "just wants to be your closest friend." Friendship is that marvelous and moving I-Thou relationship where both are willing to take a risk and reveal to each other who they are, warts and all. What had happened during those journeys to the chancel rail to pray and the conversations with Jeanette Wheaton was a process of opening my life to the presence and power of Christ. I began sensing a closeness of his presence within my life and began believing that God did literally care for me. Suddenly I realized a covenant relationship with my Lord that was going to shape and focus my life. That relationship was so important to me that I sensed how it was going to alter my other relationships. Since Billie was growing in importance, I began planning how I could share with her my feelings toward my dearest friend. I simply wanted her to know him as I felt and believed I did.

Somehow something had opened in my heart at that church and now as I worked at home on my talk for that last Sunday evening worship service, I found myself wiping my eyes. I knew this would be the last time I would get to thank those dear people who had done so much for me—Jeanette Wheaton and so many others.

That night I thanked them for their support and concern which had been so much a part of my life. I promised to try never to let them down; I promised to try my best not to let Christ down—their friendship had given me the insight I needed into my relationship with him.

After the service the people filed by to wish me well, and my heart beat faster when I saw Billie waiting at the end of the line. I had hoped she would come, but I was too shy to extend a personal invitation. It had, however, been announced in the local newspaper. And there she was!

We walked out of the church together into the cool night air and headed toward her car. As we got in, I grinned, "It's nice to be back in the Black Tank again, even if I lost a year of my life in it the last time."

We headed for the one and only drive-in hamburger stand in Fort Valley, and then drove to a lovely spot overlooking a small lake.

"I'm glad we're not delivering any babies tonight," I laughed as she stopped the car on a small rise.

"Well," she said, setting the brake, "don't forget, you still owe me a steak dinner."

"Next time. I promise."

"And next time I promise another delivery," she laughed.

Suddenly it was quiet in the car; only the rustling of an evening breeze filled the air. I felt terrible to be leaving for New York in a few days, for I knew I wouldn't see her again all summer. I hoped she was feeling as sad as I.

"Let's get out of the car," she said. We did and she climbed up on the front fender where she sat watching the moonlight shimmer on the lake. I stood on the other side of the car feeling awkward, wondering if I could stand by her, perhaps even put my arm around her waist to keep her warm?

I thanked her for the help she gave me during the past basketball season, and then we talked about my entering the University of Kentucky. I confessed I had some worries about measuring up to the Wildcats' reputation.

I had my foot on the bumper, leaning in her direction, when she completely changed the subject.

"Why did you decide to enter the Methodist ministry, Ed?"

I was so taken aback that I straightened up and cleared my throat. "Well, that's a long story, Billie."

She looked at me, the moonlight reflecting softly in her dark eyes. "Well, I'd like to hear about it, Ed."

She slid off the fender, went to the car trunk and pulled out a blanket. I couldn't help remembering the last time I dove into that trunk for towels and cloths. I thought, *that trunk has everything in it!*

I helped Billie spread the blanket on the knoll, and we sat down on it. Then, leaning back on my elbow, I tried to answer her question.

"Some folks tell me that they are called to the ministry. Well, I'm not really sure what they mean by that." I stopped for a moment, then continued. "I think I've received that call, Billie, but it's not just one specific thing; it's a number of things."

She was watching me closely, and I felt closer to her than ever before. Feeling more open, I went on. "A couple of years ago, I attended a large youth service up in Macon at the Mulberry Street

Methodist Church where I heard a man talk about the need for
foreign missionaries.

"He asked all those who wanted to dedicate their lives for this
work to come forward. Well, I went forward along with a hundred
or so others. But to be honest, Billie, I went up there to make a
statement to God and myself that I would begin to study for
whatever ministry he wanted me to enter."

I looked at Billie, who seemed more interested than ever in what
I was saying. Heartened, I went on. "Well, since then I have
wondered just exactly what area of service God wants me to enter.
I really don't know, Billie. But I do feel that he will let me know at
the right time.

"So when people ask me why I'm entering the ministry rather
than medicine, law or engineering, I just say I want to do something
that will help people the most. Now I know that persons in other
fields help people too, but right now, Billie, all I can tell you is that
I want to be a preacher. The church and its message have been so
important in my life that I want to make them important in other
people's lives, too."

I stopped, feeling embarrassed for talking so long. I laid back on
the blanket and looked up at the stars. Billie hadn't said a word so
far. Then I sensed her shift on the blanket, and she said, "I want to
help people, too, Ed."

"You already do," I answered. "Look at all the folks you help at
the hospital and the poor folks on the farms around here."

"I know," she said, "but I feel I should do so much more. For a
long time I've thought about becoming a medical missionary
overseas, maybe go to some place like Africa and help set up an aid
station. What do you think?"

"Think? Why, I think that would be wonderful!" I said enthusiastically. "Just imagine, you could be the doctor and I the preacher."
I flushed with embarrassment for what it seemed to imply, but Billie
just laughed and said, "Who knows—maybe someday."

I began to get the same feeling I had that night at her kitchen
table after the birth of the baby. There was something about her that
completely overwhelmed me—her maturity and skill, her sensitive
beauty. I was becoming more and more fascinated with this girl who
attracted me so deeply.

Despair filled me as I thought of leaving for work in New York so soon. I desperately wanted to stay in Fort Valley and pursue this friendship; no, more exactly, this relationship.

However, I said nothing and just looked at Billie, her eyes so dark in the moonlight. We made small talk about the beautiful evening, and we promised to write each other during the summer.

As we stood up together, we both leaned against the car for a moment, taking a last look at the moonlit lake. I felt Billie's warmth, the aroma of her perfume and sensed her shoulder near me. Impulsively I reached out, pulled her to me and held her tight, not wanting to let her go, ever.

Our lips found each other and for a long, warm moment the world seemed far, far away.

7

Year of the Mongoose

It was late September and a warm, sunny Sunday—my first full day on the University of Kentucky campus. I was standing in front of the dormitory that I thought would be my home for the next four years. Cars were pulling up constantly as parents and friends brought students. I was amazed at all the boxes, trunks and hanging clothes being unloaded. I had swung off the bus the night before with a small trunk and suitcase.

I marveled at the bed in my room. All the basketball players' beds were seven feet long. Before arriving I had requested a board be placed under my mattress because of my back's condition, and sure enough, it was there. UK was efficient.

A roommate who had arrived before me was a junior college transfer from Wells, Texas—Bob Burrow. He was 6'7" also, but he outweighed me by 30 pounds. He was a raw-boned, blue-eyed blond whose handshake completely surrounded mine, and I could tell that he was destined to be a great one. I had been pleased that morning when I heard him get up very early and start dressing for church. I asked him where he was going, and he said he didn't know. He always went to worship somewhere, though. He was a Baptist, and we walked together several blocks to a large Baptist church. He kidded me about switching denominations. I liked him instinctively and felt that we could become close friends.

But as I stood out on the dorm front lawn that Sunday afternoon watching all the cars roll in, students tumbling out laughing and greeting each other, I felt homesick. It was either that or just being alone in a situation that I sensed was pressure-oriented. I vividly remembered the morning newspaper's sports section that had trumpeted the arrival of 14 freshman basketball players and one junior college transfer—Bob Burrow. How naive I had been. All of the other colleges that tried to recruit me were going to sign three to six freshmen players total. Here, there were 14, the largest number signed by UK in years.

As I had read their backgrounds, I was amazed and a little envious. High school All-Americans and all of them all-staters, several had been major stars in the Indiana-Kentucky high school summer tourney series. Summer? I felt guilty as I had not even picked up a basketball since last spring because of my construction work in New York State.

The newspaper article mentioned me as the leading prep player from Georgia. The story made several other nice comments about me, but the last sentence really caught my eye: "He is also a licensed Methodist minister and will be the first ever to play under Adolph Rupp." At first it had seemed funny to me, and at lunch Bob had laughed about it also. He said he had heard there was a bet going on with the sports writers concerning Adolph and me. "Since you're the 'first clergyman ever to play at UK under Adolph,'" he grinned, "the bet is who will leave first—Adolph or you." Coach Rupp had been there for 25 years and all the odds were on The Baron. I had chuckled a little but later wondered if I had made the wrong decision. Maybe I should have gone to Duke where Methodist ministers were at least not looked upon as missing links.

That afternoon I was relaxing on my seven-foot bed waiting for more of these phenomenal freshmen to arrive when a knock came at the door. I was startled. With so many people coming in and out, why would anyone pause to knock? Upon opening the door I was greeted by a middle-aged gentleman about six feet tall with pitch black, slicked down hair.

"Clarence Yates is my name," he said with a broad smile. "You are Ed Beck, aren't you? The Methodist preacher-boy who has come to play round ball at the greatest university in the world?"

"Yes," I stammered, somewhat overwhelmed.

"Well, I'm a Methodist preacher of a church less than a mile away. It is a new church and we're building, but someday it will be the biggest in the conference. We need all the help we can get and so I not only welcome you to Lexington, but invite you to our services."

Before he could say much more, another roommate arrived and Reverend Yates excused himself with directions on how to get to his church. Services were being held that evening. Could I come?

My other roommate was Bill Surface. He looked anything but a basketball player. About 5'7" and overweight with a ruddy complexion, he reminded me of a small-town lawyer with his tousled look and bulging belly. He introduced himself and told me that he was the basketball team manager and would be staying with us temporarily. He was the first real entrepreneur I had known, and why he was not named president of the university before he graduated four years later, I will never know. Whatever one's need—whether it be data on certain professors, point spread on a football game, odds on a favorite at Keeneland race track or the best movie in town—Bill Surface could get you the entire scoop. Before he left the university he was writing sports articles and later became an author and quite an expert on tax laws.

We made quite a striking threesome on that third floor of the walk-up dormitory at the edge of the UK campus. Bob Burrow, the big, blue-eyed blond from Texas, who would not only become the next All-American at UK, but the ladies' man to end all ladies' men; Bill Surface, the jack-of-all-knowledge and master of most; and Ed Beck, the little ol' preacher-boy from Georgia.

Registration for classes was uneventful, but I continued to have misgivings concerning my decision to come to UK. Since I had signed a grant-in-aid at an NCAA University, I could not attend another school without a year's layoff. So big schools like Duke and Vandy were out, but there were smaller schools that had continued to contact me all summer, hoping I'd change my mind. One was Murray State College in Kentucky. The coach had been most persistent on the phone and in letters. In early September he had shown up in Jacksonville, Florida, where I had traveled to visit my family, and we spent several hours together. I had liked him a great deal but felt strange about talking with him since I had already signed at UK. However, I was flattered. He said that if for some reason I did not like UK, I should give him a call, and he would see what he could work out for me at Murray. As the days progressed at UK during that first week, I felt more and more inclined to follow through on that call. I felt uncertainty mostly, I think, about competing with 14 top-rated freshmen players. I wondered if I'd even make the team. So, not really trying to analyze my reasons but feeling it was the thing to do, I placed a call to Murray State on Thursday night of that first week to see if the offer still held. It did! I was elated and felt that now I had to decide whether to stay in Lexington, for better or worse, or make the break. I promised that before the coming weekend was over, the decision would be made.

At 2 a.m. Friday, I awakened terribly sick, chilled and vomiting. By six I was wishing I could die and afraid I wouldn't. Finally, I awakened Bill and Bob who immediately took me over to the infirmary.

The diagnosis was a severe case of mononucleosis. I was in the infirmary for 10 days and lost 27 pounds. It took me more than a year to regain my weight and strength. However, something happened while I was in the infirmary that affected my decision concerning staying at the University of Kentucky.

Coach Lancaster came to see me every day, but the first day or so I was so ill I had difficulty even talking. However, on Monday I realized, though still very sick, that I would live and that I had promised the Murray State coach that I would let him know my decision by the weekend. It was already past that time, and he had called me several times. I told him my illness had delayed my decision. When Coach Lancaster came to see me that Monday morning, I told him of my impending decision to leave UK. He didn't seem disturbed or upset. "Ed, you're too sick to talk about it today," he assured me. "Our main concern now is to get you completely well. Then you can make the decision that's best for you." I was amazed and touched by his fatherly attitude but I was not aware of the seemingly diabolical plan that coaches Rupp and Lancaster were working on for my edification.

Checking with my doctors, they learned I would be released from the hospital on the following Saturday. Though I was beginning to feel better every day, I was still exceedingly weak. On Thursday afternoon, with the sun streaming in the windows of the infirmary bedroom, I looked up to see three gentlemen walking toward my bed. I immediately recognized Harry Lancaster and Adolph Rupp, but I had never seen the smaller man before. Coach Rupp introduced him as Bart Peak, the head of the local YMCA and one of the leading Christian spokesmen in the city. After a number of comments concerning my progress toward recovery, Adolph put his big hand on my shoulder and said, "Ed, Harry tells me that you are thinking of leaving the University and going to Murray. That would be an awful mistake. Why would you want to play there when you know you could play here? I've talked with my good friend, Bart Peak, about this, and he asked if he could come to see you. Bart wants to pray about your future, don't you, Bart?"

I was so taken aback by Adolph's frontal approach that I immediately closed my eyes and thus never saw the faint smile that undoubtedly crossed the lips of Adolph and Harry. With Coach Lancaster standing on the right side of my bed with his hand on one shoulder, Coach Rupp on the other side holding my other shoulder and Bart Peak standing at my bedside holding my hand, the strangest prayer meeting in the history of the UK infirmary took place. Bart prayed for my life and health and began to emphasize my wisdom—my wisdom in first deciding on UK over all the other great schools in America. And how truly wise that decision had been. And how that wise decision was being confirmed through an illness that now gave me time to reflect, re-evaluate and recommit my life to excellence. And, of course, I could only achieve excellence at UK. Those were not the exact words, but their meaning could not be misunderstood.

Then the prayer was over, with a resounding "Amen" from Bart Peak and Adolph Rupp. Harry just squeezed my shoulder and reassured me that he would see me the next day. If I needed anything I should call him. He said all my professors had been contacted concerning my illness and I would have no problem catching up on my studies. As they left the room I found myself chuckling at the psychological snow job and said to myself, "If you can't beat them, you might as well join them." I went to the pay phone down the hall and called Murray State to tell them I would not be coming.

I was released from the infirmary on Saturday. Sunday morning I went to hear Clarence Yates preach on Jacob's wrestling with the Angel of the Lord and how he had been crippled because of it. I had wrestled with three "Angels of the Lord" in an infirmary, and now, because of a severe loss of weight I felt somewhat crippled myself. However, I now knew for certain that the issue of my collegiate future rested within Lexington. In a strange way I believed that God's friendship with me had been strengthened. Little did I then realize just how much Clarence Yates, Adolph Rupp and Harry Lancaster's lives would intertwine with mine.

My first year at UK began dramatically—the rest of it proved exciting, too. My teammates had elected me captain of the freshman basketball team. Although we were supposed to be one of the finest first-year teams ever at UK, we lost three games. Some observers felt that it was difficult to mold so much individual talent into one smoothly functioning unit, and they may well have been right.

Centenary Methodist Church, pastored by the ebullient Clarence Yates, who had come to see me on my first day at school, had also become a vital part of my life. I usually attended both morning and evening services. The evenings always ended at Mrs. Helen Hunt's apartment. A spark plug of the Centenary congregation, she was a petite lady in her early fifties with two grown daughters. Gregarious and enthusiastic, she always had "open house" at her home on Sunday evenings for members of the congregation.

These were happy occasions with much laughter and practical jokes. I have always wondered if Helen ever forgave Bob Burrows and me for the excitement we added one unforgettable evening.

On this night I told the group of about 15 fellows and girls that Bob had to stay at the dormitory to take care of a mongoose which had been imported from southern India by the Zoology Department. Since most of the group had never seen a mongoose, I went into great detail about the viciousness of this animal, how its favorite prey was snakes, especially the cobra. This particular mongoose, I explained, had already killed a number of poisonous snakes including the Black Mamba, most deadly of all.

As the group listened with rapt attention, I said the Zoology Department wanted to see if there were any traces of this deadly poison in the mongoose's bite since it often ate such snakes.

Several girls expressed horror at seeing such an animal, but Helen bit.

"I've read about them, and I'd certainly like to see one," she exclaimed.

"Well, I don't know," I said, "Bob has been given strict instructions to be careful with the mongoose because it's so dangerous, but . . . would you really like to see it?"

"Of course," Helen said. By this time most of the crowd was clamoring that Bob bring it over.

At first I demurred but then gave in. Picking up the kitchen phone I loudly asked Bob to "bring over the mongoose."

Shortly Bob and two other teammates showed up at the front door. He was carrying a long, narrow box. Half of it was topped with thin mesh wire through which one could dimly make out some straw and a water container. The other half was completely enclosed with a small door leading to the "feeding area." But now he had the box entirely covered with a cloth.

Group discussion hushed as he carried it into the living room and set it on the floor. "It's covered because mongooses hate light," said Bob. "Light makes them very angry. So before I uncover the box, would someone please turn off the overhead light?"

A student flicked the switch leaving only a corner lamp dimly illuminating the room. With the open end of the box facing his entranced audience, Bob slowly pulled off the cover. "The mongoose is back in his hut," he said. "Don't anyone make a sound. It will send him into a mad frenzy. I'll gently tap the back of the box to get him out."

The room was dead still with all eyes focused on the ominous-looking box as Bob began to tap it. Along with several others, Helen Hunt was on her hands and knees peering intently into the mesh-covered opening. Every once in a while she would say, "Oh, I think I see something."

"Quite, please, quiet," hushed Bob, as he continued to tap.

As the tension in the room peaked, Bob released a hidden spring flipping open the box. Out "leaped" a furry "animal"—right on to Helen's head!

Screaming wildly, she fell backwards. Chairs crashed as people scattered everywhere with Bob and I yelling, "The mongoose is loose!"

Thankfully it took only a few minutes for most everyone to realize that it was just a stuffed piece of fur. But the room continued in an uproar, this time with Helen leaning against a wall, wiping her brow and looking daggers at us. Bob lay there on the rug laughing hysterically. Other men doubled up in laughter, and most of the women lined up at the bathroom door.

Finally, Helen was laughing more than anyone else, and the evening ended with everyone agreeing that it had been the best "open house" at Helen's since anyone could remember.

Throughout that freshman year Billie and I wrote to each other—not often, but when I'd see the envelope with her familiar handwriting my heart would leap. Her letters were filled with news of her hospital work and the Black Tank, which now seemed part of us both. Most importantly, she wrote about her dream of becoming a doctor so that she could be a medical missionary.

Billie, however, was strangely divided about her ambition. In one letter she wrote, "for reasons I just cannot understand I have to continue my nursing work." Underlying all of her thoughts was a tremendous sense of limited time. When I would urge her to make definite plans for continuing medical school, she would say she felt she should be "doing, rather than just learning."

I knew Billie was not afraid of challenges. She thrived on them, and her vision of helping a world in need was clear. She also had the gifts and graces to make her mark professionally. But she was obsessed with time. "I just don't have the time to go back to school," she would write, "I need to do more *now*."

She took an alternative course by going to Macon, where she had graduated from nursing school and worked in the cancer clinic of a large hospital there. She said she felt fulfilled in the clinic, but again a strange drive sent her back to her roots, the Valley.

"I need to reflect," she wrote. Her letters became more and more philosophical. "I know my life has meaning and purpose, but I want to know what to do in order to make it really *count*."

Later that year she spent several weeks working in a tuberculosis sanitorium in south Georgia. "It's a special program for only a short time," she wrote. But I could sense sheer apprehension between her lines. I knew Billie was deathly afraid of tuberculosis. She felt it was the worst of diseases. She described how it literally incapacitated some of her patients "to where they use all their strength to gasp for the next breath. I'm grateful for the experience, Ed," she wrote, "and feel I have learned a great deal, but I'll be glad to get back home to Daddy's farm and be with my family who love and care so much."

As always, she ended her letters by expressing how much she looked forward to our talking face to face. "And don't forget, Ed," she never failed to add, "you owe me a steak dinner."

I wasn't about to forget.

8

The Kiss at Taylor's Mill Creek

I arrived in Fort Valley late at night. *Home.* I could sense the fragrance of magnolia blossoms, and more than anything I wanted to phone Billie. However, I realized it was too late; I didn't want to arouse her family. I would call her first thing in the morning. It had been over a year since I had held her so closely that beautiful night on the hillside overlooking the pond. And now that the moment of meeting Billie again was so close, I realized even more how much I wanted to see her.

The night passed slowly, and during much of it I lay sleepless thinking about Billie, my first year away at college and what the coming summer of 1955 promised.

Everything looked promising. Though most of the Valley people were University of Georgia and Georgia Tech fans, they all seemed to believe I had made the wisest decision to play at the "best basketball school in America" under the living legend, The Baron, Adolph Rupp.

The Valley *Tribune* had reported some of our freshman game highlights throughout the year and also headlined my election to team captain. And when the UK varsity team came to Atlanta to play Georgia Tech, Coach Rupp asked me to join them, he said chuckling, "to show off the Georgia boy that got away." I felt very humble being interviewed by the Atlanta sports writer, Furman Bisher, whose column I knew would be read by most Valleyans.

This summer was also special because I would be working right in Fort Valley. I had been given a summer job at the Blue Bird bus company, the town's largest industry. It had been founded in 1927 by Mr. A. L. Luce, Sr., the kindly man who advised me on becoming a minister.

His firm's general manager was George Matthews who, in 1947, had been an All-American football player at Georgia Tech. He was a bachelor and though busy traveling, we'd often visit whenever possible. I guess there is an affinity between athletes. It had been during one of these visits that George invited me to work in the firm's customer relations department my first summer at home. I jumped at the chance. The job included living quarters in his modest home which I appreciated. George had earned his spurs under the famous Georgia coach Bobby Dodd, and as I was attempting to earn mine under another legend, we enjoyed talking about the pressures and dreams all athletes share. Soon George became my confidant and advisor.

My main job would be to care for the customers who came to pick up their buses. I would coordinate all facets of delivery, making sure that the vehicles were serviced and ready. Some customers would be met at the airport and hosted during their stay—this could sometimes mean several days of taking them to local restaurants for steak dinners.

But one of the best parts of my working agreement was full use of a company car. For the first time in my life I had "wheels."

Daybreak finally came, and it was all I could do to hold off calling Billie until mid-morning. I realized that she might have had to work the night shift, I was right. My phone call awakened her. In her sleepy but pleasant way she invited me to lunch with the family. Then, with a laugh, she added, "Why don't you get here close to 1:00 p.m., and by that time most everyone will be on their way back to work."

My heart jumped. Then Billie added, as she had done that very first evening, "Be careful of that last curve on the road."

I immediately headed to the bus company and, after arranging my work schedule to begin the next day, I rushed out to the garage and picked up a 1953 Ford 2-door, sales department auto which was not being used at the present. I wheeled it out of the garage and down to the filling station.

As I waited to fill the gas tank I noted it was 12:30 p.m., so I decided to make it a slow trip to Billie's house. In no way did I want to get there early. I remembered only too well the last time.

I drove up the lane to her farm house; she was standing in the screened door waiting for me. My heart thumping, I got out of the car as she dashed down the walk to meet me. My tongue was thick, and I couldn't get the right words out.

That afternoon we walked to a lone tree overlooking a meadow and sat down together. "This is one of my favorite places on the farm," she said, looking around at the lush grass and distant orchards.

She sat with her hands folded across her knees, a sparkle in her warm dark eyes, wetting her lips slightly with her tongue as she spoke. I could sense how much she loved to taste the outdoors.

"Maybe it's because I have to work inside a hospital, but I love to feel the breeze on my face . . . and, Ed, just listen to that brook . . . it's gurgling, as if it were talking to itself," she said smiling.

I tried to say something appropriate but could only pick at a blade of grass and watch her talk, knowing that even though the outdoors was her special love, she knew in her heart that her work would be completed indoors, helping the sick and infirm.

June found us both busy at our respective jobs. As Billie had just returned from her project in the tuberculosis sanitarium, she was working all hours. Whenever the hospital administrative staff needed her she responded, probably because she was the most willing nurse on call. Often our plans to spend an evening together would be canceled because of a double shift or call-in. When she worked at night I would usually get to the hospital about 9:30 p.m.

and wait for her in the staff lounge. She would emerge at 11 looking
drawn and weary, but we would still sit in the hospital parking lot
talking until midnight.

As we embraced and kissed, a deeply emotional moment would
often be interrupted by a sharp snapping, popping sound, and we'd
break into laughter. It was Billie's white starched uniform which
crackled weird noises in the middle of an embrace.

"How can you get so serious with someone with such sound
effects?" she'd laugh.

Sometimes during the day she was able to leave the hospital for
an hour, and if I could get away from the plant I would pick her up
for lunch. I would suggest a restaurant, but she always wanted to
drive to her own home where her mother, Thelma, had a country
meal ready with three meats, vegetables and all the trimmings.
Thelma would invariably apologize that there really wasn't enough
on the table to eat, but no matter how many people were ravenously
consuming it, there was always plenty of food left over.

On most of these occasions when I arrived at the hospital lot at
noon, I would find Billie sitting in her Black Tank, engine running.
Off she would go waving for me to follow. She was an excellent
driver but an extremely fast one. My '53 Ford was quick at the start
but on the straight country road she'd leave me far behind.

There were about six miles of narrow paved roads that wound
through the lovely countryside to the Ray farm. The first mile,
through the Basset farm, was relatively flat; then came a curve to
the right with a sharp curve down into the Taylor's Mill Creek area.
After rattling across the wooden bridge, we'd climb a sharp hill,
and then after a series of gently rolling curves we'd reach a straight
stretch for a mile until the notorious curve Billie always warned me
about would come into view.

One hot July day I attempted to beat her to the farm. When I
pulled into the hospital area, I just beeped my horn and took off,
rear wheels spinning. I hit the highway first and when I swung on
to the country road I could see her far behind me in my rear-view
mirror. Since my Ford could make the hills better than her heavier
Mercury, I kept my lead past the Bassett Farm, across the creek and
up the hills. But once we were on the flatlands, I could see her
coming up fast. Her windows would be down and her long, dark

brown hair flowed back from her face. As she closed in on me, I could see her shouting encouragement to go faster. I glanced at my speedometer to see 80 m.p.h.—my heart froze. Suddenly she was passing me, her car radio blaring out the latest Elvis Presley song, a white-clad arm waved for me to follow.

Then came the notorious curve. I would never take it faster than 45 m.p.h., which seemed life-threatening even so. But Billie had the skill of a race-track driver and swinging to the left side of the road, she careened around it at about 70 m.p.h.

By the time I pulled up to the side of her house she was standing outside her car motioning for me to hurry as she finger-combed her windblown hair.

Normally, I would have been aghast at Billie's recklessness, but somehow I sensed for her it was a freeing experience. It wasn't the speed or even the race but the feeling of wind in her face and those glorious scents of freshly-cut fields and the flowers lining the roadside. Nature exhilarated Billie, and in the dark days to come she would find solace in it.

That day, as we usually did, we drove back to town very slowly, waving to each other. I followed her, and as we approached Taylor's Mill Bridge I noticed her looking at me through her rearview mirror, and I mouthed the words, "I LOVE YOU."

She almost turned her head to look back at me but instead pulled over to the side near the creek and stopped. Her door flew open and she ran down a small hill to a shady glade near the water.

I pulled up behind her car, stopped and followed her. As I approached, her back was to me and she was wiping her eyes. Standing behind her, I put both arms around her and drew her close. We stood for a long and tranquil moment saying nothing as we watched the quietly flowing stream. I turned her around and looked into her eyes. They were red and swollen. *Tears of puzzlement or joy?* I wondered.

Billie put her soft, tanned arms around my neck and asked huskily, "What did you say to me?"

"When?" I acted naive.

"You know when," she responded, "a few minutes ago on the hill. I was watching you in the mirror."

I looked down into her deep brown eyes, at her delicate nose and high cheekbones—all the things that I knew would make me say it again and again.

"I love you, Billie," I said, my throat tight. "I love you!" I pulled her close and leaned my head down to kiss her, but she lifted her right hand to my lips.

I drew my head back, puzzled, still holding her tight.

A small tear was gliding down her right cheek. "Oh Ed," she sighed, "I hope you really mean that . . . because I love you very much."

Her hand fell from between our lips, and she reached up to meet me halfway. I held her for a long time that day as she cried in my arms. I never felt so close to anyone before in my life. It was eerie and a premonition of the beginning of oneness between us. From that moment on our future together was sealed. Little did I realize how important that moment would become in the impending shadows of our darkening future.

9

The Small Cloud

There is something spectacular about daybreak. The faint streams of first light break through the depth of the darkness and, as you watch the eastern horizon, there is an overwhelming bursting and resting rhythm of light and beauty.

Mornings have always had a strange fascination for me. Some people love the night, others the afternoon, but the early hours of first light have always been my favorite. The change is so rapid—suddenly the light seems to settle just before the clouds of nature and the invasion of humanity affect it adversely.

Billie's and my relationship, though simmering just below the horizon in a strange holding pattern for well over a year, seemed to burst forth in a radiance of color in our beautiful moments of togetherness. If our lifestyles had allowed us to be together more, our relationship might have blossomed earlier, but I doubt it. There was something about our brief meetings during the previous year which allowed positive sharing to take place. Personal dreams had been thrown into the testing pond of the other person's evaluation. For a relationship to be both trusting and depth-searching, each person needs time to respond to the warmth and sensitivities of the other.

After the encounter at Taylor's Mill Creek where our feelings had first been articulated and consummated by an embrace, our beings began to meld. We seldom went to parties or movies, and we found ourselves becoming more and more reclusive. Our moments on the phone each day and our few days off on weekends were spent together in almost total isolation. We were drawn to places surrounded with the beauty of nature that Billie once felt to be her very own and was now willing to share with me. It was part of her opening process, as if she were saying, "These places are where I am more me than anywhere else; this is where I want you to know the person beyond the white uniform."

I learned that the gregarious, compassionate and proficient human being that I had first begun to know in a hospital room was also a very insecure and lonely person. Yet, she never saw loneliness as an enemy. She referred to it as a "true gift of God." When I asked what she meant, she answered that loneliness had forced her to look cautiously at life's options and to select her vocation. "You see, nursing forced me to be with people," she explained. "And having to be with many people enabled me to move from my self-imposed insulation to a world of relatedness." Because of this, she added, she now looked without fear upon her moments alone, and saw them as her most creative periods.

As I watched her work with people of all ages, shapes and colors, I saw a person who was self-assured and totally confident. Yet inside she was insecure. It was not that she was afraid of people, she was simply afraid of herself. When she confided her self-defined high expectations for worthiness, I was overwhelmed. Her insecurity was the very area of her vulnerability that allowed me to peek into the real Billie. That glimpse helped me see a childlike quality of gentleness, and I came to realize that this was what she needed most within a relationship. She boosted my ego at times by whispering in my ear about the "gentle strength" that she felt from me.

Her very being was like a fragile flower yet uncut. A beauty so overpowering that you want to make sure you hold and behold it, yet bring no harm to its life or loveliness. At times I almost held my breath to make sure I did not impose an undue pressure or unwanted presence. I sought to create conditions of freedom where she could be herself and know she was accepted, no matter what. That was really not difficult because of her magnificent nature of receiving. I think her graciousness was one of the first attributes that caught me slightly off-guard and yet enabled me to fall more deeply in love with her.

So often giving and gracious people are motivated by the need of control. Much of that type of giving was a part of the southern hospitality style in which I had been reared. Billie had been a product of that school also. But though she had accepted the positive side of southern life, she had not bought into it totally. She was one of those rare beauties who, while receiving a compliment for some graciousness given, could look you directly in the eye and demurely, yet confidently, say, "Thank you." She never ducked her head in false modesty or batted her lovely eyes saying, "Oh pshaw, it wasn't anything." She would give a part of herself to you, and if you received it graciously, she was more than willing to receive from you whatever you would offer.

Her warmth and unassuming confidence in her capabilities was contagious. I saw this often as we went in and out of the homes of the poorest on the nearby farms. The houses sometimes leaned for lack of sturdy structure, and no indoor plumbing contributed to poor hygiene. Still Billie was at home within their homes, and they sensed her sincerity and concern. After she gave shots, or washed and wrapped wounds or delivered babies, she responded to their gratitude by saying, "You're welcome. I wish I could do more, but I will do everything I can."

How often did I see her reach within her pocket and share a financial gift with a mother or father and give strict instructions of where to go to buy what they needed for their child or themselves. Before they could refuse she would simply hug them and say, "God bless you and yours!"

Why was she so sensitive to others? "I spent a lot of time alone as a child," she once told me. Billie grew up on a farm with a caring family, but she spent hours alone walking the fields, sitting under the tree by the pond and reflecting of what she wanted to be when she grew up. "I want to do something with my life to help others," she reflected one day, tears welling up in her eyes. "I want to do something that will count for God. I don't want to waste what God has given me to share."

Those hours alone in a room or by a pond under a tree had allowed her the freedom to affirm who she was. She understood what it was to love yourself positively and affirm your future faithfully.

Billie was a high giver, but her obsession to give came from her capacity to receive from special people around her. That is why she had such a passionate love affair with her family, the farm and select persons within her medical world. Her receiving world was a small body of persons and when she opened the world to me, I was both honored and rewarded.

I learned from Billie that relationships are not pragmatically based on roles of equal give and take. Instead, I found that no matter how inadequate my gift of self, she received and cherished it. I discovered the subtle ways that she could give to me. The times of silence that we spent reading different books together and I would look up to see her smiling at me. The times that her hand was on the back of my shoulder with her fingers moving delicately across the nape of my neck. The telephone call that would come saying our plans would have to change because of an emergency at the hospital, and yet she would close with, "And you know, my darling, I would so much prefer to be with you, but I must do this." No need to ask for my understanding for she already knew she had it as I had received her compliment.

It was like a beautiful daybreak for me. How many times had I seen the sun rise and been so overwhelmed with its majestic beauty that all I could say was "Thank you God for allowing me to see this." But as beautiful as they were, they were made more beautiful by sharing the experience with Billie.

In late June 1955, I had arrived at the hospital around 10 p.m. to wait for her to get off work. Billie told me that she would have to work on into the next shift, so I suggested we have an early breakfast and take in the sunrise. It was a little after 4 a.m. when she called and said she could leave work around 4:30. I quickly showered and dressed in the eerie darkness before twilight. We decided to skip breakfast and drive rapidly to Billie's favorite spot by the pond and watch the spectacular show of daybreak.

The morning air was still and crisp. We placed the blanket and pillows to the west so we could see the first faint rays of twilight. We did not have to wait long. It worked its wonder across the highest sky, and the rim of the sun soon began to peek over the horizon. We lay side by side holding hands, saying nothing but greeting the splendor with deep sighs of delight. "Oh, what a beautiful morning," I finally said. Billie replied, "Please don't sing it." We laughed together.

Finally, I said, "I won't sing if you promise to share what your feelings are right now. I want to know if it is what I'm feeling." She paused and in a demure quietness she said, "The beauty of today is the beauty I feel when I'm with you. I love you so very much Ed Beck—so very much."

That morning there was no cloud anywhere in the sky. I wish there had been one, even a little one to symbolically alert me. Less than two weeks later Billie said, "Tomorrow I'm going to have surgery—will you come to see me?"

10

The Beginning of Fear

It was a July night and the hot, summer sultriness of middle Georgia continued. I wasn't sure whether it was the relentless heat and humidity that had taken my energy or the realization that early the next morning Billie was to have minor surgery. She had told me just before I left her home, and now I was driving the six miles back to the Valley. My car windows were wide open, and as the hot air passed around me I couldn't seem to clear my head. I thought I could read Billie very well, and though she said that the surgery would be minor, I sensed her concern about the long-range implication.

Being terrified of tuberculosis almost to an obsession, Billie had an X-ray taken the night before, and the doctor had discovered some small masses just above her right lung. The good news was that her lungs were clear, but the bad news was that the masses were less than two weeks old by comparison with her previous X-rays. Whatever it was was growing rapidly. Dr. Marshall was scheduled for surgery in the morning and, since Billie was also scheduled to work beginning at 7 a.m., he would take the mass out for diagnosis and biopsy at that time. He could do the surgery with a local anesthetic, the procedure taking less than 20 minutes, and she would be back on the floor immediately. The process sounded simple enough as she explained it, but her eyes communicated concern though her smiling lips camouflaged the truth.

As I turned onto the highway and drove back into town, I looked to the right toward the hospital where Billie would be within seven hours. Since she was unsure of the exact time of her surgery, I had told her I would be there around 9 a.m. As the hospital vanished from view, I again felt that strange love/hate sensation concerning all places like it.

I drove to our Methodist Church and parked at the side entrance. No one was on the street, and all the houses were dark. I walked up those four steps leading to the side door and pressed my hand to the knob. I knew it would be open. The police would be making their rounds by the church as they always did near midnight, but I didn't worry because they had seen my car parked outside often. They knew why I stopped here almost nightly and just waved with recognition.

I made my way to that special place on the left side of the altar where I always knelt to commune and pray. I couldn't remember why I had started kneeling there rather than the other side or in the middle. I stayed there a long time with my head in my hands—I did not say much, I just listened for a clear word from God. If it came, I was too confused to pick it up.

Maybe I was making too much of this little episode. Maybe Billie was right, that it really wasn't anything to worry about. But I knew she was worried, and that concerned me. Then again, I reasoned, nurses saw so much and maybe they always thought the worst rather than the best. I prayed selfishly that all would be taken care of—that in the morning when Dr. Smoak Marshall cut into Billie's upper chest he wouldn't even find anything but rich, red, healthy tissue. There would be no small mass, no nodes of any kind, no irregularities. I was so emphatic in my prayer that I was confident God would have to abide by my request. After all it wasn't for me, but for Billie, one of God's angels of mercy. I listened some more for that clear resounding answer from God, but all I could hear was the creaking and moaning of the old church building settling in the night. I had heard those noises so often before during evenings like this, but now I found myself searching them for some sign. I pulled at every straw; even tried to create signs rather than just wait for them.

It was late and I had planned to get to the factory early to get some details worked out so I could drive out to the hospital at the agreed 9 a.m. time. As I rose from the altar, I heard a tree branch scraping on the stained-glass windows across the sanctuary. I had heard that same branch before, but I was so sensitive to any extra noise that I made my way across in front of the pews to the three magnificent windows. One of those windows was of Jesus in a white robe and deep red cloak holding a lamb in his arms. I don't know why I had always liked that picture better than the others. It was not great art, and I understood my Lord as a fiery rather than a docile shepherd figure. Still, the striking colors within the frame drew my attention. Tonight was no different as the street light from the outside filtered through. I turned to walk away, and then it struck me that the lamb was white with dark eyes and, of course, Billie's uniform was . . . I couldn't get over the odd feeling. I felt as if I had created this charade. I mean, to compare Billie to a lamb in a stained glass window was a little much. *A "sign" is one thing, but a fabricated symbol is something else,* I argued with myself. I walked out of the sanctuary rather hurriedly, but I did look back one last time at the little lamb in the arms of her Lord and thought, *What is a sign anyhow? Who knows? I sure don't.* Within 10 minutes I was home and fast asleep.

The alarm rang extra early and I was up quickly. George, my roommate, was out on one of his many trips so I didn't have to worry about fighting for bathroom privileges. I knew that Billie would already be at work, and I started to call her. Then I realized she couldn't tell me a thing, so I didn't call. I jumped into the car and was walking into the plant within five minutes. That was one good thing about living in a small town. You didn't have to worry about traffic jams and long tie-ups at lights.

I was the first one in the office, though the plant was already running full speed. They started earlier than the office staff because the summer was the big push for maximum production. They always tried to build 15 buses a day, but when Bozeman, the foreman of the line, really got them hopping they could push out as many as 19. The assembly line was about 100 yards long. At the front stood eight of the largest metal cutting and shaping presses in the South. One stood higher than 40 feet and was operated by four men. Huge rolled sheets of steel were fed into the presses, and with one gigantic swoosh of power they would cut out a windshield frame or an entire side panel of the bus. Everywhere you looked you saw large stacks of metal shaped and ready to be put together.

The assembly of the buses began slowly enough with only six men welding together the floor of the bus body. When they had finished a floor it was placed upon a small rail car and immediately pulled to the next station. There a larger crew of men both bolted and welded the one-piece skeleton beam, a trade mark of Blue Bird. Then the exterior sides and roof were put on along with the cut out windshield. From there the crew size increased from station to station as the insulation, interior panels, interior roofing, electrical components and seats were installed. With rivet guns going over a mile a minute, men shouting and screaming instructions and country-western music blaring, the line was an amazing sight.

I did not envy those men on the assembly line. On one of those special hot July afternoons the temperature inside these bus bodies could be well over 100 degrees! But the heat was not nearly as bad as the noise. When I took the customers on a tour to let them see how their bus had been built, there was no way that even my booming voice could be heard in that part of the plant area. So I had worked out a system of explaining the assembly procedure before we left the customer area and then would simply point to the different production steps. I could always speak loudly enough to be heard in the area where the buses were painted and the finishing touches were checked out. That's what most of the customers wanted to see anyhow—that finished product.

I checked the day's schedule—no one expected until late morning. I breathed a sigh of relief but realized that someone could drop in unexpectedly. It happened all the time. Just last week two men had come in from Calgary, Canada, and one of their buses had not even begun the finish line. They had been our special guests for nearly 10 days. This morning I prayed no one would come. It didn't work. At 8:00 a group of people arrived from Florida. Thank God their buses were ready which meant only a tour of less than a

half-hour. They could pick up their buses at the front gate by 9 a.m.
and be on their way. It worked out exactly, but as they drove away,
another group from south Georgia arrived. I checked on their buses,
which wouldn't be ready until about 11:00. My heart sank. That
would be two hours, and I would miss my appointment with Billie.
I asked if they had had breakfast. I was in luck—"only coffee" was
the reply. I checked out of the plant with my south Georgia
threesome and whisked them down to Poole's Cafe. I told them to
order whatever they liked and to eat leisurely. I said I would be back
before they were finished. I then told Mrs. Poole I'd be back to sign
the check and pick them up, but I whispered to her not to hurry with
their orders. She nodded knowingly, and off I went to the hospital.
It was 9:30 before I got there, 30 minutes late.

The lobby was crowded and the nurse's station empty, so I knew
that everyone was busy. As I walked down the hall searching for
that familiar presence, I heard my name being called from the
opposite direction. Billie came walking toward me. She was carrying some charts and materials, "We cannot talk long," she announced. They were too busy. Her second comment, "It's so good
to see you," made me feel very positive. I asked her how she was
feeling, and without the slightest hesitation she responded, "Fine."
She pointed to the small bandage slightly to the left of her collar-
bone. That confused me; I had understood that it would be on the
right side, but it seemed too trivial to mention. I could have heard
anything incorrectly. Why, I had even *seen* Billie as a little lamb
with a white coat. She said she would be off duty at 3 p.m., so I said
I would call around 5:00 to clarify our evening plans. She smiled
that vivacious smile and turned with those noisy nursing shoes and
that rustling starched uniform. I smiled as I remembered how I used
to hear the noise of her uniform moving in my direction when I had
been a patient here more than a year before. As she walked away,
I admired her sheer physical beauty and grace. No wonder I loved
to hold her close to me. I left smiling because I knew later that night
I would have that pleasure once again.

I arrived at the farmhouse close to supper time. One of the Rays
joked about my becoming a permanent fixture at the house. Billie
and I looked at each other and smiled.

We had discussed permanence as a part of our relationship on several occasions, but we always arrived at the same point. Billie's dream was to do more work toward her medical degree. My dream was to complete my university work in Lexington and then work for three or four years to train for the ministry or perhaps teaching. So, though we played with the idea of marriage, it was always in the context of the time beyond my college graduation and at least my enrollment in seminary. If all the pieces of the puzzle could be worked out, we felt that both of us could be enrolled in graduate studies at a place like Emory University in Atlanta. With that scenario somewhat loosely held together by our dreams and desires, we slowly came to feel quite comfortable. It also freed us to discuss all aspects of our relationship openly and honestly. Our intentions and plans were all on the table. All we had to do was make the pieces fit together.

We left the supper table early that evening. It was usually a ritual to sit and talk with the family, then ease away to the front-porch swing or to one of our favorite little places on the farm where we could watch the day fall into the west. Tonight, however, Billie was somewhat on edge, and I knew that I needed to break the routine. The hospital had called her to work that night, but she had refused because of our plans. That was unusual. I had come to realize how truly important her work was to her. As we walked toward the front porch, I suggested that she get her little black bag, and we'd make some calls on her favorite patients in the area. She turned and almost leaped up into my arms with a bear hug and, for the first time, the sparkle came back into her eyes.

"Be just a moment," and into her room she vanished. I walked out to my car and started the engine as I waited for her. A minute later she bounced down the front steps and climbed into the car. "Don't you want me to drive?" she laughed.

I said, "No, the last time we went on a call like this together, you scared the hell out of me!"

"Good thing," she replied. "You needed to get some of that meanness out of you. I've noticed you have been a lot better person since."

She directed me down some narrow dirt roads with so many turns that I was completely lost. I said something about country gals knowing all the back roads and the good parking spots. She laughed with some reply about, "You'll never really know, will you? But you'd like to!"

She had told me often about visiting the elderly and infirm, and of course I had been with her when she had delivered a baby. But that night it was just me taking the "doctor" around on her calls. We kidded each other that this was how it would be 40 years from now when we were both old and crotchety. I would be the driver for the old, beloved doctor making her afternoon and evening rounds. We laughed and continued to joke as I drove, and she became more and more like her old self. Her tension and stress seemed to vanish, for now she was in her element, caring for others and sharing whatever there was of her to share. She loved that role, and I knew that someday she would be the best doctor in the world.

I envisioned us as a mission team. We talked of where that might be. "Africa," Billie said one day. "Why Africa?" I asked. "Why not South America or one of the islands?" "Oh no," said Billie, "It has to be Africa for that is where these people are from," and she pointed to all the rural shacks up and down that red dirt country road. She shared her medical skills with these poor and unfortunate black people of the deep South. She had grown to love and care for them as they reached out to her. I felt her dream and sensed her compassionate hope. All I could say was, "Africa it will be!"

We arrived soon at a lonely run-down shack. They all seemed to look alike to me. I wondered how the tenants survived the cold winters and the hot summers. My Ford was strange to the family sitting on the porch, but when they saw "Ms. Billie," they all got up from their rocking chairs and ran down the steps to greet her. Billie hugged the two women and several of the smaller children. She was about to ask them a question when the mother of the clan asked, "Ms. Billie, is this your man?" It caught Billie off guard, and her face flushed. On other occasions like this Billie introduced me as her boyfriend or just a friend. Being so sensitive to these special people in her life and understanding their culture better than I did, she came over to me, put her arm around my waist and said, "Yes, Ellie Sue, this is my man." Ellie Sue looked at me, turned to Billie and said, "Oh, Ms. Billie, he sure is a big one and fine looking too! But I'm going to pray for you because he is so big!" It was my turn to turn red in the face, and Billie quickly changed the subject by asking about Grandma.

Billie was ushered into the house to see the elderly grandma, and soon I had to come in to meet a fragile little lady. She was already in bed, and I was introduced to her because she wanted to meet "Billie's big man." She told me how wonderful Billie had been to her . . . how she always came to see her and gave her medicine. Billie was not a doctor, but to this little lady Billie knew more than any doctor that she had ever seen. "I love Billie like she was my own," she quavered. With that, tears came to her eyes as Billie leaned over to kiss her goodnight. As we drove to the next stop, she looked at me and said, "Youse *is* my man, ain't you?" And I knew that I was.

It was now late, and we had made four or five calls, all to the elderly. I had wanted to go back to see the baby I had helped birth, but Billie told me that since that was in another direction we would have to go there another time. We drove back leisurely toward her house. Billie wanted to stop and find a tree-ripened peach. Most of the peaches had been picked, but there were still some late Elbertas. She had heard a dissertation on the wonder of a tree-ripened Elberta peach but could never seem to find them in the stores. I told Billie it was late. We couldn't see anything in the orchard and would probably get bitten by a snake. But no argument could dissuade her from her now focused treat.

We drove into one of her father's orchards and began to walk from tree to tree looking for that one lone peach that no picker or bird had yet found. It wasn't very long before she had discovered three or four and tested each one. Then I watched her go over to a tree and ever so gently reach up to where a single peach was hanging. At the slightest touch of her hand the peach fell, as if commanded, into her palm. Billie informed me that when a peach was tree-ripened and ready, the slightest nudge of its bottom disconnected it from the branch. I watched her simply peel that peach with her fingernails in three easy moves.

"Take a bite," she commanded. I did and then I heard a speech on, "Isn't that the greatest piece of fruit you have ever tasted?"

"Sure," I said to avoid argument.

There are times when it is great just to be alive, healthy and open to that which is going on around you. That night was one of those times. Billie took off her shoes and ran among the trees. She urged me to do the same, but I kept my shoes on. The stars were sparkling and though there was no moon, there seemed to be a crystal clearness within the orchard. We were hot and sweaty when we finally stopped. Billie found a few more peaches, but none could match the taste of that first one. Since I had driven my car, there was no blanket in the trunk, so we just sat on the fenders, held hands and talked.

She did not want to talk about the surgery, but I told her I needed to know the results. She simply said, "There are no results yet. Smoak said everything looked normal to him, but he took out two more nodes and sent them to Augusta for examination. There probably won't be a report back for a week or 10 days. Other than that, I'm fine," she added. She thanked me for accompanying her to see her patients and for the beautiful night. Then we laughed again about me being "such a big 'un."

We got into the car, but before I started the engine I reached over and our bodies slid together. We held each other a long time without saying a word, just feeling each other's hearts beating and listening to the sounds of the night. I felt her tremble within my arms and realized that her movements were muffled efforts to hold back tears. I just held her as she cried. I knew better than to ask what was wrong or what was right. I wanted to believe she was crying tears of joy and love for the realization that there would be so many more times just like this one.

But I was afraid, and for the first time in our entire relationship I realized that I now sensed an icy sheet of fear. I so desperately wanted not to feel it . . . but I did. Fear that something physical within Billie was not right. Something so terrible that not even our love could answer it. Something so devastating that it might be able to come between our wonderful intimacy and shatter our dreams. She continued to cry and, for the first time in my adult life, I began to cry. We kissed, we cried, kissed and cried, and finally settled into each other's arms and fell asleep in the car. But not even sleep took away that deep, awful fear within me.

11

Three to Five Years

Billie looked up at me as the shadows from the setting sun cut dark slashes across her pained face. "Three to five years, Ed." She was saying it, but it was not registering.

I knew it would register very soon, that I would be overwhelmed by the import of her words. But that would come later. Now I was in emotional shock, listening intently, but not really hearing. Maybe it was a dream. Maybe I would awaken. Maybe if I left right now and came back tomorrow the message would change.

Billie had phoned me late that afternoon. I knew she had seen Smoak Marshall, but in the quick call all she said was: "Hi! What are you doing tonight? How about meeting me at the tree?"

I remembered the tree well. It was one of her favorite spots on the farm where we had first stood looking across the meadow, talking.

"Sure, what time?"

"About 7 o'clock, if that's all right."

"Great. I'll try to be there right at seven. I have these people in from Iowa, but I'll be there just as soon as I can."

"Good. I've got to go. See you soon. I love you. Bye," and the receiver clicked.

I did not return the "I love you" for I didn't want others in the office to hear my business. I went on with my work eagerly looking forward to the evening, not knowing that it would bring the shock of my life.

Now, sitting under the tree with the orange sun sinking in the west, I was reeling under the blow.

"Three to five years is the time that I have left to live," repeated Billie softly. I stared sharply at her, her eyes were dry, yet serious.

"Who says such a thing?" I gasped. "How do they know?"

"Dr. Marshall," she said.

"Smoak? You've got to be kidding! He wouldn't say a thing like that!" I exclaimed.

Who in the world could be that accurate anyhow? I tried to tell myself. A test from one small mass of flesh? Maybe there was a mix-up in the laboratory. One heard about medical mistakes all the time: the mother taking home the wrong baby, the appendix removed from the wrong person. Wouldn't it be easy for a small cancerous cyst to be misplaced and misidentified? After all, there would be no name on it, just a bunch of numbers.

Smoak was not my doctor, but I knew the high esteem Billie held for him. He was competent and good. Although, according to some in the Valley, he did not have the best bedside manner, when it came to medical skills he was one of the best around.

I also knew he would not hold back the truth from a patient. He would get the facts, read all the data and then tell it exactly as he saw it.

Yet, weren't most cancers curable? Wasn't early detection the key to healing? How much earlier could it have been found? Even Dr. Marshall had said that the discovery was made in the earliest stages.

"Three to five," I said slowly, sensing a dark cloud swallowing both of us. For a moment I could only stare at the ground. Then, looking up at her, I choked, "What . . . what do you think you'll do?"

For the first time she smiled slightly. "The same thing that I've been doing. I'm going to work and go to school and live as normally as I know how. I'm the same person today that I was yesterday and last week. I have something growing inside of me that is not normal. But it's not going to make me any different."

Her last comment made me want to reach out and pull her to me. But I could tell Billie was set on getting everything out on the table. Frankness was her strength. And, of course, her medical background helped. Get the data, study the information and lay out the consequences. Truth is liberating, they say.

"Have you told your folks yet?"

"No, not yet," she said haltingly. "I'm going to wait until later when they are together and tell them. Maybe in the morning. I'm not sure . . . the timing and conditions have to be right. I'll call my sister, Helen, in Macon, and talk to her. Maybe I'll even go up to see her tomorrow. I don't know just yet, but it will all work out. I just know it will. But I don't want to hurt them, and I know they will worry."

I broke in, "They love you, and they need to know soon. Can I help?" I asked.

"No. This is something I need to do alone. Thank you, though, for your offer," she said.

Our conversation shifted to the medical process and what would take place. Having worked in the cancer clinic of the Macon Hospital, she was very familiar with the treatment of Hodgkin's disease. Now she would be returning to that same clinic to take X-ray treatments under her arms and in her inguinal regions. Smoak had discovered some nodes in the area where her legs joined with the trunk of her body. She couldn't feel them yet, but he said that they were there. Then, of course, she had noticed within the last 48 hours the nodes under her arms. That would be the first place the X-ray treatments would do the job, we hoped.

It was now night, though there were some faint streaks of light still fighting for existence in the west. They just did not seem to want to give up. I could have named them Billie, but she still reminded me more of the dawn than the twilight.

We were now lying side by side on the blanket. As the sun disappeared I asked if she needed something to stay warmer.

"Don't treat me as if I'm sick," she snapped. "I'm no different

than I was last week. Don't coddle and pamper me. I will not tolerate
it and I do not like it."

I backed away from the onslaught. I denied that I was treating
her any different, but knew that was false. Already I was treating
her differently. I was with someone who was ill. How could I
overlook that? How could I pretend that everything was all right?
It wasn't. I was confused by my emotions. I was angry at something
that would attack someone I loved; I was helpless because there
was nothing I could do; and I was in love with someone who was
sick and yet wanted me to treat her as if she were well.

Neither of us brought up our relationship that night. We talked
around it, skirted the issue—everything was too close. There would
be a better time after certain thoughts had settled in, when some
information was forthcoming, and maybe hope would break
through. But it was coming and both of us knew it. We would talk
about our love. She would question me as she had never questioned
me before. In the past she had received my statements and gestures
of love without hesitation. After that first day at Taylor's Mill Creek
when she had said, "I hope you mean that, for I love you," there had
never been a questioning stare or flicker of concern that what I had
said affectionately was insincere. But I knew that would change,
because though she wanted to be treated as if she were not different,
she felt she was. She would now filter everything through a certain
system that would doubly question the sincerest expression from
the one closest to her.

That, I knew, was the curse of a terminal illness. It makes the
patient wonder whether the things people do for him or her is out
of pity or personal concern. "Do they just feel sorry for me or do
they sincerely feel for me?" the patient wonders. In some ways this
reaction may be more insidious than the disease itself. We know the
course the disease usually will run, but we never know how it will
alter the personality and mind.

I *did* feel sorry for Billie, but that did not detract in any way from
my love for her. It did not increase my love for her either. We were
two human beings reaching out to each other in deep need. I realized
I couldn't truly understand all that a person feels when she is told
she has a short time to live. But I knew that a part of Billie now
lived within me, and I cherished that part of her, even more than

myself. I selfishly did not want to have that taken from me. I wanted to enhance that part, allow it to grow and nurture it into more than it now was. But I no longer had the luxury of time to allow it to take its course. Time was of the essence.

I was 19 and she was 23, but the reality of youth had passed us both by that evening. There would be no late young adult years together. We would never see or feel the middle years of crisis and family times. We would never know the aging process and feel the body's decline. What we would know was the immediate. If we shared anything of substance and life, it would be now! If we grew any closer together, it would be the result of a cosmic explosion and not an evolving entity. I felt rising panic. Time was passing by. It was already night, and we would never be able to share this night again. How many nights were left? Oh, time is so precious, and I reached over to her and pulled her close to me and held her as if there would be no tomorrow, as if there would only be tonight. In a certain sense, that is how our relationship changed. The today was vastly more important than the tomorrow—for the memories of our yesterdays would be the foundation of our hope and our dreams of the todays.

12

Smoak and Fire

I approached the white frame, two-story house with some fear and trepidation. Less than an hour before I had received an urgent phone call from Dr. Smoak Marshall's nurse that he wanted to see me that afternoon. When I had asked, "What time?" she had just replied, "As soon as possible." So I made some quick adjustments at the bus factory, freeing myself for an hour. However, now as I walked toward the house I was almost shaking. I thought it was crazy to feel this way, for I didn't even know why he wanted to see me, though I felt sure it would be about Billie.

I was heartened by the thought of her. Over the last few days, she had seemed to blossom. She was more like her old self than she had been for quite some time. Though she did not go out of her way to talk about the results of her tests of some two weeks before, she did not refuse to discuss the situation either. Her demeanor was more resolute than anything. She was tough despite her soft femininity. In the last few days her determination to fulfill her vow to herself and to me "to live a perfectly normal life" seemed to be coming to the forefront. We had laughed, joked and even taken a trip to Macon to get one of those wonderful steak dinners I had promised her some 15 months before.

That night as we drove to Macon we discussed our relationship more openly than ever before. There were now no games to play. We both felt the pressure of time. We had talked of marriage, but it had always been in the context of my graduation from the University of Kentucky in 1958, three years away. Billie wanted to go back to school, and we thought the timing would be great to get married in the summer of 1958. Then both of us could attend graduate school together, probably at Emory University in Atlanta. But that night in the car I had the terrible feeling that time was running out. It was near the end of July and I would be returning to the university within six or seven weeks. "Billie," I had blurted, "let's get married right away."

Zooming down a highway was not the best time or place to pose such a question, but I guess I was afraid to see whatever there would be within Billie's eyes. They were the gateway to her deepest self. She was innately shy and usually lowered her eyes slightly in serious conversation. But when she wanted to reveal herself, those eyes would rivet upon you, pouring forth volumes of information without her saying a thing. I also wanted her to be close to me with no opportunity to run away.

Billie was quiet for a moment. Then, drawing a deep breath, she said: "Ed, I . . . I know the report is from three to five years, but . . ." her voice brightened, "but I've heard of many cases where Hodgkin's disease can be arrested and the patient lived longer.

"And besides," she added resolutely, "we've decided on the summer of '58, and that's what we should count on."

Billie talked on about the many other variables, her X-ray treatments which would begin soon and how these would affect her strength and work performance.

"Really," she added, hugging my arm, "if everything works out over the next year or so, well, it will be a wonderful summer for us in 1958."

As the car sped along our conversation dealt with alternatives of what could happen "if." But it all seemed to me like a camouflage, of not really looking squarely at our relationship.

After we pulled into the restaurant's parking lot and stopped, I looked at Billie, wanting now to see her eyes. They were full of fear as she looked down at her hands gripped together in her lap.

I placed my hands on top of hers. They were cold and still. She continued to look down.

"Look at me, Billie," I said softly. "I want you to look at me because I'm going to say something that is very important."

Slowly her hands loosened and her dark brown eyes looked up, not at me, but out the side car window.

"Please, Billie," I pleaded, removing my hands for emphasis.

Slowly she turned to face me. My heart pounded at the sight of her loveliness, her hair laying softly on the side of her slender face, her soft tan complexion seeming to glisten from her high cheek bones. Now her eyes were aglow with anticipation. Or was it anxiety? I wasn't sure, but I knew I had to say what I had to say right then and there, in the back parking lot of that restaurant.

"Billie, I'm not sure when it was . . . the first time that I felt I was in love with you. Maybe it was in the hospital, maybe that night when we won the state championship and you waited for me. Maybe it was that night by the lake. I really do not know. All I know is that in this moment I love you more than life itself. I'm afraid, I'm very afraid that I'm going to lose you, and I'm selfish. I don't want to lose you. I love you, and I want to be with you." I put my hands on her soft warm shoulders. "Billie, I'm asking you to marry me. I know we have planned it way into the future. But I want you to marry me *now*. Soon! Go back to the university with me this fall. Please come with me. I love you."

Her eyes never left mine, seeming to pierce my very being. It was as if they were saying, "I hear your words, but where do they really come from? Do they come from the depths of love or do they come from a pit of pity because of what is happening to me?" Suddenly, she unclasped her hands and cupped my hand with hers.

"I hear what you say, Ed, believe me, I do," she said softly, "and . . . and I thank you. But you have to understand that I now question almost everything that is said to me. I do not doubt your sincerity in the least. But I find myself wondering if what you say is said because you feel sorry for me or because you really love me."

I retorted defensively. "I don't know how else to say it, Billie! I love you, and I want you to marry me. Sure, my feelings have changed about you in the last couple of weeks, but I do not pity or feel sorry for you. I do feel helpless because there doesn't seem to be much that I can do. But all I know is that I want to live with you the rest of our lives!"

Suddenly she reached over and tenderly kissed me. I was expecting an answer as she softly blew into my ear, but she whispered, "Let's go in and eat." I knew better than to press the issue, so I helped her out of the car, and we walked arm in arm together into the restaurant.

The meal was filled with light conversation about our work and some idle gossip. As we sipped our after-dinner coffee, she looked over her cup at me and said, "Darling, try to understand. I'm unsure of exactly what I want. This has been a very difficult time these past couple of weeks. Not just for me, but for my family." She looked down at the tablecloth and continued, "I'm somewhat confused and I need time to sort things out. Believe me, I love you very much. I want someday to be your wife. I've dreamed about it and looked forward to when we can really share our lives together." She looked back up at me, her eyes pleading. "But I'm not sure that now is the right time, Ed. I'm not saying no . . . will you accept that?"

I knew that this was the time to take the pressure off so I smiled and said, "You are heard, love. I hope only one thing—that soon I will hear you say yes." She gave a quick smile, I paid the check and we left hand in hand. All was not right with the world, but all was right between us.

Now, however, that particular conversation was forgotten as I opened the front door of Smoak Marshall's house office. The waiting rooms were packed with people. The window air conditioner was valiantly spitting some cool air, but nothing could overcome the humid, hot day outside and closely packed bodies inside.

I walked up to the receptionist's desk. She was on the phone. The wall clock behind her said 3 p.m. I looked again at the two packed waiting rooms. *It'll be hours before I get out of here,* I worried. *Why did Smoak want to see me now—today? I could have come later in the evening or made an appointment for the next day.* The nurse hung up the phone and, before I could say anything, said, "Ed, follow me. Dr. Marshall wants to see you now." I did not say a word, but walked by the glaring eyes of waiting patients. We walked down the hall, passing another small waiting room where mothers were trying to calm crying and squirming children. She opened the door, told me to sit down and said the doctor would come in as soon as he could. I sat down with the feeling that the wait would be long. As I got up to read one of the diplomas on the wall, the door opened. Dr. Marshall, a heavy-set man with graying hair, entered and we shook hands.

After directing me to sit down, he thanked me for coming at such short notice, explaining that he felt it was very important he talk to me. He leaned back in his chair, but then, as if he felt that was too relaxed for the subject of our conversation, he leaned forward and said, "Ed, Billie and her mother have just been here to see me, and I want to know why you are playing with that girl's heart." His face flushed and his gray eyes tightened as he continued speaking faster and faster. "She is too fragile a person for you to trifle with—she has too many things going on in her life, too many pressures. She is a sick girl, and she is going to get much sicker. She doesn't need someone who is just going to add one more pressure."

I reeled under the onslaught of Smoak's barrage. *What in the world had Billie said to him? What had Billie's mother said? Everyone in town knew that we were dating. What right did he have to question our relationship?* Then I heard him say "fragile" and it brought me to. "Dr. Marshall, I'm not playing with Billie's heart," I said, "not at all." I wanted to go on but he quickly broke in.

"You'd better not be!"

"Listen, Smoak," I said, and I could see he was taken aback by my first name reference, but if there was to be a fight, I wanted it on even footing. "I love that girl very much. I've asked her to marry me."

Smoak broke in again, "That's what I mean. She told me that yesterday at the hospital, and we have just discussed it thoroughly a few minutes ago. You are in college playing basketball. You don't have time to take care of a sick wife. Why, if you got married you couldn't go back to school. Billie could not handle that." He tried to soften his tone. "We will do all we know how to do for Billie, but no matter what, she will get much worse and soon you will be able to see it day by day. She will need all her strength to make a fight of it. And she could not stand your not going to school! She would feel sorry for you and sorry for herself. She is too fragile for that."

"But, Smoak, you don't understand how much I love her," I replied.

He leaned toward me, as if to emphasize his message. "Listen, Ed, if you really love Billie then leave her alone. Stop talking about marriage and living together. It will never happen, even though you and Billie might want it to. Continue to date this summer. Go back to school in a few weeks. Write letters of encouragement. Be a friend, but stop this nonsense about getting married! She can't handle it. It is just one more burden that she should not have to bear."

I sat stunned. Was this Smoak talking or Billie speaking through Smoak? I knew Smoak cared for Billie like a daughter. She idolized his medical expertise. She had even said she wanted to be a doctor like Smoak Marshall. But what was all this? I didn't know whether to argue or to listen, to get angry or apathetic. I loved Billie, but I certainly did not want to burden her. Maybe the best thing I could do would be to take the pressure all the way off. Perhaps I had come down too hard on Billie. Maybe she couldn't say to me, "Get lost for the time being," so she had asked Smoak to say it. He was like a father to her in so many ways. Or, and this was a new thought, a hopeful one: maybe Smoak was just testing me? That is what fathers sometimes do. "Are you good enough for my daughter? Do you have what it takes? Are you willing to fight for her? Fight even me?" Maybe he was just trying to confuse me and see what I was made of. A thousand thoughts crowded my mind. Finally I said, "Smoak, where is Billie now? Is she here?"

"No," he replied. "She and her mother have already left."

"Well, I need to see her," I said.

"Listen, Ed," Smoak urged, "you don't need to see her now or ever again. No one would think any less of you. Just go out that door, go back to work, and in a few weeks go back to school. Play ball and get your education. That's the most important thing that you can do for you and for her. Billie understands completely. She would be the first one to wish you well. You don't need to see her."

"But Smoak, I love Billie and I want to see her," I pleaded.

He stood up, put both hands on my shoulders, almost gently. "By God, Ed, you'd better love that girl. Because believe me, son, it is going to be rougher than you can possibly imagine."

I didn't know whether to hug him or hit him. I just got up, mumbled a few words of thanks for his time and walked out the door. That was also the door I knew would lead to Billie. I knew that I would never go through the other door to which Smoak had pointed me—for any reason except death.

13

A Crisis of Confrontation

I walked out of Marshall's office in a daze. His verbal assault caught me off guard. I expected a medical overview of Billie's condition and how I could be of help. But his recommendation, no, it seemed more like an order, that I not see Billie again or slowly fade from the scene after I returned to school, upset me. Defensive, I fought back, but not very tactfully. Now my pride hurt because I'd lost my cool. One of my strengths in athletics was supposed to be control of a situation when everything seemed to be tumbling in upon the team. I had captained teams because of that supposed quality. Here, in a situation similar to an overtime contest, I fumbled the ball out of bounds instead of looking for the positive opening and moving decisively through it for the score. I berated myself bitterly as I drove back to the factory.

I wanted to call Billie immediately upon my return. But the customer's reception area for which I was responsible was crowded. After setting up a plant tour, I excused myself from the group for a few minutes and called Billie's home, but there was no answer. She was not slated to work that day, but I called the hospital anyway. They had no information of her itinerary. Well, maybe she went shopping with her mother, I thought, or maybe they were having a late lunch. A number of alternatives flitted through my mind. I returned to my plant responsibilities and performed them perfunctorily. I continued to call throughout the rest of the afternoon, but to no avail.

That evening I sat with my roommate, George Matthews, and discussed the events of the afternoon. George did not necessarily support Dr. Marshall's perceptions, but he did share his own feelings.

Leaning his huge frame back in a chair and resting his long legs on a coffee table, he looked up at the ceiling and said, "Well, Ed, though I don't know Billie personally, I sure know who she is and her mighty fine reputation."

He looked at me. "But my main concern is for you, Ed, and your academic as well as your athletic future. Believe me, I know what it takes in time, effort and concentration to succeed in both fields. And I know what it would take to play at UK under that coach of theirs."

I listened carefully, remembering the records he had set as an All-American football player at Georgia Tech in the mid-1940s. "What about Rupp's reactions to all this?" he asked. "How would he feel if you got married before you graduated?"

I stared at the floor. There were married men on our team, but I also knew Rupp didn't favor the idea. He thought marriage was too much of a diversion for a young man who already had enough to handle just making grades and playing ball. I had to admit that this fiery coach's demands along with academics and marriage might just be one straw too many.

George and I talked for two hours, and his message was the same. He wasn't against my getting married but wondered if it was really the *best* thing. "Marriage is tough enough when everything's going all right," he said, "but this marriage would begin with a strike or two against it. Billie already has only five years on the outside.

"And *you*," he said, swinging his big body toward me, "you would have at least six years of higher education facing you. Moreover, and don't tell me this isn't true, Ed, basketball has been your life for the last 10 years, and now you have the opportunity to prove your ability in it at one of the major universities in the country."

He leaned forward and put both hands on his massive knees. "If you get married, Ed, and something happens down the line where you have to give up those two things, are you willing to do it?"

I sat staring at him. The obvious truth of his declaration had hit me in the solar plexus.

George graciously didn't pursue the subject any longer, and I went to the phone and tried to reach Billie again. Her father answered. "Billie and her mother have gone to Macon for the evening, Ed," he said. "I guess they wanted to get some shopping out of the way. Her first X-ray treatment is scheduled early tomorrow morning."

I held the phone, dumbfounded. Billie hadn't said anything about the treatments starting tomorrow, and Dr. Marshall hadn't mentioned it either.

Was I being gently moved out of the picture already? Maybe it had all been decided by Billie, her mother and Smoak?

I muttered a few words of conversation to Billie's father, hung up the phone and sank into the chair. Maybe there was really something wrong with me. Was I so blind and insensitive to Billie that I didn't hear what she had been telling me? Maybe I wasn't willing to truly listen but heard only what I wanted to hear.

I glanced at George who was immersed in a sports magazine. "I'm going out for a while," I said. "Take care," he said.

"I will," I sighed as I climbed into my car. I headed out into the country; perhaps a long drive would clear my head. I didn't drive toward Billie's but headed west instead along a highway banked by miles of peach orchards. I remembered Billie's and my fun together back on that early April day when the peach trees had spread their pink blanket of blossoms across the countryside. Now, near the end of July, even the late peaches had gone.

The night was clear, and the air had cooled from the day's heat. As I drove on, attempting to sort out all the conversations of the day, my major regret was that I had not allowed Smoak to say all that he apparently had wanted to say. I wish I had just listened attentively and thanked him. I had not handled that situation well, but if I had only been warned . . . and then, where was Billie in all this? Did Smoak speak for her? I could not believe it, but I had to admit it was possible.

It was after 10 p.m. when I headed back to the Valley. I had no answers, but at least my head had cleared somewhat. I now had a perspective and an approach. I would see Billie the next evening and try to find out where she stood. All I really knew was how much I loved her and how I wanted to spend as much time with her as possible.

Entering town, I pulled up in front of my church about 11 o'clock. I felt I had to spend some quiet time with my favorite listener. Instead of kneeling at the altar, I sat in the front pew and attempted to meditate and listen. My eyes were soon drawn to the window with Christ holding the little white lamb in his arms. My only consolation was my belief that no matter what happened to my relationship with Billie, her relationship with Jesus Christ would continue unabated. There were a great many things taking place in her life, but from our conversations I knew that the most important thing was the solidification of her faith in God who not only loved her, but who would suffer with her in love.

We had discussed it a couple of nights before, and I remembered her words as clearly as if she were repeating them now: "Do you think that God afflicts people with illness and disease, Ed?" she asked. "I hear people say sometimes it is God's will. Do you think it is God's will that I have Hodgkin's?"

I was caught short by her question. "Well, Billie," I said lamely, "I've heard these questions and am still attempting to sort them out myself." She laughed at my evasive statement and concluded that I would make a "good lawyer."

"Billie, I do not believe that God inflicts any of his children with disease or suffering," I continued, trying to make up for my ambivalence. "My understanding of the Bible is that God only wants the very best for all of us. I cannot explain why certain disasters happen, either large or personal, but I so believe that God wants only the very best for you."

Suddenly, I found myself strangely empowered with words that seemed to come from deep within me. "However," I continued, "we live in a world of freedom of choice and we, as human beings, do not always make the best choices. Apparently some of our ancestors did the same and so we, as a part of the human community, must reap some of their mistakes. Some of what we reap is not very good, but I certainly do not believe that God creates it or sends it. I believe that it breaks God's heart for you or me or anyone else to suffer, darling."

I took her and held her close to me, "I do not know why you have this disease—why you do and I don't—I only know that the Christ of love, your Savior and Lord, will not allow you to go through this alone. He will do whatever he must and can do to give you the strength and love that you will need. Though I believe he did not send this upon you or give this to you, I do know that he, with your help, can use even this for a great witness for his kingdom. This may be your mission field now."

Billie had not said much but listened intently. When I finished, she replied, "Well, I'm not sure I totally agree with everything you have said, but you have said some of the things that I have been feeling but could not seem to find the words to express." She hugged me. "I love you for your thoughts."

In the darkened church as I now reviewed our conversation, I looked back up at the lamb and in my mind's eye it seemed to wink and smile at me. Funny what fantasies one's mind will play upon one at certain times. I knew it had not actually happened, but it was real to me. That was all that mattered. I smiled a little, with my eyes misting, looked back at the little white lamb and winked. I walked out of the church feeling better, as I usually did when I left those nearly nightly sessions.

Billie stayed in Macon for nearly three days and I had no contact with her during that time. I decided to say what I had to say in person and not over the phone. I learned from her father that she had spent two and a half of those days at a cancer clinic in Macon beginning her first series of X-ray treatments. I could have called her either at the hospital or her sister's home in the evenings, but I felt some dust needed to settle. When one of her brothers said that she would be home Friday afternoon, I knew that during the first weekend in August we would get to talk.

I phoned Billie early that Friday evening. Her voice sounded tired, but she seemed glad that I had called. I tried not to sound upset, but I did communicate that I felt somewhat left out over the news concerning the X-ray treatments. I did not mention my encounter with Dr. Marshall; that should be discussed in person. She was apologetic about the X-ray information, but said it had come up during her meeting with Smoak on Tuesday, and she felt she'd better get to Macon promptly. "I didn't contact you, Ed, because I didn't want to worry you," she said. "I thought I'd be back on Wednesday night after one treatment, but the doctor in Macon wanted to administer several in localized areas." She apologized again for not calling me. All I could do was just say meekly that I had been worried. Her voice weakened and, though she said she wanted to see me, she asked if she could rest that evening and see how she felt tomorrow. "I'll call you around noon, honey," I said.

The next day at noon she was much more enthusiastic and asked me to come out for lunch. I accepted with some apprehension, knowing that the rest of the family would be there. Then realized I might learn more about what was going on. I arrived a few minutes later as the meal was being placed on the table.

Billie's mother, Thelma, lived entirely for her husband and children. A marvelous cook, she prepared sumptuous meals consisting mostly of meat, home-grown vegetables and hot baked bread. She always played the typical apologetic hostess—there should be more food on the table and it could be better. Actually it was always more than adequate and marvelously rewarding.

If Thelma Ray had a favorite among her children, it was Billie. Why? Who knows? I believed that most of the children accepted it without resentment. In fact, if there was a favorite sibling among the brothers and sisters, it was Billie. It was obvious that the children had been reared in a true community of caring and loving, with a very giving mother. Many of Billie's positive attributes had come from her mother.

Yet, almost from the beginning of my relationship with Billie, I felt a subtle sense of coolness from her mother. It was not that she in any way communicated dislike, it was just that her closeness to Billie was so evident. Every time I arrived at the Ray's home I was welcomed most warmly by Thelma, but there was always that slight feeling of resentment.

It may have been that my antennas were over-extended because of my meeting with Smoak Marshall, but I felt even more of a lack of enthusiasm from Momma Ray when I arrived that Saturday for lunch. The greetings and graciousness were there, but a sense of questioning my intentions was also present. I realized that a family receiving the news they had about their daughter and sister could hardly be expected to respond to anyone normally. I'm sure that they instinctively wanted to protect Billie from any more hurt, and perhaps I was seen as a possible threat.

The meal was pleasant enough. Billie still looked tired, but she had slept late that morning and said she felt fine. In fact, to hear her say it, everything seemed right with the world, but I was not quite as positive as she. I wanted to talk with her in private.

After the meal we walked out on the farmhouse porch and sat in that marvelously large, creaking swing. It was another hot and muggy day, but sitting there with Billie, swinging slightly back and forth, made the air seem most pleasant.

I asked about the treatments, and she told me they had given her localized doses of X-ray under her arm and in the inguinal region. She did not seem too upset, but very matter-of-factly described what had taken place.

I didn't know quite how to bring up all the questions I had, but the porch was not the ideal setting for privacy. I think Billie sensed the same and suggested we walk across the road to the barns and stables. As we left the porch we passed some giant oaks and maples. Billie stopped and patted them lovingly. "They've been so much a part of my life here," she smiled. I could see there was something about the farm that fed her roots and gave her life vitality. It was a lesson that I would never forget.

We walked around the big, oily-smelling, dusty tractors, trucks and combines. The men helping her father waved as we passed by. As we stepped into the dim quiet of the barn, Billie said with some pain in her voice, "Once this place used to house living, loving animals; now it just shelters mechanical things."

I had to get to the subject of my visit. "Billie," I blurted, "I saw Smoak Marshall on Tuesday." She looked shocked, but I pressed on. "He asked to see me, and when I got there he told me that you and your mother had just left."

She stopped, faced me, holding onto a large hand-hewn beam. "What did he want to see you about?"

"You," I said, watching her closely. Instead of asking me why, she gazed out the barn door across the peach orchards.

"It wasn't a very good meeting with Smoak," I said haltingly. "I'm not sure he really said what he wanted to say, and I'm sure I did not say what I should have."

"Well," she said, turning back, her dark eyes piercing me, "what was said?"

I looked down at the dusty floor planks, not knowing exactly what to say. Looking up, I said, "Smoak felt that I was a burden for you and that to push marriage was not best for you or me." The "me" seemed to kindle her exploring spirit.

"What would be the problem for you?" she asked.

"Smoak felt that I might not complete my education or play ball any more, and that would bother you."

She was silent a moment. "It would," she said softly. "I have to say he's right." She placed her thin, soft hands on my shoulders. "Ed, that would be one thing I simply could not bear." She continued, "I know how much you love basketball and UK, and nothing must ever stop you from that. I want the very best for you, my love, and I want you to become the preacher or missionary that you have committed your life to be!"

"Did Smoak speak for you the other day?" I blurted.

She straightened her body, her brown eyes flashing. "Listen to me, Ed Beck. I love Smoak Marshall and value his opinions, but he does not live my life or make my decisions!"

"Well . . ." I responded lamely, "I didn't mean to insinuate that, but I didn't know whether you had asked him to talk with me or not."

Her eyes now blazed. "I thought you knew by now that I am totally capable of talking for myself. Apparently Smoak was concerned, but I didn't know he had called you. If he had talked to me about it I would have told him emphatically, NO! So what Smoak Marshall said to you is from Smoak Marshall, not me!" She turned and walked to the barn door facing the orchards.

"I thought you knew me better than that," she said with a catch in her voice. "Of all the things we have shared, and for you to even think such a thing!"

I stepped over and stood beside her.

Tears welled in her eyes and, as she tried to compose herself, I reached out for her. She pushed me away. "Wait! I'm sorry, but recently I find myself getting all teary-eyed. I think it's the effects of the treatments. I don't know," she began to sob. "I didn't know Smoak was going to talk with you—but I do believe that his intentions were for your benefit as well as mine. I'm upset at him for talking to you like that, but I'm also upset with you for believing that he had to do my talking for me."

Her sobbing intensified. My heart was breaking for her, but she still kept me at arm's length. "If I want to say anything to you, I will," she sobbed. "I'm getting a lot of advice from a lot of people all of a sudden, but what I say to you is from me and no one else!" She stamped her foot on the floor. "I thought you knew that much about me."

I didn't know what to say, knowing that I had already put both feet into my mouth. For a long moment I stood there, my mouth working, trying to say something. Finally, I apologized, then suggested we go to one of our favorite places to really talk this thing out.

Billie said nothing.

"Well, would you go out with me tonight to a movie?"

She didn't answer for a moment, and my heart sank. Finally, she said yes. I walked her back to the house and said goodbye. I felt hesitant about kissing her so just held her close and kissed the top of her head—she was only 5'6". Then I turned toward my car.

"I'll see you tonight," she called.

"About seven," I said.

"Seven's fine," she answered, her voice brightening. "I'm looking forward to being with you."

Suddenly all seemed right with our world for the moment. I watched her walk up the steps and wave as I drove away. As I rounded the familiar curve I wondered what really had been accomplished in our talk. The only thing I could think of was that round two would start at 7 o'clock tonight.

14

In a Small Cafe

It was after 7:00 when I arrived, and Billie was sitting on the front porch. She looked rested and radiant. Her light beige, cool-looking summer dress seemed to exaggerate her dark complexion and eyes. We walked hand-in-hand together down the steps to the car.

She wanted to drive so, enjoying the coolness of the fresh evening breeze, we drove leisurely north toward the town of Roberta. There was no speeding this night. We knew when we got there that there was nothing to see or do, but we also knew that we would be together. That would be enough. As we drove we exchanged tidbits about the lovely scenery and the evening sky. The sunset was magnificent in golden splendor with the last faint streaks of crimson fighting for survival.

As the darkness finally engulfed us, I told Billie that she reminded me of a sunrise rather than a sunset. Only the humming of the car motor and the tires on asphalt broke the silence for a moment. Then Billie sighed, "I don't know, Ed, maybe I am more like a sunset. It seems each day I'm fighting harder to survive rather than looking forward to living."

Then she gave a quick, nervous laugh. "Mind you, I'm not giving up or feeling sorry for myself. It's just that I know what's happening within me, and someday I'll be using every ounce of energy just to survive, rather than giving myself to my work and other people." She glanced quickly at me and added, "And even to you."

A turbulent sea of emotions churned within me. I wasn't sure it was because I knew I had kicked the ball out of bounds that afternoon in the barn or what. But my anger at this awful thing that had come between us was building, and I blurted out something about it "being so unfair! With all your gifts and graces for the work you want to do, even becoming a medical missionary, and then to have this sort of thing happen to you!"

My emotions began to run away with me, and I started talking about physical healing. "Maybe, just maybe, God is allowing you to go through this travesty, and soon you will be totally healed—a miracle from heaven itself." Billie's calmness did not flutter at all as she kept her eyes on the road ahead. I knew there was no doubt in her mind that God had the power to do whatever he chose to do. "Perhaps I'll be healed in other ways," she said, quickly adding that her service to God might be more telescoped than she had first dreamed.

Suddenly Billie pointed to a dingy-looking gas-station-cafe ahead and exclaimed, "Oh, let's stop there, Ed. They have wonderful desserts!"

Over my first negative protest about the looks of the place, we drove in and soon were enjoying pie and coffee. Billie was right—the pie was delicious.

We sat in the back of the small cafe. Since there were only one or two other customers and a waitress, we seemed fairly secluded. I felt this was an opportunity for a positive, face-to-face encounter. I put my coffee cup down and leaned across the chipped table top.

"Billie, a couple of weeks ago I asked you to marry me and you didn't say yes or no. I understood you to say, 'Maybe.' Well, I'm not trying to put pressure on you, but *I* feel it inside of me every day. In six weeks, I must return to school and I want you to come with me."

Billie had only half finished her pie, but she laid her fork on the plate and listened intently to me. I felt encouraged.

"I don't know how much time we have left together, but that's incidental to me." I put my hand across the table on hers. "I've learned something about myself, about you and about life during these last few weeks—it's the importance of time. Some folks live years together and don't enjoy life at all. Some live only a short time together and celebrate it."

My emotions were brimming and Billie's face clouded through the tears building in my eyes. "Whatever time that God gives us, three years, five or more, I want to spend as much of it as I can with you."

I gripped her hand. "Do you understand what I'm trying to say?"

Billie squeezed my hand tightly. "I hear everything you're saying, Ed, believe me. And I want what you want, but . . ."

"But what?" I pressed.

"But I'm very concerned about *you*."

"About me? What do you mean?"

Carefully choosing her words, she continued, "I think I know what will eventually happen to me." Her slight shoulders tremored. "It's not that I don't want you to share that with me, it's just that I'm afraid of what *you* might do . . ."

"Do? Why, you know . . ."

"Now don't interrupt, Ed. Let me go on." Her brown eyes glimmered as she looked at me across the table. The other cafe customers had left; the waitress was busy adding checks behind the register. The room was quiet.

"Ed, I'm so proud of you and what you're doing at the university and what you will do beyond. I know how hard you've worked for what you hope to accomplish. I'm afraid that if we got married you might never finish school . . . because of me."

I started to interrupt again, but she pressed her hand firmly on mine. "Smoak is right, dear, I just couldn't live with that on my conscience. I can't hurt anyone or anything, and to know that I would be hurting someone I love as much as I love you is just too much for me to handle. I can't even think of it. And that's why . . ." Tears streamed down her lovely face. "That's why I hesitate to marry you."

She squeezed my hand again and held it tight. "I love you very much, Ed Beck, and I want to be your wife, but right now there are too many other things to consider."

She dried her eyes with the paper napkin, forced a little smile and said, "Look, we can still look forward to the summer after you graduate. We'll know more then about how fast or slow it's progressing."

I shoved the empty pie plate away from me and leaned across the table until our faces almost met. "Billie," I pleaded, "you don't understand. Whatever happens and whenever, I want to be with you."

"But that's what I'm talking about, darling," she said between sniffles. "You really couldn't be with me. You'd be in Lexington, and I'd be here taking treatments and working. It just wouldn't be normal and . . . and if something happened, you'd feel pressured to come."

She dabbed at her face with the wet napkin. "You know me, Ed. I'd want you to come, and others would expect you to come. And you know you couldn't."

Crumpling the napkin into a little ball, she laid it on her plate and said, trying to smile, "Just love me as you love me now, and everything will be fine."

Something akin to anger brimmed within me. "Billie," I said seriously, "this is not a game to me. I mean it more than you seem to realize. Sure, Kentucky is important to me, and so is basketball. And some day I want to be a preacher. But you are *more* important and," pulling her toward me by her hand I added fiercely, "I want you!"

"But that's exactly what I've been talking about," she said, her eyes piercing me. "I don't want to be more important than your school, your basketball career, your preaching. Don't you see, I cannot be more important than that. That is *your* life, and that's the way it should be."

The waitress had turned out the exterior cafe lights and was now piling chairs on tables. Every once in a while she'd glance meaningfully our way. I didn't care. This was the most important moment of my life. I could feel my heart pounding in my throat.

"Billie, darling, *you* are my life," I responded. "Isn't there some way that life will give it all to both of us together?"

The cafe was dead quiet. The waitress was turning off lights over the other booths. Billie stared at her half-eaten piece of pie for a long time, and then looked up at me with sparkling, life-filled eyes.

"Darling, I will marry you . . ."

My heart leaped, and I started to rise from the booth to embrace her, but she pressed me back with her hand. Now her voice was deeply serious.

"I will marry you only under the condition that no matter what happens to me, you will never quit playing basketball for the Big Blue."

I breathed a heavy sigh of relief. "Of course, darling Billie, of course. I told you before that I would do *anything* for you, and if you need that promise from me, you have it!"

"I mean it, Ed," she said firmly. "No matter what my family or other people might say, or who knows?—even me—that no matter what, you'll never consider leaving Kentucky."

Tears streamed down her face, and she choked up.

Standing up and gently taking her hand, I said, "C'mon, let's get out of here."

We drove back to the farm—quiet all the way. I drove this time, my left hand on the wheel. She pressed her slim warm body close to me with her head on my shoulder and my right hand cupped tightly within hers.

We pulled off at Taylor's Mill Creek and stepped outside in the cool, aromatic night, heavy with fecund aromas from fertile fields. Holding each other tightly, we reconfirmed our love.

"Oh, I'm so happy, Ed. I so much want to be your wife."

I felt 10 feet tall, prouder than at any time our team had won a game, and I hungered for the day when she and I would share our total selves together.

We agreed that neither of us would say anything about our decision until she had talked with her doctors. She also wanted to talk with her parents.

"Would you like me to be there?"

"No," she squeezed my hand and smiled. "It will be better for me to break the news alone."

The late night moon had sunk near the horizon by the time we got home, and in the cool darkness crickets chirped. We stood on her front porch steps for a long time, not wanting to let each other go. She stood on a higher step, and we met face to face, which made kissing so convenient. Every time I started for the car, I'd wheel and return for one last embrace. She was so warm and soft and loving; I was completely enraptured.

Two persons had made a commitment of life to, for and with each other that night. But it was a commitment predicated on a unique and what some people would later believe a strange agreement. But at least for that night, as I drove away in the car singing at the top of my lungs, all was right with our world.

15

Warm-Up for a Game of Life

One way for a man to make certain he never sees the one he loves is to get engaged with only five weeks for his bride-to-be and her mother to get ready for the wedding. I saw Billie during that time . . . for only a few minutes here and a few minutes there.

All of Billie's doctors, both in Macon and the Valley, gave her their blessings. Even Smoak came around after he realized that this was what Billie really wanted. Smoak thought the world of her and, though not convinced that marriage was best, soon acquiesced to her hopes and dreams.

Billie had continued working at the local hospital several days a week and underwent treatments in Macon one day a week. The rest of the time she was immersed in pre-nuptial activities. Every time I wanted to see her she was on her way to some shower or party. Though the schedule was demanding, she seemed to glory in the activity and the attention. She was as alive and radiant as ever.

The discussions we did have during that time centered upon her deepest desire to live as normal a life as possible. Even so, a monkey-wrench was thrown into our plans almost from the beginning. Although we would be married September 11th and school began a week later, Billie would not be able to join me in Lexington until late October. Her treatments would continue until that time, and we felt it the better part of wisdom not to change them. We were confident, however, that before November she would be with me in Lexington.

We were both being bombarded by recommendations from friends and colleagues. By this time information of Billie's illness had spread through the small community, and naturally the gossip mills rumored that Billie would be dead before the ceremony. Another rumor was that her family had fabricated the illness to "catch the basketball star of the Valley." According to one story I had forced Billie into marriage so that Adolph Rupp would feel sorry for me and put me on the first team. The other side said that I really did not even care for Billie but that I was willing to sacrifice my life for a person who needed love desperately. The most irrational tale was that the cancer clinic in Macon had contacted me and strongly recommended that I marry Billie as part of her therapeutic program!

Billie and I would call each other every time we heard "the latest rumor." Some of them were so insane that they were sick, but Billie's sense of medical humor always seemed to come through. In my dead-pan expression I would tell her of how great a martyr I was, preparing to sacrifice myself for this love-starved nurse. In many ways the gossip brought a morbid type of humor into our relationship, but it also helped us keep everything on the table between us, keeping us from drifting off into fantasy.

It wasn't that our relationship had slipped into a cold, logical transaction. It was just that we could not escape too far from the basic reality of the illness that was both a curse and a blessing. A curse because of what it was doing to Billie from within, but a blessing because it had accelerated our marriage. We now realized that time was of the essence, and we did not take for granted the few remaining moments that we were experiencing.

One night, a couple of weeks before our marriage, we talked about how long five years really was. We counted the days, the minutes and even the seconds. It seemed like a long time from that point. Then we did the same with four years and three years. The more we talked about our precious gift of time the more I knew I wanted to spend every moment of it with her. But with all the functions of pre-marital bliss in a small community, I soon found my ideals not becoming realities. However, we talked on the phone every day we didn't get to be together.

Billie's family had mixed feelings about the forthcoming event. Billie's father was matter-of-fact as we talked alone together one day out by the barn. He said he wanted the best for his daughter, and if marriage was what she wanted, well, that was all right with him. It wasn't an overwhelming endorsement, but I felt I knew how he meant it.

Thelma, her mother, was another story. She continued to be very gracious and even joked a bit about my being her son-in-law. She hugged and kissed me when I arrived at the farm and when I was leaving, but I knew it was breaking her heart to see Billie get married. Billie's illness had only reinforced what I and other members of her family knew and understood—that she was very possessive of Billie's talent, time and tenderness. Cancer had exaggerated the feelings she had for her terminally-ill daughter. I was seen as a threat because I was taking some of the time and tenderness that before had been directed to the family. Yet, it was to Thelma's credit that she loved her daughter enough to desire for her the very best life could offer and never once set up any kind of block. In fact, if anything, she was overly nice in every way, and I tried to reach out to her in her time of hurt and disappointment. I knew that the closer the wedding day came, the more difficult it would be for this lovely woman.

Billie's brothers and sisters were ecstatic. The brothers, in particular, treated her more normally than any other group. They kidded her about no longer being "an old maid down on the farm" and about getting married just before receiving her retirement pay and social security check. The sisters, especially Helen, seemed to reach out to her through the coming event. They were so pleased about Billie's happiness that to them her marriage was all that really mattered.

I continued to receive my share of advice. When I asked my roommate, George Matthews, to be my best man, he took me to the drive-in hamburger place in town, bought me a meal and made me sit in the car and eat with him. Every time I took a bite of food, when he knew I could not speak in my own defense, he urged me to re-think my plans. It had nothing to do with Billie as a person, he reiterated; he saw it as a real threat to my future.

However, as we drove back to the house, he told me that he would never bring up his arguments again. He just wanted to be honest with me and make certain I knew where he stood. From then on, his support for Billie and me was firm in every way.

I never mentioned to anyone my promise to Billie concerning "my completing college—no matter what." I felt as if this was a part of our covenant, and I put it in the back of my mind, though every now and then Billie would bring it up for emphasis.

My mother and father, living in Jacksonville, Florida, were somewhat shocked, but totally supported my decision. They had met Billie the year before at the basketball tournament but never really had the opportunity to get to know her. Still, if she was the one their son chose to be his wife, that was good enough for them.

I had called UK to discuss my decision with Coach Rupp, but he was out of the country for a week's lecture tour. I then phoned Coach Lancaster who, though not overjoyed, was quick to say marriage would not affect my standing with the team or any of the coaching staff. He said he would be talking with Adolph in a few days and would communicate the news. During our conversation I told him that I would be staying with the team in the dorm rather than getting an apartment—I had to let him know something of Billie's condition. That was when I discovered another side of Harry Lancaster, one that would be reinforced in the months and years to follow. A very compassionate human being, he wanted me to know that UK would work with me in every way possible. They would continue my scholarship package as if I were a single person until the time Billie arrived in Lexington. Then my status would change. But whenever that occurred, it would be all right with the UK athletic officials.

So now I waited for the big event. At times I would get those funny butterfly feelings in my stomach—like waiting in the dressing room for the biggest game of the season to begin. And, in a way, that's what it was, the biggest event of my life. I did not realize then how many time outs, discussions, troubling defenses and overtime periods I would experience. I was going into a game that would demand every ounce of physical strength and every fiber of emotion, wit and faith that could be asked of a person. I began my season of love as a boy and would emerge some 18 months later as a full-scale human being feeling that I had lived several lifetimes. That development process would be filled with both pleasure and pain.

16

And God Made Them One

My arm was wrapped tightly around Billie's shoulders, and she clung to me as we walked slowly down the Atlantic beach just hours after our marriage. It was nearing midnight, and we had been walking in the surf for nearly an hour. It was cool, but our windbreakers kept us free from chill, and the salt air on our faces was invigorating. Every now and then we would pause and look out over the sea. The brightness of the nearly full moon sparkling on the waves was almost as captivating to me as her presence. Every now and then Billie gave me a squeeze of contentment and peace.

At times she would break away to run laughing down the beach. I would soon catch up with her. Eventually, wanting to run no more, we held each other close with our arms and our lips. A ship's lights twinkling on the horizon revealed a serious mood reflected on her face. "Someday we'll be on a ship like that," she sighed, "when we go to the mission field together."

I said nothing but just pulled her to me once again. I did not want to discuss the future. The present moment was too precious to disturb. The dream had become a reality, and here at midnight on September 11, 1955, we stood, ran, walked and played on our Creator's sandy beach.

It had been a busy day and we were both tired, yet buoyed up by the feeling of our oneness. I reached down, picked her up and swung her around, then gently placed her on the sand. We fell together on our knees. She lunged and knocked me over on my back. I held her close as she, now on top of me, struggled to get away. At last, almost exhausted, she quit struggling and looked down into my eyes. Hers were as dark as ebony, but the sparkle within them belied the night that engulfed us.

"Oh, Ed, I'm so very happy and so much in love with life."

All I heard was the "in love," and I did not analyze the "with life." There are times to speculate and times to participate. This was no time to speculate, so I said, "Thank you, darling, for being you. I love you so very much, my dear Billie."

Her body totally relaxed in mine as she snuggled reaching out for the warmth of my physical presence. We stayed that way for a long time and then walked toward our honeymoon cottage.

"Is it customary for the husband to carry his bride across the threshold?" I asked.

"Why yes, it is, and that is why I have lost weight, just for this special moment," she laughed as she literally leaped up into my arms with her salt and sand-caked body.

We showered together and later enjoyed God's exciting, unique gift to newly married couples; then fell asleep in each other's arms—at least I did. I was aroused by a wide-awake Billie wanting me to see the sunrise of her first full day as my wife. She was so much in love with life, and every moment was so precious. We walked the beach, ate breakfast at a surf-side cafe and visited all the shops.

In mid-September Brunswick, Georgia, begins to close down for the winter. The beach was not crowded. Some of the residents were still there, but we basically had the area to ourselves, no waiting in line at restaurants or shops. It would have made little difference though, for we spent most of our time in closeness walking the surf and lying together in each other's arms.

We had planned to stay there for only a few days and then drive back to the Valley. I was scheduled to return to Lexington on the weekend, and Billie would stay in Georgia to complete therapy, arriving in Kentucky no later than November 1. So, on our last honeymoon afternoon we drove the short distance to St. Simon's Island. We went there for only one reason.

Located on the island is a statue and a shrine honoring John Wesley who, in the 1700s, arrived near that place as a missionary for the Church of England. He later would seek reform within that church, and the reform movement would historically become The Methodist Church. Billie had heard me talk about Wesley and the monument, so she wanted to see it. We walked within the area for about an hour as I described Wesley's missionary work in America and the defeats of his inner spirit that led him back to England, a broken person. Out of that humbling defeat his "hour had come," as he had preached at Oxford on an Easter morning. His awakening had arrived, and it revolutionized his life. Billie listened intently and then remarked, "I can see that when he came here his intentions were positive, but his life was not properly centered."

As we walked toward the car we discussed "being intently focused." How do you know that you are pointing in the right direction? How can you be assured that you are doing what God wants you to do with your life? Is there a feeling, a sign? We finally came to an agreement that there was an awareness—probably picked up differently by each person—but an awareness, nonetheless, of knowing when your intentions are purposefully focused.

"Our actions might not always measure up to our intentions, but that's the reason for the day-by-day quality of our hope," Billie said quietly as we walked down the sandy path.

"I know there have been times that I've felt so close to God," she added, "and the other times I feel as if God does not exist or, if he does, he either just doesn't care or doesn't have much time for me."

"But all true followers of God, through Jesus Christ, have had those desert times," I responded. "There has never been a saint of God—Wesley, Luther, Calvin or anyone else—who didn't have his dark night of the soul."

With that, her face brightened and she said, "Dark night of the soul . . . that's what I've had, I guess. I really went through some times of doubt and uncertainty over these past two months, Ed. But I'm better—much better now. And thank you for helping me through them—and for loving me!"

I held her close and kissed her. "Billie, you have added to my life what I so desperately needed—you!"

With that, we vowed again the help that each of us would need until "death do us part." Now, Billie's pensive look returned, the same look that I had seen just a few days before when we stood at the altar and repeated the words about love that never really ends, but is adjusted drastically when death parts the two. When she repeated those words, a tear came to her eye and a squeeze of her hand let me know that death would be held off for as long as possible and love would be given in every way.

The wedding ceremony was a moving experience for all. We stood at the Methodist Church's altar, the altar that meant so much to me and had slowly come to be important to Billie too. Her loveliness had been accentuated by the whiteness of her long wedding gown. The wedding had progressed to the point of the spoken vow, and the audience was gripped with the words "til death do us part." There had been no outward gasp, but the inward empathetic, silent groan was evident. The tears in both our eyes were expressive enough for those nearest us to know that we had truly meant each word.

Now, slipping into the warmth of our car, we drove back to the beach and spent our last night of love in the cottage of our oneness.

We arrived back at the farm late on Friday afternoon, rested and relaxed. The family greeted us with relief and joy. We were to spend that one night of our first week together in Billie's room. I was scheduled to leave the next morning for Kentucky. When we were getting ready to go to bed, I was sitting on the bed beginning to undress. She sat down next to me and whispered, "We've got to put the mattress on the floor."

I looked at her incredulously. "What in heaven's name for?" I blurted out as she placed her hand over my mouth saying, "Sh-h-h." She wrapped her body around my side and whispered again, "My bed makes funny noises."

"What kind of funny noises?"

"Some day I'll let you hear them, but not tonight. My mother and father's room is just on the other side of that wall, and I'm not about to worry about keeping them awake. Now, like a good boy, won't you put the mattress on the floor, just for me?"

With that, she kissed me on the cheek and started to walk toward the bathroom. When she got to the door she turned toward me and winked.

When she came out of the bathroom the mattress was on the floor. In fact, it was there the next night too. I decided to be just a little late returning to school, for what I experienced those nights was not taught in any class I ever took at college.

17

A New Covenant

It was late Sunday afternoon when I arrived at the dormitory. Bob Burrow and some of my teammates were standing out front. I got out of the car to greet them.

Bob said, "Understand you got married, Beck? Where is your wife? I want to meet that southern belle!"

I pointed toward the car where Billie sat and started to walk over with him.

Bob said, "I don't need you. You stay here. I want to talk to this special lady all alone." Bob so enjoyed being a ladies' man, I stayed behind and talked to the other fellows about the summer. Pretty soon Bob and Billie walked over to us and Bob, in his magnificent Texas way, introduced my wife to the team, giving a scenario on each team member.

Billie had not planned to return with me to the university, but she later decided to join me for just the first week of school. Her plan was to return to the Valley on the following weekend so she could resume therapy. I'm not sure whether she felt a premonition of some kind, or just curiosity, but I was so pleased that she was willing to make the journey. She had called her doctors in Macon about the delay of the treatments. Several delays had already occurred because of the wedding and honeymoon, and although they were not pleased with her decision, the doctors asked "How in the world do you argue with a young bride who just wants to be with her husband?" They realized that in a few more days she would be separated from me for more than a month.

I was so pleased that Billie could meet my teammates as well as Coach Rupp and Coach Lancaster and my friends at the church. All knew I had married. I knew that some of them felt it was done under questionable circumstances so I believed that once they met Billie some of their thoughts and/or suspicions would be allayed.

Though tired, we attended the Centenary Methodist Church that evening and heard Clarence Yates give a beautiful sermon. "I *like* him," whispered Billie after it was over. We all gathered back at Helen Hunt's house, as was our regular ritual. I was still welcome there despite the "mongoose." There was a larger crowd at the house than usual because Helen had spread the word that "Ed Beck's wife is here and you'll want to meet her." And they did. Billie, though very tired, won them over with her beauty and grace.

The next morning we headed toward the UK Memorial Coliseum, home of the Wildcats basketball team. I had to go on to classes, but Billie had wanted to walk around the campus and get the feeling of her new home. As we were approaching the coliseum I heard my name. I turned around to be greeted by Harry Lancaster.

"Is this the pretty young lady you told me so much about?" he graciously asked. Before I could answer, he continued, "Well, you did not lie to me in the least. She is even more beautiful than you said." And with that, he extended his hand to a blushing bride. Harry was always a master psychologist, but I felt that what he said was not expressed just for emotional impact—it was how he actually perceived Billie.

I quickly explained my schedule. Harry said, "Ed, you go on to class. Adolph is here, and he wants to meet Billie. You come back at noon and take your little lady to lunch." He waved me away, took Billie by the arm and escorted her into the building for the round of introductions. I never found out what happened in the next three hours because Billie refused to relate anything except, "we just talked." However, from that time on, it was obvious to me that Harry

Lancaster and Adolph Rupp felt very close to her. She became a part of the team in a unique, inspirational way. Billie's well-being and her dreams had been imprinted upon their hearts.

We decided to leave Lexington before the end of the week to return to the Valley. The trip was uneventful. Billie had met most of the team members and had conferred at length with the UK coaching staff about which she felt extremely positive. She had even interviewed for a nursing position at a local hospital. Everything seemed to fall into place. We arrived in the Valley convinced that she would return to the bluegrass country on or before November 1.

We never dreamed of the devastating event that would alter our plans.

Basketball practice was to begin officially on October 15, but no Kentucky athlete ever started without having conditioned himself consistently for several weeks. My sophomore year, in the fall of 1955, was no exception. The pre-season rankings had placed UK in the top five nationally. A veteran varsity team was returning, and of course the strongest sophomore members were now the strength of the bench. Enthusiasm ran high on that first day of practice.

I felt both humbled and honored when I was placed as the center back-up for All-American Bob Burrow. Everyone felt that a great deal would be riding on his pivot play. If he got into any difficulty I would be called to fill the gap. I approached the season with high expectations. Bob and I continued to be roommates, and now and then he would joke about how glad he was that he did not look like Billie because he wouldn't want to be attacked while he was asleep. He realized how desperately I missed her, and through his compassion we developed a special closeness. He became my spokesman about Billie to the team. Whatever I shared with Bob, I knew he would pass on in the most tactful way. Thus none of the team members ever asked me about Billie's progress, for they knew that whatever I wanted them to know, Bob would share. We found this a workable and positive solution to a potential headache for all of us.

Billie's treatments resumed upon her return to Georgia. She also went back to work full time at the hospital, which did not please me. Yet, I understood that she would rather be working than sitting.

Then too, I knew she felt she had to help put "hubby through school," which was really not necessary with my full scholarship and the money I always saved from my summer employment.

About a week before basketball practice was to begin, I received a letter from Billie saying that she was scheduled for further exploratory surgery around the middle of October. I called her the night her letter arrived, and she explained that some nodes had been discovered in her left breast. Dr. Smoak Marshall felt it best to make a visual examination. She assured me that it would be similar to the ten-minute surgery she had experienced previously. I either accepted her explanation without question or was insensitive to the potential outcome, I'm not sure which.

On the afternoon of October 15, a fellow dorm resident rushed breathlessly up to me. "There's an emergency phone call waiting for you, Ed!"

I raced to the phone to find Helen, Billie's sister, on the wire. It was obvious she had been crying, and her voice broke as she told me what happened.

Billie had had her "exploratory" surgery that afternoon. "It turned out to be a total mastectomy, Ed," sobbed Helen.

My head whirled and I sank into a chair, gripping the phone. "You . . . you mean they had to take both?" I gasped.

"Yes, Ed, both breasts," she choked.

"Is she all right?" My hand was shaking, and I could hardly control my voice.

"Yes, Ed, Dr. Marshall said everything went just as it should, and she'll recover."

"How is she feeling?"

"That's the point, Ed. Billie's not taking it well at all. Before the surgery she had told Dr. Marshall that no matter what he found, he was to take out only enough for a biopsy and then sew her back up. After the biopsy results, she would decide what to do."

"But Smoak didn't do that?"

"No, he felt it was too far gone to wait."

Tears filled my eyes and dropped to the phone receiver. "What's Billie's reaction?"

"Not good at all. When she awoke in recovery, still partially sedated, she was confused by all the tubes in her arms and by her

chest being so tightly bound. When Smoak entered the room and
told her what he had found and what he had to do, Billie exploded."

My heart broke as I envisioned her terrible discovery.

"She told Smoak that it hadn't been his decision to make,"
continued Helen, "and reminded him he had promised not to do
anything until they discussed it." Helen broke into sobs, as she
recounted Billie's crying out, "You had no right! You had no right!"

"Smoak did his best to convince her that time was of the essence,
but Billie was too wrought up to understand," continued Helen.
"Before they could calm her with sedation, she had yanked out one
of the needles from her arm and tried to get out of bed."

Helen again broke into tears, and then recovering, said, "Oh Ed,
I'm so sorry, so sorry for Billie and for you. I know what you must
be going through."

"Helen," I said quietly, "I'm coming home right now."

"Oh no, Ed! No, you can't. Remember what you promised
Billie."

"Helen, that doesn't mean anything now. Billie needs me and
I've got to be there."

Her voice became quietly serious. "Ed, I have to tell you the last
thing Billie said to me when I left her bedside before the operation.
She said, and I'm quoting her word for word, 'If anything out of
the ordinary happens, make sure you remind Ed of our agreement.
He is to stay at school until I really need him.'"

I was silent for a moment, remembering our promise to each
other.

"Ed? Ed? Are you still there?"

"Yes, Helen, I'm sorry. I was just thinking about what you said.
Yes, I had promised Billie that, and I guess I'd better live up to it."

"I'm glad. To be frank, I worried that your breaking that promise
might make Billie feel even worse."

"When do you think I can talk to her on the phone?" I asked.

"Tomorrow, I'm sure she will be able to talk by then."

Hanging up the phone, I found Bob right away. I had to share
my grief with someone close as soon as possible. Bob didn't say
much, which was helpful. He just patted my shoulder and listened.

Then I called Coach Rupp at his home. "Ed, you get to Georgia
and be with her," was his quick response. But when I explained the

reason for my not going, he didn't argue. Finally, he said, "Whatever you decide to do, you know we will back you in every way."

I couldn't sleep that night—just lay there and prayed for Billie. I knew the terrible trauma she was going through. I had studied enough psychology to understand the awful sense of loss a woman feels when she loses such a meaningful part of her body. There is not only heartbreak of surgery, but also the terrible feeling that she is no longer a complete woman.

The next day at practice everything went as usual. The only comment was a supportive word from Harry Lancaster as we walked to the court. He and Coach Rupp were deeply sensitive to my need and yet, on the court, they never treated me any differently than the other players. If at any time I had felt I was specially favored, it would only have added to my agony.

The same went for my teammates, who already knew about Billie from Bob Burrows. Instinctively, they let me know their sympathy in little meaningful ways off the court. My room was immediately off the hallway near the dormitory entrance. Almost every evening one of my teammates would stick his head in the door just to see how I was doing. They often asked, "Have you heard from Billie today?" Whatever my response, it was never questioned or elaborated upon. They never said, "We're pulling for you, or we are in your corner, or if there is anything I can do. . . ." All of that and more was understood.

Whenever the time came for surgery or hospitalization, the team members' interest intensified, but they followed the unspoken agreement that one of my roommates would convey the details so each team member did not have to ask me the same questions over and over.

My teammates showed great concern, but on the court, either during practice or a game, it was strictly business. My fellow Wildcats were highly trained and tuned athletes, conditioned to compete and play their very best. They gave no quarter, and I expected no privileged position. That athletic dedication molded us into a nationally ranked and powerful team on the court. The crisis of the human tragedy that was unfolding knit us together as a community of caring and sensitive human beings off the court.

I had heard about community concern for a brother all my life from the pulpit, but I believe my first experience of its pure reality came on the basketball court with the men I lived and played ball with.

I could hardly wait to call Billie that next day. I waited until the afternoon when I felt she would be more able to talk. Our conversation was erratic for she was not fully lucid as a result of the medication. I could understand her anger at what had happened, but it hurt me to hear her say how ugly she was and that I would never want to see her again.

"I just don't want you to see me like this!" she sobbed. She didn't add "never," but the meaning flashed across the wire as strongly as an electric shock.

There was little I could say to help her, and I ended up fumbling for words. After a tearful goodbye, I immediately called Helen and told her that I felt I should see Billie right away.

She again reminded me of the promise. So I continued to talk daily with Billie on the phone. In a few days she was more like herself and apologized for her angry words during our first call, blaming it on the sedation.

"But there's one thing you must promise, Ed," she said. "Don't come back to the Valley until I'm out of the hospital."

When I began to protest she reminded me of our "covenant." She said that my wanting to be with her was enough for her right now. She knew that basketball practice had just begun and said, "I'd worry, Ed, about your missing it and maybe not making the team."

Finally, I agreed to wait. After hanging up the phone, I stood in the hall a long time fighting two conflicting desires, one to jump into my car and drive to Billie now, the other to abide by our covenant.

Finally, I decided on the latter, a decision which I would come to regret. As the days passed by, Billie continued to heal and we were in constant telephone communication. Each time we talked I told her I planned to leave immediately for the Valley, and each time she reminded me of our agreement.

The inner conflict within me began to take its toll. I found myself becoming very unsure about what I really should do. It reached the point where I began to wonder how realistic our covenant agreement really was. It was not that I felt untrue to Billie in wanting to disobey it, it was simply not knowing what was right. Finally, the real issue seemed to be whether I was going to be true to my inner self. The war within me began to hinder my focus on whatever I was doing, whether in the classroom or on the ball court. My self-confidence and inner integrity were slowly eroding.

Finally I analyzed my dilemma. There were two Ed Becks. A vital part of me, my mind, was in Georgia at Billie's bedside; and the other vital part, my body, was in Kentucky. I wanted desperately to be in both places and that, of course, was impossible. It was beginning to consume me, and I knew that soon I would be no good to myself or anyone else.

To find peace I did what I usually had done in the past—I turned to the Scriptures. I reread the story of how God had made a sacred and trusting covenant relationship with his chosen people of Israel. The entire Old Testament is God's revelation of the uniqueness of his personhood to this special body of humanity. Israel at times responded in faith and at other times in miserable failure. Then, when the revelation of God's presence began to reach its zenith, his son—our Savior—burst into human history. One of the New Testament writers, expressing his boundless joy in this reality, penned, "The new covenant has come in Christ Jesus, our Lord."

As I sat on my bed reading these words with the late afternoon sun stretching its rays across the floor of my room, a new thought struck me. Yes, a covenant can, under the right circumstances, become new and different and can express an even more meaningful relationship!

Neither Billie nor I ever took the importance of this colossal word "covenant" lightly. But where was the total responsibility of the covenant between God and his chosen people? Was it God's? Or the Jews? Of course, it was God's! At the moments when the people of Israel were in need, God came to them in different and unique ways. He even sent messengers to inform and support his people.

Now I related this understanding to Billie and me. I viewed her as a unique person, my chosen wife; I, her chosen husband. However, in our situation we had drawn up certain interpretations of our covenant in the context of difficulty. Had we agreed upon them in too much haste? Had they truly been thought out? Had our emotions overruled logic?

It is easy to agree to such a covenant while two healthy people are driving through aromatic peach orchards. But what about now? Hour after hour of analysis seemed to sap my body and mind. Finally, as the dorm lights were turned on by someone entering the darkened room, the revelation came. The danger of any human covenant is that one can analyze it to death and suffer from the paralysis of analysis. There comes a moment when one must cease such mortal meanderings and go to the feet of the One who understands all, who knows what is best for everyone. There comes a moment when one must act on the true feelings of his heart as given by his Creator.

The God of Israel was a moving and an acting God; the Jews thus became a moving and an acting people. It was time for Ed Beck to pray, to hear God's answer and to act.

I did just that and then, without even phoning Georgia, I drove out of Lexington late one Friday afternoon right after basketball practice. My goal was simply to be at Billie's side. Our covenant had to be renewed in each other's presence.

18

'You're No Different, Darling'

The mountain scenery of southern Kentucky and northern Tennessee is lovely in the fall. My entire route, from Lexington to the Valley, lay through the Great Smokies. As beautiful a drive during the daylight hours, it could be treacherous and lonely at night. The two-lane roads with hair-pin turns demanded total concentration. The trip took 12 to 13 hours and was very fatiguing.

However, I had no trouble staying awake knowing that each mile brought me closer to Billie. I wanted to be as close to my destination as possible when dawn arrived. Despite rain all through Tennessee, I made good time, and by the time I got to Dalton, Georgia, with approximately 200 miles to go, the night was still pitch black. The sky had cleared, though, and I estimated I would arrive at the farm in time for breakfast.

South of Atlanta the first light of morning showed in the east, and I was again overwhelmed by its radiant beauty. There was always something about the dawn that reminded me of Billie.

I knew that she had been released from the hospital a few days earlier. I had talked to her Thursday night, and I knew she would wonder why I had not called on Friday. But we had also discussed the cost of so many phone calls; I had promised to cut back on them and write more letters. She would be surprised when I arrived at the farm.

I had envisioned my stealing into her bedroom and kissing her awake. My romantic notion was dashed, however, when, upon my arrival, I found her sitting at the breakfast table sipping a cup of coffee. As I walked through the back door she nearly dropped the cup. She stood up slowly, and by the time she was out of her chair, I was by her side wanting to hug her tightly, yet knowing that I should not. She tried to put her arms up around my neck, but could not raise them that high because of the stitches. So, awkwardly, yet warmly, we embraced. Brushing the tears from her eyes, she finally looked up and laughed.

"You can hug harder than that—I won't break."

I answered with silence and a continued embrace. I soon took my arms from around her body, cupped her face with my hands and tilted her head toward me. Our lips met very tenderly. The kiss was lingering, until I sensed the embarrassed movement of her mother behind us. The rest of the family was already out in the fields.

"Oh, I feel a little light-headed, I'd better sit down," said Billie.

Trying to be humorous, I said, "Well, I see I have not lost my sex appeal."

But it was a poor choice of words, and there was little response. The awkward moment passed, and we sat down together. I soon was answering the questions: Why hadn't I called; what prompted this sudden visit; did I cut practice; and a dozen more. I handled them quickly by bringing greetings from the team and the coaches. I discovered that Billie had received a lovely bouquet of flowers from the Athletic Department of the University of Kentucky. Naturally the colors were blue and white.

I had planned to leave late the next morning to return in time for some rest, classes and practice the following day. Since I had not slept because of the drive, Billie and I soon retired to her room. I began to place the mattress upon the floor, which had been our regular routine, but she suggested that it stay on the bed. I nodded understandingly, and we lay side by side holding hands and quietly talking. As I started to apologize for not coming immediately after the surgery, she stopped me. "I would have felt that you had not kept our promise and that would have hurt me more than the surgery," she said. Then we talked about the operation. She told me how she had completely lost control of her emotions when she learned what had happened, but as the days passed she reflected on her reactions. She realized that they were normal when a woman loses such a vital part of her body, and she knew in her heart that the entire surgical staff had done what they believed to be in her best interest. From that moment I never heard her question any of the procedure.

She told me she would not be able to put her arms over her head for several months and that she would be unable to lift any heavy weight for nearly six months; "Then, for nearly a year I will have difficulty touching anything higher than the top of my own head." She laughed and continued "So, I won't be able to smooth your hair like I used to."

I then approached the sensitive area that I knew she and I both were uneasy about. How did she feel about herself? "I feel ugly and unwomanly," she sniffled. Billie had always been proud of her figure, and now she was full of scars and X-ray burns. It was not just the loss of her "appendages" (a term that Billie used to refer to her breasts), but what was happening to her body, she told me. She was losing weight. Also, the X-ray treatments had made part of her body rough as horsehide and had discolored it as if it had been burned. The straw that almost broke her back was the jolt she received when she awakened from supposedly minor surgery to discover that her breasts had been removed.

"They took everything except the nipple. I feel that I am no longer feminine. The woman you married a month ago is no more, Ed," she sobbed softly. "I was afraid this might happen someday, but I never dreamed that time would come so quickly."

No amount of assurance that it would make no difference in my feelings for her seemed to have any impact. "What has happened, has happened, Billie," I soothed, "but the real personhood of the woman I love has not been touched."

The words sounded good, but she was not buying. I sensed that her physical self-image had been completely altered, and it had done something to her as a person as well. Her confidence had been totally shaken.

Despite her depression, the more we talked, the more I realized that she was already looking forward to going back to work and joining me in Kentucky. But she still seemed to have worries about how I felt about her.

Though I was trying to verbally communicate my love and devotion, my sleepless night was beginning to take its toll, I realized the subject of our conversation was monumental in importance, but I was not as sharp as I should be with my responses. I asked rather sheepishly if we could continue the discussion later in the evening. She rose from my side, leaned over to kiss me and said, "Get some rest, my darling. Thank you for coming, but I'm still upset that you did not call."

"I was afraid you would not want me to come," I responded sleepily.

"Oh, I wanted you to come so much, but I knew you shouldn't," she said. "I want you to stay, but I know you must go. That is the way it has to be, for I will get well soon and come to you. Now, get some sleep." Before she reached the door I was asleep.

That evening we continued the subject in the same vein. How many different ways can one express his love and devotion verbally without it soon becoming mechanical and empty-sounding? So, I changed my approach and we began to talk about the future in Lexington. I told her of some apartments that I had discovered near the Methodist Church and the Baptist Hospital where she had been interviewed. One, on Limestone Drive, was going to be vacant in November. Her response struck me like a thunderbolt.

"I will not be able to come to Lexington this year, Ed. I'm so very sorry, but I will need to stay here until the healing process is over, and I must take some more treatments in Macon."

My mind reeled with shock and confusion. *What is she really saying*, I asked myself? Is this her way of telling me that she will never come?

In medical terminology she began to explain what would have to take place before she could go back to work. She did not want to come to Lexington until she could work. She did not want to sit around the apartment all day while I was in school and at basketball practice. She did not want to change doctors. She wanted to complete her treatments before she left the Valley. When she did come to Kentucky, she just wanted to be my wife. She wanted us to be able to go places together. She did not want to be sick any more, especially while she was at the university with me.

Despite my shock, I began to see her fighting spirit of determination and self-confidence returning. As she determined what was going to happen in the next few weeks, she began to believe again that the best was yet to be. She believed that she and we, and whoever else was involved, were going to lick this cancer one way or the other. No longer feeling sorry for herself, she began to feel the spirit of life and the courage to overcome. She began to believe that obstacles could become opportunities for life and purpose. All the old clichés of faith and positive thinking began to take on personal meaning for her. They were no longer words in a book; they were being written upon her heart and mind. My shock turned to admiration for this woman I had married.

In high spirits, I put the mattress upon the floor, and she laughed. We both knew that no sexual involvement could take place because of her post-surgery condition, but that was not the issue. It was symbolic; our lives were pulling back together. Our relationship had been slightly torn, and the separation of miles had exacerbated it. But we were learning how to trust one another, though separated. We were learning how to care and grow together, though we were apart. It had been a painful trip physically and emotionally for Billie, and a painful process for both of us. But now the mending was taking place, and although we somehow knew that the future would hold more of the same type of distressing experiences, we felt that, together or apart, we would be able to handle them a great deal more positively. We fell in love in newer and deeper dimensions as we lay there side by side into the night, holding hands, touching, caring and loving.

When God said, "The two shall be as one," I'm sure he knew how truly beautiful married love can be.

19

A Covenant Renewed

Billie's determination to join me in Kentucky before the first of the year was powerful. Less than two weeks after my return to Lexington she called to say she would arrive there before Thanksgiving. "My X-ray treatments have come to an end for the time being, darling," she said excitedly, "and I've regained my strength." No more surgery was contemplated in the foreseeable future, she told me, as I fairly danced with joy.

Despite Billie's exuberance, I knew some of her medical advisors had urged her to stay in Georgia where she could be watched more closely, but she wanted to be in Lexington for the basketball season. Too, she was getting tired of all the medical exercises and felt she needed a break. Her plea to me was, "Ed, I just want to lead as normal a life as possible for as long as I can. I can't do that here. I'm your wife and I want to be with you. So get ready—here I come!" And get ready I did.

Just before Thanksgiving I acquired that little apartment on Limestone Drive. Billie had written the hospital and they informed her she would be hired the day she arrived. All, for a change, seemed right with our world. It was not perfect since we were not yet together, but now there was a small light at the end of a very long and dark tunnel.

When Billie arrived in November, I found her a little thinner and slightly more pale than I remembered. But her scars had healed, and she was able to reach a little over her head. She reminded me of how wonderfully she had progressed when she greeted me by placing her arms around my neck and saying, "Go ahead and hug, you can't hurt me now."

I did, and fell more deeply in love with her than ever before. One of Billie's biggest decisions was whether or not to wear a padded bra. She had actually adjusted so well that she could joke about it.

"Just think, darling, I can now make myself as large or as petite as I want." She really did not want to wear that type of garment but decided it might eliminate stares and awkward moments for others. Her positive feminine feelings had returned, in spite of the departure of her "appendages." She knew beyond a doubt that the real woman and the real person had not been touched at all by that surgery.

Thanksgiving holidays were always the roughest days of practice at the University of Kentucky. Except for "turkey day" itself the varsity team practiced twice a day in preparation for the opening of the season. The team members looked forward both in dread and excitement to those three days. We would practice on Thanksgiving morning and get the afternoon off, then come back on Friday and Saturday for the killing schedule of both morning and afternoon practices. Lord help the player who wasn't in shape by that time. If he wasn't, he would be by Sunday or Adolph and Harry would know the reason why.

The season opened in early December in Baton Rouge, Louisiana, against LSU. We would play in the Cow Palace, a mammoth, barn-like arena. The veteran varsity team would start, and, though all the sophomores were eager to play, we were very nervous. No matter how many high school games and freshman college games one plays, it's a big leap into the varsity huddle. We seemed to handle the warm-up drills well, and we felt we were ready. The pre-season rankings still placed UK's team in the top five, and we meant to stay there.

Of course I had prayed before the game as I had done all the previous years—I prayed not so much to win but to be able to do the best I could.

I was the backup center for Bob Burrow, and I knew I would eventually get in the game since Bob would need a breather in each half. Playing center in the Kentucky style of man-to-man defense also meant that you were the stopper. If one of your teammates got picked off and his man was coming in toward the basket ready to score, it was the center's responsibility to stop him. That meant a brilliant defensive move to block the shot or using your body to take him out of play all together. The latter, of course, drew a foul, and therefore Kentucky centers always played on the edge of fouling out of most games. I knew that Bob would get tired, would get in foul trouble or would sometimes not play as well as he was capable. Adolph Rupp, the great coach he was, would substitute me for him every game. I knew before that first game I would see action. The question was *when?*

I knew also that Vernon Hatton would play in every game. He was a sophomore like me, but most observers of that 1955-56 Kentucky team felt he was very capable of playing on the starting squad. So I knew that if either of the guards did not play their best, or if they did not control the game tempo as Coach Rupp demanded they do, Vernon would go in immediately.

On the way to the Cow Palace the sophomores all sat in the rear of the bus. I was sitting across the aisle from Vernon, and though we were not supposed to talk before the game (Adolph believed silence helped you to concentrate) Vernon and I did some whispering. "You're going to get in the first five minutes of the game," I said in hushed tones. Vernon just shook his head and looked up as if to say "Really?"

Later, when a lot of street noise filtered into the bus, he leaned over and said, "You will go in before me." I immediately responded, "Oh no, you will be the first one." Fearing that we might be overheard and reprimanded in the dressing room for not taking this game seriously, we ceased our whispering.

We arrived toward the back of the Palace and began the long walk down the corridors. Now it was safer to carry on a conversation, and we bantered back and forth about who would go in first.

It made no difference. We both knew that tonight in the first game of the season, we would open our varsity career as subs.

As the game opened our varsity was tight and shaky. They did not play well to begin with, and as the quarter continued they began to fall apart. I was sitting next to Vernon. We looked at each other and knew that it would not be long. I think we both were confident in our abilities but scared of the inauguration. I said to him as one of the other Kentucky guards made a bad pass out of bounds, "I hope you go first," since I was more than a little nervous. My hands stayed wet with sweat no matter how I dried them on the towel.

The name "Hatton," rang out from assistant coach Harry Lancaster. I patted Vern on the back, "Good luck—go to it, Vern." I sat back with a slight grin on my face as, with a worried look, he trotted toward Coaches Rupp and Lancaster. He had no sooner received his instructions when I heard "Beck" ring out. I almost froze but forced myself to run forward to receive the words of insight. As I arrived at the scorer's table Vern was waiting to go into the game, and I said "Beck in for Burrow." Then I sat on the floor with Vernon. He turned to me and said quietly, "We both win, and we both lose; let's go in and show them that sophomores can play with the big boys." With that, we both entered our very first varsity game.

Vernon scored the first time he got his hands on the ball, and I cleared seven rebounds the first six minutes. At half time, soaked with sweat and panting heavily, I was still nervous. Still, Vern and I both knew we had helped bring the game back to proper perspective. The first team entered the game to begin the second half, went on with the lead that we helped gain and demolished LSU. It was great to feel the thrill of victory at that level of competition. I knew that Billie, listening to the game on the radio in Lexington, would be even more pleased than I was.

I spent December practicing and playing basketball. Billie worked at the hospital and organized our apartment, and we both looked forward to spending our first Christmas there together.

UK won the Christmas tournament in Lexington, and the team went home for a 48-hour holiday break. Billie and I stayed at the apartment. On Christmas Eve we attended worship service. The lighting of the Christmas candles has always been a very meaning-

ful experience for me, and as Billie and I went out into that night
with our glowing candles, everything seemed perfect.

That Christmas would be our first together as husband and
wife—it was also the first time that Billie would be away from her
family for the holidays. So, her family brought the Christmas
celebration to her.

Thelma, Billie's mother, and two of her brothers, Dickie and
Jimmy, left early Christmas morning from the Valley and brought
us a bountiful dinner from the farm. It was a lovely thing to do, but
more important, it buoyed Billie's sagging spirits.

Though Billie had been in Lexington for only a month, I was
concerned as she was becoming more pale and thin and noticeably
weaker. Christmas Day I took her mother aside to share my concern.
We agreed that if Billie continued to fail, she should return to the
Valley for more treatments. I knew that would be easier said than
done since Billie was determined to stay in Lexington until summer
and "live a normal life."

Our team wasn't scheduled to play until just before the New Year.
In January we would begin our march through the SEC (South
Eastern Conference) schedule and, we hoped, on to the NCAA. I
hardly let myself think about the title—it meant so much to me. And
now we were closer than ever before. Billie's excitement about it
almost matched mine. We still ranked in the Top 10 but we had
dropped a couple of pre-conference games through a very tough
schedule. The coaching staff of UK always believed that the way
to get the team ready for the post-New Year conference grind was
to play the best competition in the nation in December. Usually that
was the case, except for the season opener. That game, most of the
time, was against a weaker opponent, though Vernon Hatton and I
still laughed about our first experience under fire.

Vernon had broken into the first five because of his outstanding
play. I was still the backup for Bob Burrow. However, I took solace
in having started one game when Bob was hurt and unable to play.
My emotions ran sky-high at the opportunity. The game was against
Dayton University, and I was to go up against Bill Ulh, who up to
that time was the only person I had ever played against that was
over seven feet tall! I so wanted to do well that I did not do well at
all. My moves were poorly coordinated, and after the first 10

minutes I was benched and Jerry Bird, who usually played forward, replaced me. Though we lost the game, he played brilliantly, scoring 36 points.

I felt terrible over my poor showing, but it soon slipped into the back of my mind. That's the way it had to be, otherwise you could adversely affect your future by dwelling on the past.

Bob Burrow was back in the line-up for the very next game, the opening of the Christmas tourney, and we swept through to victory. My role again was back-up to the All-American from Texas on the court, and to the little brunette from Georgia off the court.

Our neighbors were all recently-married students. Though we were all busy studying and working, a community of mutual concern grew rapidly among the tenants. Dick and Nancy Rushing, a very gregarious couple, had lived there several years. They went out of their way to make sure everyone knew each other. Dick had been a star football player at UK, and he would soon be graduating and heading for the beginning conflict in Southeast Asia where he would distinguish himself as a fighter pilot.

We found our days in that apartment both lovely and loving. Billie functioned as one who was perfectly healthy. She worked 40 hours a week as a registered nurse, cooked, kept house, helped me with my studies and saw all the home basketball games. Our first five months there were as near a normal home life as we were ever to experience. The one exception came in late January when she returned to the Valley for more treatments and blood transfusions.

Billie had continued to grow weaker, and I had called her mother to contact Dr. Marshall. Smoak called Billie one evening and convinced her to come home briefly. She left Lexington only on the condition that she return within two weeks. Smoak was true to his word. She was back for the end of the basketball season.

Upon her return to Lexington in February, Billie's self-confidence really bounced back. Now she believed that eventually she would lick the cancer, and though she was still very thin, her healthy, light-bronze complexion was returning. She fairly glowed. We believed her cancer was in remission, and we rejoiced.

Spring that year was magnificent in beauty and mild in temperature, and Billie and I loved to walk leisurely across the campus. We spent our weekends enjoying parks and driving through the bluegrass regions near Lexington and Paris. She loved the horse farms, and soon we found favorite places with huge trees and lovely bodies of running water. They were not her farm back in Georgia, but they were as close as we could find. We took books and spent long, lazy hours reading, napping and just talking.

The basketball season continued into early March. Kentucky won the SEC championship and traveled to Iowa City to play in the NCAA tourney. I played a great deal as back-up center to Bob Burrow. We lost some very close games but were still considered one of the top 10 in the nation. We kept moving up and down the charts, from fourth to seventh, and dropped to number 10 once. However, after winning the conference championship, we landed in the number six slot until after the national tournament. In the quarter-final championship game against The University of Iowa, we lost in the last few minutes. My dream had come so close, but there would be no final four NCAA shoot-out for Kentucky that year. We returned to Lexington a dejected team. The University of North Carolina would eventually be crowned the champions for 1956.

Though Billie enjoyed watching the games played in Lexington and listened to the road games on the radio, she was as glad as I when the season ended. Now our afternoons and evenings would be free. Because of our tight budget, we did not go out much, but spent our evenings in our small, comfortable apartment.

The Rushings had decided to move to a house and leave their apartment, so they sub-leased it to Jack and Sue Butler who planned to get married over the spring holiday. Jack was a 260-pound football tackle, and Sue was a diminutive girl of approximately 100 pounds. The Rushings had given us the key to the apartment, and we waited for the honeymoon couple to arrive from Jacksonville, Florida, where they had been married.

Several hours before they got back, Billie and I made one last perusal of their apartment. Friends had brought gifts of food and small furnishings. We wanted to make certain everything was just right, "as if," as Billie commented with a wry smile, "they will really care or even notice." Nonetheless, we were diligent, having planned a small neighborhood "welcome to the newlyweds" party that evening in our apartment. The party guests were present by the time the Butlers arrived. They were very tired since they had driven most of the day. Some of the fellows unloaded their car, carrying everything up the three flights to their apartment. Ours was next door, and we shared common walls. This was not very private, but at least you got to know your neighbors well.

Jack and Sue were delighted with the party, and the festivities were in full swing when Billie announced that it would only be proper to allow the newlyweds privacy for the evening, and we would excuse them. The other guests were invited to stay. The girls quickly picked up on the idea and pushed it. I discovered later that Billie had alerted them, feeling that Jack would leap at the bait, but Sue might have to be convinced that they would not hurt our feelings by leaving early.

When Jack and Sue went to their apartment and we heard the bolt being set in place, Billie divulged her plan. It would probably take the Butlers an hour or less to get ready for bed, she said. We were to continue our party until that time. Billie would monitor the new couple's activities through the common wall between our kitchen and their bedroom. When they went to bed we would adjourn quietly to the kitchen to listen. Some of the fellows lamely protested that it was an invasion of privacy, but Billie explained her diabolically simple plan.

She had noticed that afternoon while making their bed that the mattress and box spring rested on slats. She arranged the slats so that persons lying motionless would have no problem. However, any unusual or prolonged movement would allow the slats to soon work loose and the mattress and spring would go crashing to the floor! Everyone laughed at the thought of the potential happening.

Our party, now somewhat subdued, continued. Soon Billie stepped into the living room to report that the Butlers had just gone to bed. As silently as mice, we all moved into the kitchen to take up listening posts. Some even put the open ends of water glasses against the wall and pressed their ears to them. There really was no need for that. Suddenly we heard a blood-curdling yell and the crash of the collapsing bed, quickly followed by some loud expletives from Jack.

Our entire party rushed out of our apartment to the Butlers' door and beat on it until a very disheveled Jack, wearing a robe, non-

chalantly opened the door. That was a mistake. The group streamed
into the bedroom to see Sue on the mattress covered with a sheet,
her mouth open in shock. Suddenly, she and Jack caught on that it
had all been planned and began to laugh as hard as the rest of us.
Sue scampered into the bathroom to get her robe as the fellows put
the bed together, this time under Jack's careful supervision. When
it was done he tried to extricate us from their apartment, but he
finally gave up and the party continued into the wee hours of the
morning.

Jack Butler always blamed me for that night's set-up, and no
matter what anyone else said, he "knew that Billie was too nice and
innocent" ever to do such a thing. Everyone admitted, however, that
the episode "broke the ice" in bringing new neighbors together, and
the Butlers found themselves very much at home in their new
apartment on Limestone Drive sooner than they expected.

"Oh, Ed, it's so beautiful."

Billie was sitting beside me as we drove through the bluegrass
countryside at sunset. It was early May and spring had blossomed
in God's full glory. As the white board fences of the horse farms
flashed by, Billie exclaimed in delight at a group of mares racing
across a field. "Oh, Ed" she exclaimed, "look at them running.
Aren't they beautiful?" This drive from Lexington to Paris was
Billie's favorite, and we had timed it to coincide with the setting
sun, the time of day when the famous bluegrass almost glowed in
cobalt brilliance.

It was to be the last drive we'd make to Paris; the girl beside me
was not the same Billie who had come to Lexington full of vitality.
During the past several weeks her strength and her enthusiasm for
life had begun to wane.

"Darling, quit your job at the hospital," I had urged. "You don't
have to put yourself through that." She did cut back on her hours,
but she would not leave altogether. "I promised them I would work
until the end of May, Ed," she said, "when we go home for the
summer." Yet, even knowing we would be home in a few weeks did
not seem to excite her. Dark hollows spread around her eyes which
were becoming more and more lifeless. That was why I had
suggested this drive to Paris.

The sun disappeared behind clouds banking into the west and we turned back toward Lexington. It was still beautiful at night with the white fences glowing in the light of the full moon. We talked very little, only the hum of the motor and the slap of the tires on tar strips broke the silence. Billie had rested her head back on the seat cushion, her hands folded lifeless in her lap. I knew she was dreading the three-flight climb to our apartment.

Reaching home, I let her out at the front door and quickly parked in the rear. Then I bounced up our stairs catching up with Billie a little over halfway. She had sagged against the stair railing, breathing hard, trying to regain her strength. Five months before, when we had moved in this building, we had both dashed up the stairs time and again, chasing each other in excitement. Now her every step was sheer agony.

With my arms around her shoulders, I almost carried her up the last flights and helped her into our bedroom. As she lay on the bed, breathing heavily, beads of perspiration covering her forehead, I felt her pulse. It was racing.

"I'm going to call a doctor or take you right to the hospital's emergency room," I said.

"No . . . no, please, Ed," she sighed, her eyes imploring me. "All I need is a little rest and I'll be all right." I knew that both of us realized this was a fallacy; Billie would get better at times, but she would never be all right. For her slight remission of the past few months had now given way to the onslaught of the deadly cancer advancing within her. Her sparkling eyes had dimmed, her bronze complexion had paled. Billie was now beginning to fight for her very life. I sat on the side of the bed and took her hand.

"I'm going to die, darling," she said softly.

I was startled and surprised; a chill swept through me. "Sure," I floundered, "sure, we're all going to die someday."

"That's not what I mean, and you know it," she said quietly. Her voice, despite its pained fatigue, was dead serious. "I'm losing the battle, Ed. All of a sudden I'm so tired, more than I have ever been. And I can feel something awful happening within me."

She squeezed my hand lightly and smiled weakly: "I'm going to die, and we need to talk about it."

I braced myself. If this is what Billie wanted, I'd do my best.

"Okay," the word came out sounding husky, "let's talk about it. Do you think you're going to die soon?"

"I . . . I don't know," she said. "I don't want to think so, but I do think it will be sooner than the doctors said at first." Tears glimmered in her eyes.

"Oh, Ed," she sighed, "I don't want to die. I want to live but . . . but I don't know how." Now she was sobbing, great heaving sobs wrenching her thin body. "It's not that I'm afraid to die, Ed. I really don't think I am." She bit her lips. "It's just that I don't want to. I don't want to leave you."

"And I don't want you to leave me," I cried. "I need you so very much." As her slender, pale arms reached up to me, I picked her up gently and held her close. "Honey, we can lick this thing together," I blurted. I kept repeating the words again and again. " I know we can, yes, we can." But Billie said nothing, just weeping, softly now, in my arms.

Finally, we lay side by side on the bed. She had stopped crying and had wiped her eyes with a tissue. "Ed," she said firmly, "I always promised you that I would be honest, and you promised me the same. Well, I'm *not* giving up, believe me. But I know that I'm losing. I can feel my strength leaving me, and I had to tell you because I knew you sensed it. I just can't stand a false silence between us, and I know what you see because I can look in the mirror. I know what you're thinking because I'm thinking the same. It's just that the time is getting here faster than I thought it would."

"Do you want to go home now?" I asked. "I could take you home before exams and return to Georgia right after them."

Billie raised up and sat on the edge of the bed.

"No," she responded, "I promised the hospital that I would work until the end of May, because I just have to do that—for me."

I said nothing for I knew that her continuing to work was symbolic of not giving up. For the next three weeks she would minister unto those less ill than herself.

"What do you want me to do?" I felt bewildered, helpless.

"Remember the covenant? Don't forget it, Ed, for anyone, including me."

"Now what do you mean by that?" I asked. I thought we had

forgotten all about the covenant we had made at another time, another place.

Billie reached out and took my hand. "Well, darling, this disease may reach the point where I don't know what I'm doing. I may say things that I really do not mean to say. There may come a time when I'll even ask you to come and be with me, but that will not be what I really want."

She studied me imploringly. "Do you understand what I'm saying, Ed? I may even ask you to come in front of others, even get angry if you don't. But I need to know now that you will never leave the university for *anything*, even me."

I sat down beside her and held her close. "Billie, darling, I made that promise to not leave the university, and I now affirm it again. I will try to come when I can, but I promise you that I will stay here and study and stay with the team."

Nodding her head in agreement, Billie then turned to me and in a voice that trembled, said, "Try to be with me when I die, Ed. I know I will not be alone because Jesus Christ has promised me his presence. But if you can be with me and hold my hand like this, and pray with me . . . ."

I held her very close, tears streaming down my cheeks. "I'll be with you, I promise," I choked.

For several moments we clung to each other, our silence confirming my promise. And then our conversation shifted to some practical things.

In a lighter tone of voice Billie said that she wanted to set up a system of hand signals so that if she could not communicate verbally, or if she went into a coma, I could communicate with her. I would hold her right hand and one long squeeze from her would be "yes." Two short ones would be "no." We practiced one of them as I leaned over and whispered in her ear, "Do you know that I love you?" Her squeeze was long and tight as we kissed goodnight.

I pulled the covers up to her neck, kissed her again, said "Goodnight, my love," then turned out the light and went into the living room to study. As I sat at my desk with a book open in front of me, I could only wonder what would come next. How could there be so much pleasure and so much pain at the same time? I laid my head down on the desk and began to pray. The next thing I knew, my neck was being gently rubbed . . . by Billie. She was standing behind me in her white nurse's uniform. I had slept at the desk all night. It was 6:15 a.m. and she was on her way to work. She still looked tired, but radiant.

"Did you get much studying done?"

"Not much," I tried to smile.

"Remember," she smiled, "part of our covenant is that you can't flunk out either." And with that she laughed and kissed me goodbye on the cheek.

20

Bittersweet Summer

Our departure for the Valley at the beginning of summer was made with mixed feelings.

Dear Helen Hunt, in her inimitable way, had given us a wonderful going-away party. She had taken Billie under her wing like another daughter, and I knew that Billie loved her. Many of our old gang from church were at the party along with Reverend and Mrs. Yates, who had also become very close to Billie during the past months.

However, as hard as everyone tried to make it a joyous scene, the obvious change in Billie's appearance couldn't help but be noticed by our friends. An underlying mood of compassion and concern struck a somber note through the whole evening.

Billie, of course, sensed it, and when we returned to our apartment she broke into tears. "I know I look terrible, Ed, and it just kills me to know that others notice it." She wiped her eyes. "I wanted the party to be fun for everyone, but I had to spoil it."

I pulled her over to our lumpy, old sofa and drew her down. "Honey, no one wanted to be obvious about it, but it's just human nature. People are uneasy in the presence of illness. For one thing, it reminds us of our own human vulnerability. That's probably a good thing because we all play the part of God at times, thinking we are immortal. Then we are confronted with our mortality mirrored in the presence of another, and it can be shattering."

"I guess so, Ed," she sighed, "but I just don't want people to feel sorry for me."

"But you must remember that they are really feeling sorry for themselves, Billie," I said. "They may project their grief on to you but it's *they* who are scared. We're all such frail creatures, and we know it. The trouble is that too many people don't have enough faith in God to accept their mortality for what it is."

I drew her close to me, put my hand under her chin and turned her face toward me. "But you, my brave little one, have that faith. In fact, you're very strong, Billie. I saw it in you when you first took care of me back in the hospital so long ago, remember?"

She smiled at the memory.

"Well with your faith, just be more sensitive to other folks who feel so vulnerable, accept their fears for what they are, will-o'-the-wisps, and let them know that love can win out in any situation."

Her face brightened. "I think I'm beginning to see what you mean, Ed."

"Yes," I responded, becoming more excited, "As you have changed your own fear into faith, you may just be the catalyst to help them do the same." As we talked about her opportunity in this, I found myself becoming excited about the parallelism between Billie's suffering and Christ's.

"Billie, I believe in Jesus Christ as our Lord and Savior, not just because someone told me he is God's Son but because he was also a human being like you and me, yet so different. Remember how he hung on the cross that Good Friday from noon until three in the afternoon, and after all that torture and loneliness he cried, 'My God, my God, why hast thou forsaken me?'"

My wife nodded, snuggling closer to me.

"Well, that for me wasn't so much a question as it was a declarative statement. For three hours Jesus had been totally alone, 'forsaken,' as he said, but he won out against all the odds. For even without having God with him, he had shown that love conquers. He had become the God of all gods."

I looked into her shining brown eyes. "Oh darling, don't you see that Christ has shown us that love can withstand whatever, can overcome whichever and can make all whole when everything else crumbles?"

Stopping for a moment for breath, I smiled and said, "Please forgive me, darling, I didn't mean to preach a sermon."

"No, Ed, go on. I like what you're saying."

"Well, then, if I understand the Scriptures correctly, there is nothing within us that is immortal. The Greeks thought immortality was what lived on within us no matter what, that it could not come to an end. But Christianity does not teach that, as I understand it. Jesus has given to each of us in faith the gift of eternal love. That's our gift from God. It is not an innate entity within us no matter what we do or how we live. But I believe that somehow that gift of faith, of eternal love which comes to us totally and unconditionally from God, activates us for an eternal journey beyond the imprisonment of our humanity."

In my enthusiasm I stood up and placed my hands on her thin shoulders. "Oh, Billie, there will be those who will come into your presence with whom you will have the opportunity to share the truth. They will see it in your confidence of faith and your certainty of love. And you will give them the greatest of all hope."

Billie seemed to fairly glow as she considered this, and we talked about it long into the evening. Now it seemed to her that her illness was not a dead end, but it might well have some purpose in helping others.

"When I get back to the cancer clinic in Macon, Ed," she said enthusiastically, "I'm going to talk to the doctors about experiments they may wish to do with me to find out more about this disease. I've gained a good bit of medical knowledge in school and work, so maybe as they try out new treatments or medicines, I could let them know in their own medical terms what's happening to me."

Now Billie was excited. "Just think, Ed, it might not help, but maybe, just maybe, it could help others." She became somber again. "And even if it doesn't help, I'll at least have the peace of mind in knowing that something positive might be happening because of my illness."

In a way our talk that night helped her look forward even more to returning to her beloved farm. Like a cut blossom in the sun, her body was wilting each day, but now her attitude was becoming stronger. Somehow there had to be a purpose throughout all of this; she vowed she would either find it or create it.

Our return to Georgia that June was joyous and jolting. Billie heaved a deep sigh as we drove through the familiar peach orchards. But immediately upon our return she had to go to the hospital for blood transfusions. The trip and the preparation for it had taken its toll. In a few days, however, she returned to the farm refreshed and with new vigor. It was probably a combination of the new blood which helped fortify her and returning to the home she loved.

She wanted to return to nursing at our local hospital, but we all finally persuaded her to take the summer off to regain her strength.

"You just have to relax and get ready for our move back to the university this fall, Billie," I said in company with her family. But there was an unspoken awareness among us that unless something drastically improved she probably would not return to Kentucky in the fall. However, it was something not one of us wanted to think about, much less discuss.

June was rushing by quickly. My job at the Blue Bird bus company had picked up exactly where it had left off the previous September. The company had grown and, of course, that meant more customers from farther areas of the country and the world. There was more responsibility for me, and we had to do things in a more efficient manner.

Billie became active too. Despite family pressure she did some hospital work—a day here, a day there. She filled in for a sick nurse or was called in on a special case. She loved the work so much, we soon ceased remonstrating with her. But at least Billie was more realistic about her schedule. She no longer worked regular hours or late at night. If the hospital called and she felt like it, she would do it; if not, she told them "not today." And she never worked double shifts now, which were her forte when I first met her.

She was elated that the doctors in Macon had become intrigued with her offer to let them experiment with her case. Thus, she would relay into a tape recorder in medical terminology her minute-by-minute physical reactions to the medicine and treatments. Later a number of these experiments were studied, not only in Macon, but also at Johns Hopkins Research Center.

Early in June when Billie was in the Macon Hospital for a few days, I would drive up to see her every night after work. One evening I left a little later than usual for the 30-mile trip. There was a light rain, the highway was slick and I was not as cautious as I should have been. About six miles from the Valley I zoomed over a hill and suddenly came upon an old farm truck moving very slowly. I could not pass because of oncoming traffic. I could not pull to his right because of a narrow shoulder. Applying my brakes sent me into a fight for my life.

My car skidded and fish-tailed, and then I lost control completely. As I felt the centrifugal force pulling me toward the door, I instinctively pulled my feet and legs up into the front seat and covered my head with my hands. My tires screamed as other car horns blared. Then there was a thud, the car stopped, its motor still running. I shut it off and got out. The car had spun twice in the middle of the road and then shot backwards off the shoulder into a huge mound of red dirt. All the other cars and trucks on the highway had miraculously avoided my deadly merry-go-round.

Astonished people rushed up to see if I was all right, and one older farmer said, "Young man, somebody up there sure had his hand on you."

I called Buddy Luce, the president of Blue Bird, and told him of the accident. He was a good friend and came within 15 minutes. I apologized for wrecking one of the company cars, but he was not upset. Instead, he was grateful that I had not been hurt. After looking at the wrecked car, he gave me the keys to his own car and said, "Ed, go on and see Billie. Tell her hello for me. Don't worry about anything; I'll get the car back to the plant."

As I drove away, I thought of all the marvelous friends that we had. Those people who wanted to help in any way, and yet maintained their distance so that we could live our lives as naturally as possible. I thanked God for all of them in Georgia and in Kentucky.

Billie was quite upset about the accident. I had tried to minimize it, but Bobby, one of her brothers, had come by the scene shortly after I had left. He discovered I had not been hurt and called Billie to convey the good news.

As I was leaving her that night, I leaned over to kiss her goodnight. She held me around the neck and said she was going to be released that weekend. Then she added, "Remember the covenant."

I said, "I am!"

She said, "A part of the covenant is that I'm supposed to die first. If you get killed, I will be very angry at you." She began to laugh, and I laughed with her. What in the world can you do but laugh when you are with someone who can find humor within the very shadow of death?

21

'Just Some More Time'

It was nearing the end of July. For the past couple of weeks Billie cycled through good and bad days. There were very few days that were in-between. She felt either very well or very ill. Moreover, although she did not smoke, Billie had developed a persistent cough, almost like a smoker's cough. There was a hoarseness in her voice, and she jokingly called herself "Gravel Gertie."

On one of her good days we sat with her entire family around the noontime dinner table enjoying conversation. Helen had come down the evening before from Macon, and Billie always looked forward to her visits. In many ways they were alike, and Billie felt that Helen really understood what she was experiencing. Whether she did or not, one thing was certain: Helen listened to her, cared deeply for Billie, and she and I knew Billie appreciated that.

Someone told a joke at the table, everyone laughed and the story really hit Billie's funny-bone. As she continued to laugh, she began to cough. As it became more persistent she excused herself. The rest of us continued with our conversation. Probably 10 minutes passed before Billie's mother noted that she had not returned to the table. Suddenly we heard Thelma's call for help, and we rushed out to the front porch where she had found Billie crumpled on the floor against the door screen, motionless.

I carried Billie to her bed, and though we were able to revive her, she did not respond completely. She was unable to walk without support, and her thinking was unclear. We all felt it best to rush her to the hospital. She resisted the idea at first, but soon she sat in the front seat with her head back and her eyes closed. Her hands were pale and folded on her lap. Helen sat next to her and supported her as we sped over the country roads. Dr. Marshall had been alerted, and he met us there. Billie was admitted to the hospital. Ironically, she checked into the same room that I had stayed in some 18 months earlier.

They discovered that she was slightly dehydrated and needed intravenous nourishment, but her blood count was within the normal range. Nothing specific seemed to have caused her blackout and the resulting dizziness. But Smoak Marshall felt that she should stay in the hospital over the weekend. It was then late Saturday afternoon.

The weekend passed without any real clue as to what had happened the day before at the farm. Billie remained in a semi-coma most of the time, yet there were moments that she was quite lucid. However, on Tuesday morning she took a sudden turn for the worse. Her cough became more persistent, and her breathing labored. By now she had been catheterized and, of course, the feedings continued via the veins. An oxygen tent helped her breathing. All of these efforts apparently brought no progress. She seemed to be headed in a downward spiral, and even the medical staff was very concerned.

Smoak Marshall had to leave town on Wednesday morning for an important medical meeting, and Dr. Frank Vinson took over the case. The three of us met late Tuesday night, and the doctors told me they had consulted with the Macon Cancer Clinic as well as some medical advisors at Grady Hospital in Atlanta. They had come to the consensus that if Billie continued to fail over the next 24 hours, they could not reverse the trend, and she would die. One of the doctors in Atlanta had recommended they try a mustard gas injection directly into the veins, but when he heard of her weakened condition he withdrew his suggestion.

However, something made me pursue the mustard gas idea—I persistently asked questions about the treatment and what it was designed to accomplish. In 1956, there were still many concerns about its validity and effectiveness. But one thing that all the doctors agreed upon was that anyone taking the treatment needed to be in fairly strong physical condition. In most cases where the gas had been administered the patient became violently ill—I knew that Billie's weakened condition would not allow her to withstand that kind of onslaught. After hearing all the negatives, I asked if there were any positives. Smoak spoke up with, "Well, I have to say that it would be doing something that may help. It is better than just standing and watching her die."

I thanked all of them and told them I would let them know the next morning. Before I left the meeting, I asked once again if they thought there was anything else that could be done. Not one of them replied.

Now it looked as if Billie probably wouldn't live through the weekend. Tuesday night she was in a primary coma. There were moments we thought she recognized us, but those were few and far between. I left her hospital room late that evening and made my way to the altar of the Methodist Church. I had not been making the nightly sojourns as I had the previous summers, but I was still getting there at least twice a week. This night I needed some special insight. If the decision to give the mustard gas was incorrect, then I would be accelerating her death. I recalled several conversations that Billie and I had had concerning mercy killing or euthanasia. She had seen many hopeless cases and felt there needed to be a time when you allowed a person to die with dignity. Yet, she also knew the difficulty of that decision and its awesome responsibility.

Billie had made me promise that, once there was no hope in her case, I would allow her to die in dignity. "Not with all those machines and apparatuses attached that keep people alive, when they don't want to live anymore," she had pleaded. As I remembered my promise, I felt very restless. I believed emphatically Billie's time had not come. It was not only that I loved her, but there seemed to be so many things left undone—her concerns for medical science and the experimentation and for her family and what she wanted to share with them. Even as much as we had shared, it seemed there

must be more to our life together. That night while kneeling in the
dark church I knew that Billie would eventually die, as we all
would, but I could not believe that this was the time for her. Yet, I
found myself doubting my own belief.

As I rose to my feet, still very unsettled concerning the next
proper step to take, I stepped across the quiet sanctuary to that
stained glass window with Jesus holding the little lamb in his arms.
No sound had drawn me to it. I just had the feeling that I needed to
view once again the symbol that had helped me so much in the past.
After communicating with Jesus, I walked out of the church feeling
that no matter what decision was made, it would somehow work
out best.

The next morning I asked Dr. Vinson to proceed with the mustard
gas treatments. He felt it best to wait for 24 hours and see if there
was any change in Billie's condition. He had never administered
this gas before, so he called Grady Hospital in Atlanta to see if one
of the doctors might come to the Valley. That was impossible, so
they suggested she be transported to Atlanta. I said no to that—she
was too weak to make a 100-mile journey. Finally, a compromise
was arranged. They would send the mustard gas by the highway
patrol with instructions for injecting it. Dr. Vinson then would call
them at 7:00 Thursday evening and clarify any directions. They
would stay near the phone for the next hour to hear of Billie's
immediate reactions, and they would give emergency numbers
where they could be reached throughout the night, in the event of
some violent reaction. One of the doctors from the Grady medical
staff carefully explained to us what would happen, "Within two or
three hours after the administration of the gas, the patient becomes
violently ill; this becomes her crisis." He stopped for a moment and
continued. "Until it happens, we don't know whether it's for better
or worse."

"You mean . . .?"

"Yes," he said compassionately, "she could die, or, she could
become much better. We don't know right now."

The next day was grim. The stress of the last week, plus continuing to work at the bus company, was taking its toll. Family members
were taking turns being with Billie during the day, but we all felt
helpless in her comatose state.

On Thursday evening Dr. Vinson called Grady and received instructions. Smoak Marshall was still out of the city, but Vinson had conferred with him earlier, and he had concurred with the decision to use the gas. Beginning at 7:30, as we sat next to Billie's bed, the gas was injected in her right arm. There seemed no indication that she felt the needle or cared one way or the other. The procedure took about an hour, and by 9 o'clock the tension began to build—when would the violent outburst take place? The nurses were alerted, and we were told to press the help button at the first sign of Billie's distress. Ten o'clock came and she seemed to be in a deeper sleep than usual. At 11 o'clock I sent the family home and told them that if anything happened I would call. Dr. Vinson also left, leaving word that he be called at the first sign of change.

The lonely minutes ticked away endlessly. Billie lay motionless, silent. I had not really talked with her for more than six days. There was so much I wanted to say. I began to pray for Billie at her bedside, kneeling, standing and sometimes just sitting and holding her hand. I asked God to let Billie stay with me a little longer. "Just some more time, Father," I pleaded, tears burning my eyes. "Just some more time."

It was now 1 a.m.; several hours had passed since those violent seizures were to have occurred. Billie continued to lie motionless, breathing evenly under the oxygen tent as the intravenous feeding continued, the clear liquid monotonously dripping into her veins. Then it was 2:30 and I was feeling the tiredness and stress in the depth of my bones. I fought to stay awake and began to walk back and forth in the room. Still, Billie didn't move except for the rising and falling of her chest.

The nurses stopped in regularly and just before 3:00, with still no change in Billie, a nurse urged me to take a walk. "It will refresh you," she said compassionately. She assured me that she would check Billie regularly and that they had placed a call buzzer in her hand for extra insurance in case she awakened.

Just before leaving, I checked Billie one last time. The oxygen tent was still in place. Her head was raised slightly to make her more comfortable. The intravenous feeding was still dripping into her left hand. Everything seemed to be all right, so I bowed my head, prayed for her healing and walked out. I was gone less than five minutes when I decided to return. Still no change. Ten minutes later I came back to find her the same.

One of the nurses said, "Ed, we'll check on her. You must rest."

I walked toward the doctors' lounge where there was a sofa and a refrigerator with some beverages. As I entered the lounge, I met Dr. McKee, a friend from a neighboring town, waiting to deliver a baby. He immediately asked about Billie as he had heard of the mustard gas injection. "I think her calm condition is a good sign, Ed," he said. I was feeling better, so we talked about 30 minutes before they called him into the delivery room. During our conversation, one of the nurses had poked her head into the room to say that Billie was the same.

I read a magazine and drank another cup of coffee to help me stay awake. I looked at my watch; it was 4:15. I went back to Billie's room; she was exactly the same so I returned to the lounge. I dozed in the chair, then woke with a start and looked at my watch. It was a few minutes before five! I rushed toward her room.

As I approached, I thought it strange that the door was closed. I had left it ajar. Maybe one of the nurses had closed it on her way out.

As I hesitantly pushed the door open, the first rays of morning sunlight were beginning to brighten the window. I glanced toward the bed and stared dumbfounded. It couldn't be! And then I heard, "Darling, what are you doing here?" Billie sat on the side of the bed, fully dressed in the clothes she had worn to the hospital some seven days earlier. I did not know whether to rush over to kiss her or support her so she would not fall or caution her about getting out of bed. "Why are you here so early?" she asked. I stumbled through some words as my mind raced for clarity. I could not believe what I was seeing.

"I . . . I had some things that I had to get done at the office, so I'm a little early," I lied haltingly. "Do you feel all right, Billie?" I asked.

"Why, yes, I feel fine,"she said pertly. "I'm just a little tired. But I could not believe it when I awoke a few minutes ago—the oxygen and the needle. I had to go to the bathroom, so I shut the oxygen off and took the needle out. They shouldn't have had all those things on me—that's for sick people. I feel fine. So I decided to get dressed and wait for Smoak so he can dismiss me and let me go home."

I was still in shock. Here, a lovely woman who just hours before had been fighting for her life, was sitting on the side of the bed, fully dressed, saying she was fine. She stood up to walk over to the mirror to comb her hair, and I moved quickly to her side to make certain she would not fall. She glanced at me strangely.

"Are you sure you feel all right, Billie?" I asked

"I feel just fine, Ed. Really, darling. I am a little weak, but believe me, I'm fine."

I wanted to believe her but could not. We pray for miracles, but when they happen we question them. We pray for new strength to invigorate a weakened body, but when it happens we wonder whether or not it really has taken place. Humans are so ridiculous. We assume that God can do anything, but when something extraordinary does take place, we doubt if it could actually happen. I guess that is where God gets most of his laughs. He must have a tremendous sense of humor to tolerate the things we mortals do.

Billie combed her hair, brushed her teeth, then drank a glass of water. I was still watching her in disbelief. She walked toward me, "Now I can kiss you. I had to get rid of that terrible taste in my mouth. What have they been feeding me?"

"You know how hospital food is," I said, not knowing what answer to give. I took her in my arms and kissed her gently. She looked up at me and said, "That was so nice, but I will not break." With that we pulled each other close and kissed passionately.

In a few moments we sat down together near the window. Sunrise was now blooming in all its golden splendor. My favorite time of day, and certainly my most favorite day that summer. Here, Billie sat with me, as alert and sensitive as I had ever seen her, where just hours before the doctors wondered if she would live until morning.

I leaned forward and took her hands in mine. Her head rested back on the cushioned chair.

"Billie, you have been a very sick girl. Very sick. There was a time that we did not think you were going to pull out of it." I allowed the words to sink in for effect. Her look turned to consternation.

"What day is this?"

"It's Friday morning."

"Friday?" There was a long pause. "Why, I don't remember anything. I do remember you and Helen bringing me to the hospital on Saturday, but nothing else. What has happened to me?"

I began to relate the last six days of her life in detail. I tried not to leave anything out, for that had been my promise to her. She listened in rapt attention. I ended by apologizing for my lie about going to work.

"I was not going to work, darling," I said. "I've been here all night. When I saw you sitting on the side of the bed, I just did not know what to say. I had prayed for it to happen, but when it did, I could not believe it. It's like a miracle!"

She raised her head and leaned toward me. I leaned forward to kiss her once again, ever so gently.

"Do you think I've been healed?" she asked.

"Yes, I do. How much and for how long, I don't know, my darling, but God has touched you and made you well. I can't get over it. You are well!"

Then we just sat there in the brightening sunlight, gazing at each other, holding hands and basking in a miracle.

Billie and I had often discussed miraculous healings. From her medical perspective, she had witnessed hopeless cases rise up from their beds of affliction to go out and lead new lives. She believed in physical healing, as well as healing of the emotions and the spirit.

We had even discussed traveling to a famous "faith healer" who was conducting a crusade in the neighboring state. She had not laughed at the thought, but her comment was so very succinct.

"If God wants to heal me, God can heal me here, as well as there. I see no use making that kind of trip."

I agreed completely, but I still would have taken her if she had wished. As for gifts of healing, I feel most doctors have this gift, too. I have always admired these people—it is not just their skill and dedication but the fact that they are co-laborers with God, whose concern I also believe is to make all persons whole and well. The word "salvation" particularly makes sense to me in the context of wholeness or wellness of body, mind and soul.

I also knew that many apparent physical healings happen when a person with emotional or psychological problems manifested in physical ways are handled in a positive manner. Billie had discussed with me the hypochondriacs within the Valley and how a word of assurance from a doctor or a prayer for healing from an authoritative person seemed to work miracles. So I had no problem with that type of healing process.

But Billie's illness was not psychosomatic or emotional. It was cancer, deadly and deep, with cellular growth and division going wild within her body. She had had slight remissions before. A few days later, after her return to the farm, she sat with me planning our day. She seemed to have more pep and energy and love of life than she had had since early spring. She wanted to visit all her old cherished places on the farm and to call on her favorite patients in the Valley. Her physical energies were undoubtedly on the rise.

The doctors were amazed at her rapid turn-around, at her overwhelmingly positive response to the mustard gas treatment. Interestingly, though they would have liked to have taken credit for her rapid recovery, they were reluctant to do so. We all came to the conclusion that a combination of things had resulted in a miracle. How long the miracle would last, no one could begin to guess. Still, a gift of time had been given.

In one of our early conversations upon Billie's return home, I had used the term "borrowed time."

She looked very thoughtful when I said that. "You're right, Ed, I *am* living on borrowed time. My doctors have made it very clear that I still have Hodgkin's disease. But for some reason it has gone into remission."

We were standing at her favorite tree and a summer breeze ruffled her lovely chestnut hair. She brushed it back and continued, "Why have I been given this 'borrowed time'? Why have I regained so much physical strength?"

I murmured some attempt to answer, but she continued, "Maybe I have been given this because of the experiments I still must undergo at the Macon Clinic. Maybe there are people that I should talk with, I mean really talk with about things we have never really said. And that includes folks in my own family."

She looked up at me, her eyes bright and alive. "One thing I know, Ed, I'm not going to waste any more time or take it for granted. I've walked through the Valley of the Shadow, and though

it didn't frighten me, for reasons I can't explain I think I was allowed
to return to begin the most productive part of my life."

"And what is that, darling?" I asked, holding her close to me as
we both looked down the windswept meadow.

"I believe I now know my true mission field. It is not in darkest
Africa working among the natives. It's right here where I have been
reared, with the people I know and love. God has called me to be a
missionary, I know, and it took my walk through the Valley of the
Shadow to be awakened to what and where it really is."

The girl I was holding seemed more at peace with herself than I
had seen her since that first day she told me about the "minor
surgery" more than a year ago. She seemed to be in total control of
herself, and her softly spoken words were stated with clarity and
purpose. It was clear to me that Billie had discerned the purpose of
this tragedy and I could almost see her glow with triumph of the
spirit.

Billie had been healed completely that early morning in the
hospital; I felt certain of that. True, she still carried the seeds of
cancer within her. But through it she had been given the joyous gift
of peace of mind. Her attitude toward life had been renewed and
glorified. I came to believe that this kind of healing is the greatest
one that God can give.

Billie had first been broken, then she had been blessed and only
then had she been made completely whole—mind, body and spirit.

How truly blessed can any person be?

22

An Angel
Named Woodie

The day arrived for the celebration of our first wedding anniversary. We had spent the time leading up to the middle of September attempting to live as normally as possible after the mind-boggling events of late July.

Billie seemed to possess a new sense and purpose in life. The "borrowed time" theme kept cropping up in our conversations, but the real change was that we no longer talked about long-range goals. We mentioned nothing about what would happen after my graduation in the summer of 1958. Today was the most important day of our life together. I tried not to think about the UK fall semester which would begin in mid-September. Basketball officially began on October 15, and the first game was in early December. We now discussed these imminent dates and other things that were to happen in the near future.

Billie and I accepted the fact that she would not be returning with me to Lexington in the fall. We talked about her coming to the Christmas Tournament, and every now and then we flirted with the idea of her returning to Lexington in the spring. However, we always left that thought hanging as an option. Everything depended, of course, on her health. So we began to fortify ourselves against the reality that we would once again be separated for a number of months. I would be at the University in Lexington, and she would remain on the farm with periodic excursions to the cancer clinic.

For our anniversary we had discussed going back to the beach at St. Simon's Island where we had spent our honeymoon. But, as a substitute, we decided to spend an evening in Macon. We made it a sentimental journey, driving toward the downtown restaurant on the same route we took more than a year ago. A morbid blanket continued to hang over us. In unspoken ways I know we both sensed that this might be the only anniversary we would ever celebrate together.

We returned to the farm very late. Instead of going directly to the house, we parked in one of her father's orchards. It was the first time we had parked like that since our marriage. It was as if we were hungrily reliving our early moments of unfettered togetherness.

I began to share my deepest feelings of love and thanksgiving for Billie and how she had enriched my life. She listened intently, and as I leaned over to kiss her, she put her hand up to my lips.

"Ed, this may sound funny to you, but I must tell you that I have enjoyed being your wife," she said seriously. "I must admit that there have been moments I felt maybe it was not the best thing for you or me. At times, I'm sure, you probably have had that feeling. But darling, you have made me very happy, and if it's possible, I love you more tonight than I ever have. I want you to know that. I don't know how much longer I have to live and how much longer we have together, but thank you for being my husband. I have loved being your wife."

Time seemed to stand still that quiet night in Georgia. It was as if the moon and all the stars had hushed to listen to us.

I lifted my right hand from her lap and brushed away a tear that began to slide down her cheek. Her eyes, though tired, were sparkling with light and love in the brightness from the evening stars. I slid over to be as close as possible to her, and very gently laid her head on the back of the car seat. I held her close and could feel the beating of her heart. Every soft breath of Billie's heightened my consciousness that I was holding the dearest and the loveliest person I had ever known. Time was beginning to slip by and an inner knowledge came over in waves that these moments of oneness would soon be no more. It was difficult to believe that day would ever come, and I kissed her harder and clung to her even more fervently, as if to forestall it. I fought to think of only this moment, our closeness, our kisses and our laughter.

Billie seemed to sense my fight to enjoy the existential present. "It is good, isn't it!" she said. It was not a question, it was a declaration.

"Very good," I sighed, "as it has always been with you, and will always be."

"I wish," she said with a poignant note in her voice, "that I could have been the healthy wife that I wanted to be; that we could have shared more completely what I wanted—but was unable—to give."

"You have given me *you*, darling," I replied, "that is all I ever wanted."

"Oh, I know that, but you know what I mean, don't you?" she asked.

I hesitated, then replied, "I know, but I'm so grateful to God that he has given us this long. But I'm selfish, so very selfish, and so I pray that this year will be better for you than last."

"Ed, I'm on borrowed time. We both know it. I don't know how much longer I have—I feel that it may all end soon. But I don't want you to worry about me. I mean that. Please. I will be all right. I just wish I could be with you in Lexington and see you play this fall. But, even though I can't be there, I will be with you all the time. I'll pray for you and reach out to you, and love you as I do now." With that, we said no more. We kissed and held each other for dear life. For life was dearer to us in that moment than it had ever been, a gift to be shared, and we enjoyed it fully.

We drove home very late. All the lights were out in the house. I carried my one-year bride up the stairs. "Sh-hh," she hushed, "don't wake the others." We walked into our bedroom and held each other once again. Later she emerged from the bathroom prepared for bed and began to giggle. I was lying on the mattress, on the floor. She came to me and said, "You do take a hint so wonderfully well."

My arrival in Lexington for the fall semester made me feel schizophrenic. Already missing Billie terribly, I found myself look-

ing forward to the challenge of school as well as the basketball
season.

I realized that I now had an opportunity to be one of the starting
five players and was well aware of the rugged demands I would
have to meet to make that select number. My former roommate,
Bob Burrow, All-American center, had graduated and was playing
professional basketball. That left me a clear shot to take his place,
and I felt that this is how the coaching staff had planned it. The final
decision, however, would not be made until late November as we
prepared for the season opener.

Coach Lancaster, in consultation with Coach Rupp, had arranged
for me and my two new roommates, John Brewer and Don Mills,
to live in a large, three-bedroom suite with private bath on the first
floor of the dormitory. However, the main reason that I had been
selected to live there was that it was the only dorm room that had
a private phone. Both coaches felt that it was a necessity for me.
Even though all calls went through the university switchboard,
Coach Rupp had kindly arranged that I could make long distance
calls to Georgia and the bills be sent to the athletic department.
Realizing that this was a departure from NCAA rules, they had gone
through red tape to have this cleared with the NCAA executive
committee. They made the exception because of the unusual nature
of the case. Later, the same executive committee would allow the
fans of UK to make donations to help off-set a $30,000-plus medical
bill for Billie's care and treatment.

My new roommates were a godsend. John Brewer assumed the
same role that Bob Burrow had filled for me. I would share with
him whatever news I had, and he would convey it to the team. My
teammates were concerned, yet courteous. I sensed them reaching
out to me in love and support, but very few words were ever said
concerning Billie's condition.

Don Mills, a freshman, was my same height and would turn out
to be my substitute the following year. He was a happy-go-lucky
fellow who was madly in love with his hometown sweetheart, also
a freshman at the university. John and I would counsel with Don
for hours concerning his roller-coaster love-life and the temptations
and complexities of university life. These diversions would always
end up in laughter because of all the crazy and sometimes dumb

things Don would do. But he had such a keen sense of humor that he brought some frivolity into my life, which was turning more and more serious with the pressure of school, basketball and the terrible illness within Billie.

One of the new people I met at Helen Hunt's Sunday night gatherings would prove to be a rock in the time of storm. Woodie Ballard was an auburn-haired lady in her early 30s, whom I wished Billie could meet. She had been a friend of Helen's for several years and Helen, in her sensitive manner, had urged Woodie to meet me.

Woodie Ballard had been married for seven years. On the night of their seventh anniversary her husband had been killed in a tragic accident. A surprise party had been planned for that fateful evening, and Woodie, with a number of friends, had decorated the house in preparation for the celebration.

Woodie's husband was a Public Service worker who specialized in installation and repair of the power lines and generators. Severe electrical storms in the area had disrupted the power to entire neighborhoods, and apparently he was rushing to complete a repair job. As the people gathered for the surprise party, the male guest of honor did not arrive. Fully an hour after the party was due to start the phone rang. Woodie answered and heard the searing news that her husband had been instantly killed by inadvertently touching a high power line.

I met Woodie two years after this terrible accident, and though still encountering some tough times, she had worked through the primary grief cycle in a marvelous way. We had many long conversations concerning loss and love, grief and grace. I now believe God gives people like Woodie to us in time of need, to share our sorrow and to help us through dark days.

Woodie often ate in the university cafeteria, and I would sit with her and just talk. She was an amazingly sensitive and warm person. As she shared her life story one evening in the cafeteria, I came to know a woman who had experienced deep pain, yet had discovered her own inner power through it. "I never thought I would make it," she said. "There were times that I knew I could not go on, but then I was aware of some source of power, of some energy helping me go on. My belief in God and awareness of God's constant presence had not been cultivated," she continued. "Oh, I went to church and was a believer in Christ, but actually there was not dailyness to my faith. But when the crisis arrived, and I was shattered and cut to the quick, I began to evaluate what is and is not important in life. I came to see how very important my faith and trust in God really was."

Woodie talked of the pain of not sharing love, the aloneness without closeness, the longing for a touch and embrace that special person could no longer give. She instilled within me the certainty that I should never miss an opportunity to touch and hold Billie when we were together. She made me realize that our moments were limited, and therefore special, and to intentionally make sure that those special times were celebrated meaningfully.

Woodie's experience was different from mine in that she had seven beautiful years with her husband, and, of course, no indication of an impending tragedy. Then, on a night focused on joy, a phone rang with a message that completely changed her life. She spoke longingly about dreams that would never become reality. Although my time with Billie was limited according to the medical prognosis, we still had time to make practical wishes and dreams come true. I determined not to miss the little things—a touch here, a word there, a stroking of the hair or a beautiful embrace. Those were the things that I would remember after the separation when the pain and the grief bore in.

Again, my situation was different because Billie and I both knew the probable outcome of our marriage. I thought I had begun to prepare for that separation from almost the first moment, but the crisis in the hospital in July had shaken my confidence. Now I was beginning to see that there was no adequate way to prepare. Woodie was able to help me see that my anxiety was valid, and that, prepare as I might, there would be a devastating sense of loss, guilt and anger that I would have to deal with openly after Billie died. *If* she died, I kept telling myself.

Woodie was not only a great listener, which I desperately needed at that time, but one whom I trusted implicitly. Our common tragedy—even with differences—helped me in discussing my feelings and fears and also helped bring to the forefront some hidden needs within Woodie's life which she had not dealt with completely. These would be brought to light during our conversations and not without tears in her eyes and mine.

When basketball season opened, the four tickets that I received as a team member were always shared with my friends. The year before Billie had always come along with Helen Hunt and a various selection of friends from the church. This year, Woodie Ballard would sit with Helen along with couples that had become a special support team of mine. It was a small way of repaying her compassion.

23

'Get into that Corner and Throw Up, Ed!'

I dreamed of being a great athlete since boyhood. I also wanted to go to college and be a great student. I was motivated by the townspeople to excel in sports because of my 6'7" size. But I was trained and equipped to be both an athlete and student in high school by one man—coach Norman Faircloth.

Coach Faircloth was the only coach at Fort Valley High School. He coached football, track, girl's and boy's basketball, plus teaching a full class load of physical education. He had no assistants and no helpers except a few student managers, but he had the avid support of the townspeople and the admiration of every athlete who ever played under him. He and I were especially close. He saw within me the raw materials of an outstanding basketball player, and I saw within him a teacher, motivator, big brother and adviser.

"Remember, Ed, if you're good enough as an athlete you can get a scholarship to college, and that allows you to prepare for your chosen profession," Coach would say. "You have got to keep your grades up. So study and get your work in on time."

There were times that he called me into his office because he had been talking to one of my teachers who determined I was not fulfilling my potential. "If you want to be an average ball player, just goof off," Coach Faircloth would say looking into the distance and listing a litany of ball players that were potentially great athletes but were slothful (one of his favorite words). He would then mention one or two who had worked long and hard and had been rewarded. They had not returned to the farm to work as laborers; they were not driving trucks for a living or working in the factory. They were rising stars in their professions because of the lessons they had learned on the sports field and in the classroom. "They go hand in hand you know, Ed. How you study is how you will practice is how you play," Coach Faircloth admonished.

So every week during the basketball off-season he would meet with me and work out a schedule of what I needed to do on my own time in the gym—how many runs up the gymnasium stairs; how many laps; how many sit ups; how many hook shots from the right, from the left, from the foul line; how many free throws; how many rebounds. Every week he recited a new litany of rigors, expectations, hopes and dreams that would come true if I did what I should. But the work I demonstrated on the court was also expected in the classroom. There was no excuse for non-performance in either arena. Non-performance on the basketball court was traced to laziness, a sign of lack of commitment; low grades and undone school work was traced to slothfulness, a sign of lack of commitment to excellence. Coach Faircloth gave me the whys and hows of achievement with excellence. His coaching and caring stamp was left indelibly upon my life.

Few men have been honored in any sport like my head basketball coach at the University of Kentucky, Adolph Rupp, The Baron, the man in the brown suit and the winningest basketball coach by percentages, in the history of the sport. He was one of the most remarkable human beings I ever met. From the first day, until just two months before he died years later, I kept in close contact with "The Man" and benefitted from every conversation with him. Many of my long letters to Billie mentioned how much he was helping me.

Adolph had been a great high school and college athlete from the plains of Kansas. He had played under the legendary Fogg Allan, and though they were later bitter opponents, a great deal of Fogg's philosophy had been adopted by Coach Rupp.

My sharpest memories of him do not involve games or his famous half time speeches and tirades, but revolve around the practice sessions, or "labs," held every afternoon from 3:15 to 5:00. The labs were brief by some coaches' methods, but for those of us who wore the Big Blue it symbolized why he was one of, if not *the* most successful college basketball coach of all time.

Situate Adolph Rupp in any large corporation, and you would have a well-oiled, smooth-running operation. He was a planner, a conceptual thinker and an astute implementor. He was also probably the finest practical psychologist that I have ever known, a master at motivating highly talented and ego-strong young men and demonstrating that the team was always greater than the single player.

I did not find Adolph Rupp to be a particularly religious man, at least not outwardly. Of course none of us can judge another's relationship with God, and, for all I know, Rupp may very well have had a strong faith. I do know that when he was young his mother often read the Bible to him, which explained why he could quote vast quantities of Scripture. However, the context in which he used it was not always completely scriptural. I remember when a teammate, Jerry Bird, had one of those unfortunate days in practice session when he did everything wrong.

Coach Rupp finally leaped up from the bench and, approaching Jerry, shouted: "Jerry, you have just broken one of the Ten Commandments."

"What . . . uh, which one?" gasped Jerry, his face white.

"Thou shalt not be stupid!" barked Rupp as he wheeled and went back to the bench.

Though a strange mixture of a man, he always respected another person's beliefs. I'll never forget the time during my freshman year when our team was asked to meet in the stadium on Sunday afternoon to set up offensive plays for Monday's game. He approached me in a confidential way and said, "Uh, Ed, you don't have to come if it interferes in any way with your religious beliefs; you know that."

"No, it won't, Coach," I said, "that will be O.K."

He seemed, however, to take delight in my beliefs when we played a Catholic university. One night while playing DePaul in Chicago, he said, and I was never sure if he was serious or not, "Now you boys probably have noticed DePaul has some priests there praying for them, but don't worry, we have Ed and he'll be praying for us."

Somehow I became fixed in this man's mind as the only religious person on the team, which was far from reality. One night during a particularly hot session on the floor, an opponent and I squared off and almost came to blows.

The next night while playing Notre Dame, Coach Rupp sounded off about our team's lack of aggressiveness and finished his tirade by shouting, "Seems the only guy on this team who's willing to fight is our preacher."

His comments never bothered me. In fact, I was amused and knew he meant no disrespect.

If there was anything outwardly religious about Adolph Rupp, one would have to say it was in the context of seriously adhering to the strict rules of practice session. Players could arrive on the court any time up to 30 minutes before the beginning of practice— 3:15 p.m. In fact, you were urged to get there early if at all possible, and the amount of urging usually depended on your shooting percentages, both from the field and the free-throw line. Anyone shooting free-throws under 75 percent would certainly find it advisable to come early. If you did not, you were warned in subtle ways.

At exactly 3:15 p.m. the gates leading to the gym floor were locked by the manager, and woe to anyone who came late, except for the best of reasons. From 3:15 to 3:45 each player on the team rigorously practiced "game shot" situations. Heaven help you if, as a center, you were found shooting from a guard position. You were to carefully handle each shot as if it were the game-winning one. You were never allowed to walk after the ball, you'd better dash after it. "Hustle" was the motto for the Big Blue.

From 3:45 to 4:00, a number of things happened. If Adolph or Harry wanted to review the team's past efforts, they spent at least five minutes offering compliments or constructive criticism. You learned to be doubly on your toes for the next hour because that would be the area on which to concentrate.

Academics were also seriously reviewed. This did not occur everyday, but Coach Rupp always received a grade progress report on each athlete. Again, heaven help you if you did not have a valid excuse for a missed class or if you were failing any course! Every scholarship athlete at UK had to pass every course, and no excuse was accepted. Private tutors were available, all monitored and supported by the athletic department.

Coach Rupp's philosophy of academics was summed up in several comments I never forgot:

"Boys, if you're too dumb to pass classes here at the university, then you're too dumb to play basketball.

"Basketball is a game of intelligence. It is not a stupid man's game. Any man that can play basketball here is capable of graduating from this university. If you don't, it has nothing to do with intelligence; it has to do with laziness."

Coach Rupp was extremely proud of his athletes who went on into various walks of life, and he gloried in their achievements. I was just one of many that he kept in touch with over the years.

Sometimes during the 15-minute break in practice, which consisted of three to 10 minutes of conversation, the whistle blew and the team automatically went into the patented UK warm-up drills. We would run these drills every day, the same drill that we would run through without error on the floor before every game, to the amazement of the fans. If they only knew how many thousands of times we had practiced that entire drill they would not have been so impressed.

When the practice whistle blew again, it was 4:00 p.m. The next 60 minutes would seem like climbing the Matterhorn. The whole hour might be spent on half-court offense, defensive patterns or drills. On another day it might consist of a half- or full-court scrimmage, but whatever, you could bank on the one fact that every minute had been previously thought out and discussed by Adolph and Harry. There never was a lost minute, never a look of puzzlement on either of the coaches' faces that would suggest, "Well, what do we do now?" When the closing whistle blew at 5:00 p.m., you needed no encouragement to move to the showers. Panting heavily, you had been pushed from within as well as without, for the potential that lay somewhere deep within you. The coaches had motivated you to reach that potential, either through praise of a good move or shot, or criticism that stung to the quick. They were masters at every phase of the game.

We always dreaded the scrimmages. Adolph would position himself on one end of the court where you would be playing offense. Nine out of ten times when you come down court, whether your team scored or not, criticism rang out concerning the sloppiness of the play, an inadequate pick or a play that had been run too slowly. Harry would stand under the other backboard and criticize every rebound that you failed to hustle for or every time you didn't help a teammate in trouble as he tried to guard his man.

I recall a time after one difficult practice where the criticisms came hot and heavy concerning our poor defenses. Afterwards we ate together at the training tables, all tired and dejected because the verbal abuse had hit us hard. That night Jersey Joe Walcott and Rocky Marciano were squaring off for a televised major heavyweight fight. One of the team members blurted, "I know where I wish Coach Lancaster was tonight. Right in the ring with Walcott and Marciano, both beating the h___ out of him!"

Bill Smith, our jokester, said dryly, "Well, all he would do is criticize them as they beat him to death."

Silence was paramount to success in practice sessions. You could holler for the ball or discuss some technical side of the game that two of you needed to work on, but you never uttered an idle word about anything else. Coach Rupp would say, "This is a two-hour lab session that meets every afternoon. You don't talk in your classes unless asked a question. You are there to learn. You are here for the same reason. If you want to talk, go up in the stands where the fans sit and talk. On this court you do not talk unless it is about basketball."

Thus, there would be long periods of time when the only sounds heard at UK Memorial Coliseum were the drumming of basketballs on the maple floor and the deep breathing and grunts of athletes doing their utmost to impress a mentor who had seen the best athletes in the world.

It was easy to see why my letters to Billie were so lengthy. Writing her offered a welcome release from the continual pressure.

Adolph Rupp had coached 25 years by the time I arrived at the university. UK celebrated his silver anniversary during my freshman year, and I remember that night when all of his old athletes came back to honor him. Some of the all-time greats were there. Fifteen years later I would return to honor his 40th year in coaching and would be humbled by being allowed to stand on the court with some of those same men that I had viewed with awe as a freshman.

Since Rupp had coached so long by the time I arrived at UK, we all felt he had experienced every possible game situation. So, when he spoke, we listened. He often said, "If I tell you to do something that does not work out and we lose, I'll take the blame. But if I tell you to do something and you do something else—well, all I can say is that it had better work. Because if it does not, *you* take the blame!"

There were times that his directions did not work and, true to his word, he took the blame. But most of the time when we did what he told us to do we won. The few times we went native in the fracas and it backfired, we found out the next day what hell must be like.

An interesting thing that I learned about after my graduation was the intense psychological study that Coaches Rupp and Lancaster made of each team member. Several weeks before the season opener they would spend a morning discussing each team member's emotional and psychological make-up. They felt they were aware of the boy's basketball ability, but it was the inner person they felt they needed to know. They spent a three- to four-hour session on each player. The coaches reserved 10 to 12 mornings for this study, depending upon how deep they planned to go in the line-up.

Their discussions involved each man's stability. Can we depend upon him in the tight situations? When he needs discipline, who does it and how? Do we talk to him personally, berate him in front of the team, pull him off to the side during practice or call him in the office the next day? Can he take criticism, and if so, how much and by whom? Do we shout at him or just talk to him, man-to-man? At the half time, to motivate him, do we talk to the team as a whole, or do we single him out?

For instance, Vernon Hatton, my teammate for four years and one of the most highly disciplined athletes I've known, was handled by the coaching staff in a way totally different from John Crigler, another teammate. They never spoke with Hatton directly, except with praise. He was one of those few players who put out one 100 percent at every practice and in every game. During a practice session when Vernon was putting out his usual effort but was having one of those days when everything went wrong The Baron criticized his play. Coach Rupp simply said, "Vernon, you are simply awful to day. What is wrong with you son? Did you have a fight with your wife?"

Vernon played for about one more minute and then simply walked off to the sidelines and sat down. Coach Rupp was caught short for a moment. Finally he said, "I've been coaching here for nearly 30 years, and I've never seen an athlete just give up and quit."

Vernon's reply was, "My best apparently is not good enough for you today. And all I can do is my best."

Nothing more was ever said or done. The next day Vernon was there putting in his full effort again, and this time there was no criticism.

John Crigler, on the other hand, excelled under verbal abuse. That may sound strange, but the coaching staff was actually addressing the entire team as they blasted Crigler for poor playing. He was usually the focus of much of the analysis of what was wrong with our play. When Crigler was not under attack, then Johnny Cox, the other forward, was the recipient. Every so often Adrian Smith or I would suffer a comment or two. But the rest of us did not receive half of the verbal tongue lashings that Crigler did.

One night we played a very difficult game against Auburn. We had won by the skin of our teeth through some last-minute shooting by Cox. Crigler had made the unforgivable mistake of allowing his man to score uncontested just before half time. For some reason he did not try to block his opponent! I was walking with Crigler up the ramp to the dressing room, and I could hear Adolph behind us mumbling to Harry about how badly we had played. Half time provided a tongue lashing to end all tongue lashings. Adolph began with Crigler, and seven minutes later he was still on him. He ended his tirade with the now famous statement,

"Crig, 100 years from now this coliseum will be no more. One hundred years from now this university will be no more. One hundred years from now there will be no more life on this planet. Do you know what is going to be right here where I am standing? A grave, son. A grave. There will be a small tombstone. Do you know what the writing on the tombstone will say? It will say, 'Here lies John Lloyd Crigler—killed by Adolph Rupp!' And, son, that is exactly what I'm going to do to you if you don't begin to play better this second half!"

Vernon and I were standing in the showers after the hard-fought ball game when John Lloyd came in. No one said much, and finally Crig looked over at me and said, "Ed, Adolph really took notice of me tonight, didn't he?"

"Yes," I said, "he certainly did."

Crig understood any comment from the coach was good, and, as long as we won, it was all right with John Lloyd Crigler.

One memorable night during my junior year Crig was not the target. The first half of our game with the University of Mississippi had not gone well, and I kept missing an obvious defensive switch with my teammate, Johnny Cox. Mississippi had scored three goals just before the half. It had obviously given them new life, even though we were still ahead by a few points.

Harry Lancaster had confronted me while I left the court to demonstrate what I was doing wrong. After that brief coaching lesson, I felt fairly confident that I would not have any problem with the same move during the second half. In the dressing room I took my place on the bench with the rest of the first five sweaty, steaming bodies. Towels had been dispensed and we were wrapping them around us to prevent a chill when I heard Coach Rupp call my name.

"Ed, do you see that corner over there in the toilet?" He was pointing to the adjoining room. His face was red as fire.

"Yes, sir," I replied, "I see it."

Adolph continued, "I want you to get up and go over there and throw up! I want you to lose everything you have ever eaten at this university. You have been here for two and a half years, so you need to get rid of a lot. When you get through, I want you to go to our hotel and sit down in your nice comfortable room that we are paying for and write me a letter. No, it will have to be longer than a letter. Write me an English theme paper. No, it will need to be more than that. I want you to write me a doctoral dissertation on this subject— 'Why Adolph Rupp Was Crazy Enough to Go to the State of Georgia after the Likes of Ed Beck.'"

He stood there trembling, his eyes blazing. "Now, son, before you leave this dressing room, I want you to do your job over in that corner," and he pointed his finger again. "I'm going to let you play the second half. You are terrible, and you know it, and Mississippi knows it, and every fan watching and listening knows it. But I want you to get beat bad tonight. I want your man to continue to run over you all night, just as he has done in the first half. But, at the end of this game, I want you to come up to me and say, 'Coach, I did something in this coliseum tonight, even if it was over there in that corner.'"

We won the game handily and, at the end of the game in the dressing room, Coach Rupp approached me. With a twinkle in his eye he said, "Good job on the court, Beck!"

We both grinned as we looked over at the empty corner.

I wished I could have told Billie about it that night but I had to content myself with a long letter. I hoped it would make her laugh.

24

Victories of Life and Death

Harry Lancaster had been Coach Rupp's assistant for 16 years before I arrived at the University of Kentucky. I am uncertain who discovered whom—whether Harry found Adolph or Adolph found Harry. Either way, they were an unbeatable team! Much of the coaching success of Adolph Rupp—as great a coach as he was—belongs at the feet of this unique human being.

Harry had been another outstanding high school and small-college athlete. His first love was baseball, and for years he was the head baseball coach at the university. But when Harry became a part of the basketball staff, he added his strength of excellence to that part of the athletic department.

There are few people who can work in the shadow of a legend, realizing they will never receive their due recognition. Harry Lancaster was one of those unique men. I had heard about dedication all my life, but my association with him for those four years showed me what it actually meant.

Again, as with Adolph Rupp, Harry Lancaster wasn't a man to demonstrate his faith . . . and neither could I judge him on it. But I'll never forget one evening when our freshman team played at

Morehead, Kentucky, and we all sat down to dinner. It was one of the first times Harry had eaten with us.

As usual, I bowed my head in a silent prayer of grace when Harry leaped from his chair, dashed to my side and anxiously inquired, "Ed, are you all right? Are you feeling sick?"

"No, Coach," I looked up, "I was just giving thanks."

"Oh, uh, oh," his face flushed with embarrassment, "I'm sorry, Ed, I thought you weren't feeling well," and he slipped back to his chair.

But the old saying, "How you act speaks more loudly than what you say," certainly held true with Harry Lancaster. For though I had heard many sermons on humility, I saw it lived in Harry's life.

My images of humility used to be of praying monks and barefoot saints. However, as I wrote Billie in a letter, I began to learn what real humility was from watching Harry Lancaster coach under the shadow of The Baron. When we traveled, the press would invariably crowd around Rupp. They never sought out Harry. When his photo did run in the newspaper, he would always be standing next to or a little behind Coach Rupp. Sometimes he'd even be cropped part way out of the photo; but he never seemed to mind.

Once our team plane landed in Memphis, Tennessee, for refueling. We were slated to play the University of Mississippi there within a couple of weeks. Local reporters wanted Adolph to get off the plane and pose along with the players and coaching staff. The plane ride had been a little rough and some of us were rumpled and pretty sad looking. Coach Rupp got up and said, "Come on, boys . . . whoever wants his picture taken, follow me."

Several of the team got up and went outside. I was sitting across the aisle from Harry and leaned over to say, "Coach, why don't you go?"

Harry said, "No, Ed, that's Adolph's bag. He likes it. I'll stay in here with the rest of you boys."

And that is exactly where he liked to be, with the team on every level.

The partnership style of Rupp and Lancaster was psychologist-motivator coupled with strategist and teacher. It was apparent during those brief one-minute time outs when they alerted the team to a new direction or strategy. As we arrived at the bench, Coach

Rupp would invariably tell us what we were doing wrong and/or leap on someone for their lack of play or lazy style. Then Coach Lancaster would lay out what should take place. In the last 10 seconds before the horn blew for play to resume, Rupp tried to motivate us with some kind of challenge. One memorable experience occurred in the 1957-58 season against Temple University.

Temple had three stars that year, Guy Rodgers, Tink Van Patton and Bill Kennedy. They actually outplayed us most of the game but at the last minute we tied the game. The first overtime swung back and forth until they were two points ahead with one second left on the clock. We received the ball at half court. The time out session was gloomy, and Adolph was fuming because of our lack of defense. All of a sudden, Harry stepped forward and said, "We're still in this game, so don't give up yet!"

Our heads jerked up. "This is what we are going to do," he continued. "Smithy, you are going to take it out and throw it to Hatton. Hatton, make sure you have your feet planted facing the basket. You have only one second, so the moment it gets to you, shovel it toward the basket. Ed, you get right under the basket and, if it is short, try to tip it in. Who knows, the clock might be late starting. Now, go do it."

Even Adolph remained silent. We all lined up. The ball flew to Vernon, and he shoveled it toward the basket in what must have been the funniest looking shot in the history of the game. I could not see it because I was trying to draw a foul under the basket. Then I saw the ball falling toward the rim and positioned myself for the final jump. I had already heard the horn go off, but Coach Lancaster said "*tip*," so that's what I was going to do. The next moment, pandemonium broke out in the packed coliseum as the ball swished through the net! We tied the first overtime with that spectacular 47-foot shot by Vernon Hatton with one second to go! In the third over time, we went on to win!

In my junior year we played Duke University at Durham, North Carolina. As I confessed to Billie that night in my letter, it was a strange homecoming for me, I had originally wanted to play at Duke. We got an early lead, and with about three minutes to go we were ahead by nine points and coasting. Suddenly, Bobby Joe Harris, with whom I stayed when I visited Duke that time a few years back, ignited his team. The Duke Blue Demons put a full-court zone press on us, which we had never seen before. Bobby Joe stripped Vernon of the ball four times in a row, and we lost the game by three points. We were a dazed group in the dressing room that night. "Harry," I asked, "what kind of defense was *that*?"

He simply said, "You'll know everything about it tomorrow."

We flew back to Lexington in gloom that night in the private plane. Early the next morning I dropped by the coliseum and there was Harry, bleary-eyed, with basketball books and magazines spread all over his desk. He had stayed up most of the night investigating the phenomena we had witnessed the night before. In our next game we not only knew how to break it, but we also knew how to run it. Two solid days of practice had been devoted to an intensive seminar on zone press conducted by "Professor Harry Lancaster." It was as if he had devised it and written all the articles on it himself.

The team used to call him affectionately, and sometimes non-affectionately, "the Bear." With his bulk, he looked like one. I always thought that if there were ever a fight on the court away from home and local fans descended from the stands to get us, I would stand right next to Harry. I felt he could beat almost any man alive. However, there was another side to Harry that not too many people knew. He was as sensitive and tender-hearted as they came. He reminded me of a certain piston-ring magazine advertisement in the 50s, showing this big burly-looking man holding a tiny piston ring in his hand. The caption: "So tough and yet so gentle." That was Harry.

The University of Kentucky had been such a perennial power in basketball that in the pre-season rankings it was usually in the top 10. Sometimes rankings are given to coaches more than players. This was true at the beginning of the 1956-57 season. Most of our scoring punch had left with Bob Burrow and several other graduates. Even though Rupp and Lancaster would have to mold a team mainly around juniors, the sports writers had seen them do that so many times previously, they ranked us in the top 10.

The fall schedule was very difficult. We played some of the top teams in the nation in the Christmas tournament. On successive evenings we played Southern Methodist (ranked number three) and

Illinois (ranked number two). As we approached the late December match-ups, it appeared that the University of Kentucky might, for the second time, lose its own Christmas tourney. We had a fairly sound pre-conference season, but we had dropped a couple of games and were heading into the tournament ranked number seven in the nation. Now we were the underdog.

SMU was highly touted with their All-American center, Jim Krebs. When the opening whistle blew, they leaped out to an immediate lead, and we valiantly attempted to keep within striking distance. With approximately four minutes to go in the game, try as we might, we were 10 points behind. During time out, Adolph and Harry went to work on us. It is one of the few time outs I wish I could recall clearly, but for some reason it remains fuzzy in my memory. What does remain extremely clear is the next three and one-half minutes of play. From a 10-point deficit, we moved like the Big Blue of the past—five men playing furiously as if they were one—and scored 18 uncontested points! It was the most effortless and flawless few minutes of basketball that I had ever witnessed or been blessed to experience! With less than 30 seconds to go in the game, and Kentucky now a sure winner, SMU called a time out.

For the first time in my basketball career I could not hear either of the coaches. The roar of nearly 12,000 partisan fans in Memorial Coliseum was deafening! Kentucky had roared back from seeming defeat to total command against the number three team in the country! Harry Lancaster, shouting at the top of his lungs, told us to just hold the ball another 30 seconds. I remember standing there waiting for the game to resume and looking up in the stands at the fans' reaction. I had never done that before, but at that moment I was caught up in their emotion. I could feel the excitement of impending victory and the thrill of adulation. It was intoxicating. I saw people standing, cheering and waving their arms. Fans were hugging and kissing. I even saw a lady hitting a man standing in front of her with her handbag, and he seemed to be loving every single swing! A few moments later, victors, we walked off the court amid the deafening roar of appreciative supporters. It was the first time in two and a half years that I really felt I was a Kentuckian and a vital and contributing member of the team.

All I needed was for Billie to be there.

As we got to the dressing room, Harry, who was usually the last one in, now stood at the doorway shaking our hands. Adolph came in and said, "Boys, I just want you to know—that was not a clapping game, that was a shouting game!"

Now, we had the renewed confidence that we could beat anyone we wanted to. The next night Illinois was only in the game for the first few minutes, and we were crowned the tourney champion. I had played two of the best games I could remember, matched up on successive evenings against two All-Americans. I felt awed and appreciative, yet, my elation was shadowed by sadness as I headed home for Christmas.

Billie was losing her battle. She had been unable to make the trip to Lexington as the disease was moving relentlessly within her body. The opponent she had fought so well was now wearing her down. We did not sense it completely at the time, but our fourth quarter had already begun.

Billie had gone to bed the night before, trying to listen to our game over WHAS, a powerful Louisville station. On certain evenings she would get the signal very clearly, and that happened the night of the championship. She was excited by our victory and because we would be spending a few days together. I arrived at the Macon airport the next afternoon. Billie had rested most of the day to be strong enough to drive to the airport by herself. As the plane taxied up to the small terminal, I looked out to see her standing there waving. A strange feeling swept over me as I knew that this could be our last Christmas together.

Coach Rupp had suggested I return to practice a day or so later than scheduled. I had told him it would depend on Billie's progress—she had just been released from the clinic in Macon. Her skin had that weather-beaten, burned look again, and she was so thin, her high cheek bones were even more pronounced. Her eyes had the familiar hollow look, and I often would find her staring off into space, even during a conversation. Yet, her indomitable spirit was as alive as ever. If possible, she had fallen more deeply in love with life, perhaps because she was realizing there was so little of it left.

Billie needed numerous blood transfusions and had several just before my arrival. They gave her renewed strength, but I noticed that she rested more during the day and moved even more slowly than usual. As much as we had enjoyed the candle-light service the previous Christmas Eve, we felt it best not to attempt that type of excursion this time. Just being together was the most important thing.

We went to our room early that Christmas Eve and had our own little service as we sat side by side on the floor, holding hands. We talked simply about the marvelous first Christmas night and the miracle of love incarnate sent into our world. The symbolic gifts that had been given—there was no response when I mentioned gold, but frankincense and myrrh caused her to look up. "Those last two gifts were sometimes used in the ancient world to place upon the bodies of the dead," I commented. The baby Jesus, symbolically, through those gifts, was born into this world to die in our behalf. So, even in a stable of life we see the reality of death and the gift of love."

"It is getting much closer now, my darling," she sighed. "I know it, and I am worried about you."

"Worried about me?" I responded hesitantly.

"Yes, about you," she reached up and patted my face. "So many people are reaching out and praying for me, and I feel so blessed. I ask them to pray for you. I think this whole thing is harder on you than it is for me. So I pray for you."

"Thank you, my darling, thank you." Tears flooded my eyes.

We had a long wooden match that we held together to light our one Christmas candle. Its golden glow flooded the little area where we were sitting. We sat together on the floor looking at our candle as it burned into the night. We embraced each other and watched the flickering candle burn down. Somehow it symbolized our wedding candle, but the light was so close to going out.

Billie asked me to put the mattress on the floor, and I did. We lay there close together and she cried. Once again she said she was not afraid to die, but she did not *want* to die. We talked on into the early morning hours, when finally we fell asleep.

We heard noises in the morning as the Ray clan gathered for their Christmas celebration. Billie was not in a hurry to get up. We lay there, cuddled together, knowing somehow without saying it that these moments would be very few and far between. At times like this one relishes the simplest things of life—a touch, an embrace, a kiss. We reached out to each other as best we could, and the love given was our gift to each other.

It was later at lunch that I presented the special invitation from the athletic department of the University of Kentucky. We were scheduled to play in Atlanta against Georgia Tech in late January. Billie was invited to come as their honored guest. She replied cautiously, but her eyes sparkled for a few moments as she told me to tell Coach Rupp, Coach Lancaster and Bernie Shively, the athletic director, that she would be there if at all possible. She mentioned the invitation several times that day—I could sense her hope to see that game.

I left early the next morning for basketball practice. I was happy to have had those few days with my wife, but I was extremely upset also. I could not overlook the tell-tale signs; the exhausting game that Billie was playing had been long and hard. She had become more worn than I had ever seen her. Her hope was beginning to wane and those far-off looks broke my heart. It is a certain look on the face of the suffering that indicates they are seeing what others of us cannot see—as if they are looking through this earthly dimension that imprisons, into a world beyond that frees. I believe they are aware of something that gives them a different kind of hope, not a hope to stay here but an expectation of total freedom. It is the longing for release, for the end of a struggle, for not having to fight for the next breath or a pain-free moment. They could be looking toward a passage to where there is no more human frailty, no more disease or deterioration. My darling Billie was now beginning to visualize her freedom, the same freedom that she had heard her black friends sing about so often, "Free at last, free at last— Great God, Almighty, I'm free at last!"

I guess if we who love these valiant persons were more sensitive, we might make their passage much easier. As I left to return to Kentucky I knew that Billie was so very tired, tired of pain and perhaps even tired of hoping. If I had been as aware that Christmas as I would become during the next 90 days, I would have released Billie that night. I would have told her she could go and be free. But I had not. I had told her to hope, to fight, to hang on, no matter what. But she had a very soft spot in her heart for those she loved—she did not want to hurt any of us in any way. So she would fight to live a little longer, more to help us than herself. What she believed we wanted, she sought to fulfill.

How very selfish we are at times. We rationalize by giving pep talks to the terminally ill when actually we are the ones who really need help. We are the leeches that will not let go. We are the lepers of faithlessness. They have been blessed in a special way for they have time to review their priorities and accomplish what they can. Once they do, we are the ones who hold them back. We want their one last ounce of strength, that one last touch, that one last kiss, that one last word. We are insatiably insensitive. All we have to do is say, "Darling, you are free to go. You do what you need to do. I release you with my love." But we don't. I was still too selfish to give her that special gift of love. For I looked forward to the special game in Atlanta honoring Billie. It was only a month away.

25

Scarlett and Rhett

We were scheduled to play Georgia Tech in Atlanta on the last Monday of January. It was semester break for exams so we had not played for more than a week. Coupled with that, nine days previously I had had minor surgery for an infected cyst on my left shoulder. The cyst was deeper than they first realized, so to hold the incision together, they had wired it. I was unable to practice, though I did continue to run to keep my legs and lungs in shape.

We flew to Atlanta on Saturday, arriving late in the afternoon. We worked out at the coliseum and then had a team meeting. The next morning the team trainer, Rusty Payne, and I drove to the Valley to pick up Billie so that she could make that trip she had talked so enthusiastically about last summer. Billie had grown weaker during January and had to have several more blood transfusions. She had been released from the hospital that very morning. We left the Valley in mid-afternoon for the two-hour drive back to Atlanta, with Billie lying on the back seat.

We arrived at the hotel about 5:30 p.m. Rusty Payne ducked in ahead of us and, as expected, found the team together eating their evening meal. He alerted Coaches Rupp and Lancaster, and when

Billie and I walked into the dining area, the entire team and coaching staff stood up, greeting Billie as if she were a princess. It was quite a sight, all those young men in their blue blazers emblazoned with the big UK initials, standing and applauding my wife. A big lump filled my throat, and Billie, though so very thin, held herself high, as regal as ever. In her gracious southern manner, she thanked them for their concern and prayers.

Then, just as she had admonished me that first time in the hospital, she added, "Now please sit down, boys, and enjoy your meal."

We sat down with them at the table, and for the first few moments conversation was a little tight. No one really knew what to say, understanding how awkward the usual things, such as, "How are you doing?" or "Golly, you look great" would sound.

Finally, Harry Lancaster in his understanding way, broke the embarrassment with, "Billie, I'm sure I speak for all of us when I say that we're so pleased you could be with us tonight and tomorrow. We've looked forward to this for a long time." The he glanced at me and winked. "And we all know Ed has been excited."

That loosened things up, and easy conversation continued at the table. Then, as my teammates left for their rooms, they came over to Billie. One by one, they introduced themselves again and told her how happy they were she had come to cheer for them. Some even added they would try to win the game for her. That night Billie Beck became the mascot of the Big Blue. Her fight to live seemed to inspire the team to want to do even better than its very best.

Coaches Rupp and Lancaster, Rusty, Billie and I stayed in the dining area to eat our meals. It was nice for Billie to be within the athletic family again. She did not realize just how important she had become.

Finally, the others excused themselves, leaving Billie and me alone at the table. Even the waitresses seemed to sense it was a special time for us and kept their distance, checking only periodically for our needs.

We laughed about being so special that we had the entire dining room to ourselves. By this time Billie's eyes were dark hollows, but she still wanted to dine leisurely before going to our room. So we ate and continued to talk for well over an hour after dinner.

I joked about how we had come up in the world. "Remember how I asked you to marry me as we sat in the restaurant parking lot, surrounded by hungry people?" I asked, taking her hand. She squeezed my hand and smiled. Tonight we sat in elegance in one of the loveliest and oldest hotels in Atlanta on Ponce de Leon Avenue. Knowing that one of Billie's favorite literary figures had supposedly lived in this city, I leaned across the table and said in my best Clark Gable accent, "Ms. Scarlett, even in those clothes made of drapery material, you are as lovely as the South itself. I wonder, Ms. Scarlett, if we might go upstairs to our room and look out across the city?"

Her dark eyes sparkled in the dimly lit restaurant as she replied, "Rhett Butler, you wouldn't take advantage of an innocent little ol' southern belle, now would you? You Yankees have ravaged our land, and now you think with some sweet talk and a meal you can do the same to its women. Well, I want to ask you something, Mr. Butler—where is your room?"

And she laughed, and for a moment her joy in life flooded the room and my heart.

We made our way slowly through the lobby to the golden elevators. On the top floor we opened the door to what must have been the finest suite in the hotel. I was flabbergasted! The Kentucky team always traveled first-class, but usually we stayed in the regular hotel rooms. Now here was a huge suite overlooking the city. My heart flooded with gratitude. It was the Athletic Department's way of saying, "Welcome and thanks!"

We stood together at the windows and looked into the night at the city. It was aglow with millions of lights. Neon signs winking in the distance reminded Billie of the fireflies on the farm, she said. We stood there with her head against my chest and my arms wrapped around her thin body, basking in the quiet beauty of the evening.

Shortly, we unpacked our belongings, showered and prepared for bed. She was wearing her honeymoon nightie with all its lace and finery. Her face was slightly thinner, but the elegance of her profile and the darkness of her hair against the white nightie bathed her in loveliness. I took her in my arms and kissed her. We made our way to the king-sized bed that was raised on a slight pedestal.

We sat on the side of it and embraced. Billie finally looked at me and said, "Aren't you going to put the mattress on the floor?"

"We don't need to," I grinned, "This is a seven-foot bed and there is no noise." I bounced up and down to prove it.

"Oh, you insensitive man! You just don't know how to be romantic and win a girl's heart, do you? Rhett Butler, you put the mattress on the floor this instant!"

The thing seemed to weigh a ton as I huffed and puffed dragging it onto the floor. All I had to do was hurt my back lifting this thing, I grimaced to myself, or pull some of the wires out of my incision, and I would have had it. I could just see myself explaining to Adolph Rupp. "Well, Coach, you see, it was like this . . . I was pulling a king-sized mattress to the floor when . . ." And he would ask, "Why, Ed, I got you the finest room with the biggest bed available—why in the world did you need it on the floor?" And I would say, "Well, Coach, there is this gal who thinks she is Scarlett O'Hara, and she called me Rhett Butler, and . . . oh, well, you just would never understand anyhow."

Billie's lovely nightie was soon draped over a chair. She remarked that she never really got to wear that "thing" very much, but I told her how nice it looked hanging on the chair. We held each other for so long. We embraced, kissed and cared. I was shocked at the weight she had lost since Christmas. I could feel almost every bone in her back, but the strange configuration of swelling in her abdomen had begun. She looked four months pregnant. The fluids were beginning to back up and the nodes were now immune to all the X-ray and mustard gas. But, at least for that night it made no difference. The night of hope had turned into the night of love, and she knew how very happy I was that she had been able to come to the game.

I arose early and ate with the team, but Billie stayed in bed. Breakfast was brought to her, but she just picked at it. She was feeling slightly ill when I reluctantly left for shooting drill. At the coliseum I was interviewed by Furman Bisher, the great sports writer of the Atlanta paper. He asked me specifically about Billie. I told him she was with me in Atlanta, but I requested he not print anything concerning her condition. He was true to his word, but he did run a large article about my playing days at the University. I returned to Billie as soon as possible, and we spent a leisurely afternoon in our room. Billie wanted to eat with the team at 4:30, where Coach Rupp graciously welcomed her. It was unprecedented action on his part since team meals were for players only. But I guess in a way Billie was considered as much a part of that team as any one of the players and, in certain ways, more so.

A little after 5 o'clock Billie's family arrived for the game. They were introduced to some of the players and coaching staff in the lobby. I went with Billie to our room to pack and say goodbye. I knew that after the game we would have only a few minutes since out team would be whisked to the airport for the flight back to Lexington.

It was a touching moment for us. We sensed that these might be our last moments of togetherness under what might be termed a "normal" situation. The room was quiet. The mattress was back on the bed. We stood for a few moments at the window with the back of her head on my chest and my arms wrapped around her. I leaned down and said, "Billie, you have made me so happy. Thank you for being my wife. I love you more than life itself."

She began to sob, turned to put her arms around my neck, and we clung to each other.

"I love you, my darling Ed," she said, " I love you so very much. I'll be pulling for you tonight. Play well."

I left the room and met Danny, one of her brothers, in the lobby. He promised to help Billie pack and take her to the coliseum.

The team dressed in silence. We ran out onto the playing court and went through our drills as the fans cheered and applauded.

What was wrong with us as a team that night, of all nights, I do not know. We played with total effort, but without control. Maybe it was the week's lay-off for exams, maybe it was the tightness of trying to do our best for our Georgia Princess. In the fourth quarter I over reached for a rebound and felt the tearing of flesh from the incision on my left shoulder. I could feel blood running down my back, and the referee stopped the game for the trainer, Rusty, to check it. He wiped the blood, we continued the game. Though it was a struggle we prevailed and won the game!

Afterwards I was examined by the Georgia Tech physician, and he pulled out some of the wires. He felt that there was no damage to the shoulder. The only effect would be that some of the wire had broken off inside, but it would work itself out in time. Weeks later, little bits and pieces of metal protruded from my shoulder, and they were pulled out easily.

I was the last team member to shower and dress for the airport ride. Billie and her family were standing near the taxi line, and the team members came and said goodbye. Adolph suggested that I ride to the airport with Billie, so we followed the taxi caravan. She was concerned about my shoulder, but I told her what the doctor had said. That seemed to relieve her.

When we arrived at the hangar where our university plane waited, I sat in the car with Billie until I saw the last team member enter the plane's door. Then I held Billie very tightly and whispered in her ear, "I love you."

She put her hands up to my lips as I began to kiss her and said, "Stay well, my darling, stay well. Come to me as soon as the season is over. Win the title for me. Tell all the boys I want them to win it for me. I love you."

One engine of the two-motored plane had already sputtered into life. We kissed, and I got out of the car and ran to the plane. I climbed the steps and waved to Billie. The aircraft's door was closed and I found my seat. The plane was silent except for its roaring engines. There was something about sealed planes just before take-off, that always reminded me of tombs.

26

Light in a Dark Room

The rigors of beginning a new semester, with the demands of academics as well as basketball, were enervating. The push to fight through the rest of the SEC opponents and move into the first round of the NCAA march for the crown kept every team member constantly on his toes. The realization that my wife—my only love—was in the last stages of her life consumed my every waking moment. More than ever I depended on that extra strength that can come only from beyond, from our Creator.

I had pondered Billie's words, "Come to me at the end of the season." The end of the regular season was a little over a month away. Certainly we were out to win our conference race; it would be a close one. If we won that title, we would go to the NCAA tourney. The first round was slated for Lexington, and if we won those games we would then go to Kansas City to play in the final four. North Carolina was picked as the favorite to repeat their exploits of the previous year. We believed that we could win if, as a team, we could just put it together. But we were up against other formidable teams within the SEC who wanted the title just as desperately.

On our next road trip to Nashville two blows applied more pressure. The first happened when Billy Thompson, a sports reporter for a Lexington newspaper, came to my room the Friday night before we were to play Vanderbilt. He had been selected by the other sports writers of the Kentucky papers to ask me about Billie. Thompson, a close friend, traveled with us on all our trips. He knew that most reporters wanted to get the jump on others, and he was afraid that unless some information was coordinated an article might be released prematurely that would hurt me and the Ray family. He discussed this potential problem with the other Kentucky writers, and they had asked him to talk with me about Billie's condition.

In confidence I told Thompson my personal feelings, that Billie would be re-entering the hospital soon (a fact he already knew) and that I wondered if she would leave it alive. I told him that I appreciated their cooperating with me since Billie's family would be upset concerning any premature release; and, by all means, I did not want Billie to read anything about the seriousness of her illness.

Thompson agreed to share the information with the other sports writers and ask them to hold it until the appropriate time, or to use it in clarifying any premature releases from other writers in Georgia or elsewhere. "As I travel with the team," he said, "everywhere I go the first question they ask me is, 'How is Billie Beck?'" He said that he had been trying to handle all of it in a low-key manner, but he added, "Ed, you never know what a writer might put in his paper."

Thompson asked for a picture of Billie, and I agreed to give him the one I had on my desk back at UK. He could make a negative and send it to the other writers for their use at the appropriate time.

The other blow was the very rapid degeneration of Billie's condition. It was now clear that she had forced herself to go to Atlanta at all costs, and upon her return had declined very fast, re-entering the Macon Hospital's cancer clinic.

I had been talking with Billie daily by phone, and every three or four days I would call Helen Newby, Billie's sister. The news was always negative. Billie had begun to lose interest in so many things. The one thing that she seemed to want to know about was the team's progress, and she kept up with the scores as well as she could. "I'm not really sure whether they always register with her," Helen told me on the phone, "but she at least wanted you to know that she really cares. I think your team winning that NCAA title means more to her than any of us realize."

The team was heartsick over Billie's deteriorating health, and every one of them now seemed to be fighting for her harder than ever. We battled furiously against Vandy, and I pulled down a season high of 23 rebounds. We had played as a unit, which had been a far cry from our miserable Tech performance in front of Billie and her family. The very next weekend we were scheduled to play the University of Mississippi in Memphis, and Mississippi State on Monday night in Starksville. Then I received a telegram from Helen on Saturday, just before our University of Mississippi game. It read, "Billie needs you! Please come." We won the Mississippi game handily in the second half, even though my mind was far away from that basketball court.

I showed the telegram to the coaches, and after the game I left immediately. I flew to Atlanta and drove to Macon, reaching the hospital early in the morning. My heart pounding, I rushed to Billie's room, where I found her alert and somewhat distressed that I had come. Her immediate response was "Who called you?" "No one," I lied, "our team is on a southern swing, and it was easy for me to come out of Memphis. I'll get over to Starksville on Monday for the game that night." She did not accept my story completely, but once she was convinced that I was really leaving the very next day and not going to break our covenant, she seemed to be relieved.

Billie's condition had worsened a great deal since I'd seen her in Atlanta. Her stomach was very bloated, and she was having difficulty retaining food. There were times when I would have to hold her head to comfort her. She had begun to vomit the refuse of cancer. Now, I found myself reaching out to her sister, Helen, who had vowed to stay with Billie "as long as she needs me." I appreciated what Helen had been going through after I had been at Billie's bedside less than a full day and found myself exhausted. Helen had been there for nearly two weeks.

I drove back to Atlanta the next morning and caught a plane to Starksville, Mississippi. It was a horrendous trip, with the plane landing at five airports before we reached the hometown of Mississippi State. I had never played there, but its reputation of hostility to opposing teams was legendary. I remembered Adolph and Harry talking about the clanging cowbells swung energetically by the student body sitting directly behind the bench. You could not hear yourself think during a time out. State had beaten an excellent Auburn team on Saturday night, but we had just whipped another very good Mississippi team ourselves.

Rusty met me at the airport, and we drove to the gym for a late morning workout. The team was already winding up their shooting time, but I put on my basketball togs and went onto the court. I had a brief 30-minute workout alone, just shooting and running, and though I felt tired, I believed an afternoon nap would set me up for the game that night.

Earlier, as I had arrived in the dressing room, Baldy Gibb, UK's head scout, and Harry Lancaster cornered me. "I saw Mississippi State play Saturday night," said Baldy, "and I am really impressed by their sophomore center. He has some good moves and a good shot, but his lack of experience shows. He has good potential," he added, "but I feel he's still a year away."

"What you will need to do, Ed" Baldy advised, "is jump on him early. Play him very tight and don't let him shoot from in close. He's not too good from the outside, so I wouldn't worry too much if he goes out to the side or past the free-throw line. He shoots from there, but his threat is speed, and I'd rather give him a low percentage shot than the possibility of a drive to the basket. You won't have any trouble with him this year, but beware next year! But then, he laughed, "of course, you will have him in Lexington."

Baldy was astute in assessing opposing players. The UK players used to say that when Baldy scouted a team, he knew what they ate for breakfast, lunch and dinner, and how many times they went to the bathroom. He was thorough, but sometimes the best of us don't see things clearly, or maybe Baldy just did not want to terrify me with the exploits of this budding sophomore star.

Babe McCarthy was the Mississippi State coach and, though Adolph and Harry thought he was a loud-mouth, we all respected his ability. The newspaper I read that afternoon had quoted him concerning "a few surprises" that he had cooked up for the Wildcats. This was the biggest game of the year for Mississippi State in many ways. Kentucky was still ranked third in the nation and State was not even ranked in the top 20. In fact, they had not been listed in the top 10 in the school's history. The more comments I read by Coach McCarthy, however, the more I felt we were really the underdog.

The warm-ups were run flawlessly again. The game started with my shaking hands with their very handsome, young-looking, 6'7" center, the one Baldy had told us about. He returned my handshake warmly and wished me well. That was the last thing he did that night for my benefit. The first seven shots he took, four of them from above the free-throw line and one from the very corner of the court near the in-bounds line, hit nothing but the bottom of the net. He did not bank them in or even allow them to bounce on the rim, they just went "swish." It made no difference whether I played close or far away, he always seemed to be in just the right place at the right time. At the half, as I wearily trudged toward the dressing room with my head down and the cowbells clanging, Mississippi State was 13 points ahead. That nice looking kid I was guarding had made 20 points. No one had ever made 20 points on me during a full game, and he had accomplished it in one half! Here, I was supposed to be the best defensive center in the league. What I did not realize was that I had been the promoter of the best offensive center in the league.

The second half was not much different, although we played quite well. Mississippi State just played better. We lost the game by seven points, and the man that I was assigned to guard scored 37 points. I shouted at him, hung on him, made faces at him and did everything else I had been trained to do on defense. The only thing he did was score.

As we walked off the court that night with the screams of the loyal Mississippi State fans ringing in our ears, I found myself walking stride-for-stride with Adolph. He turned to me and said, "Ed, *you* will never make All-American, but you made one tonight. Tomorrow every New York sports writer will know about that boy. He should write you a letter of congratulations."

As I was dressing and packing my gear in the locker room, Baldy Gibb walked over to me and patted me on the back. "Ed, I really thought he was a year away. I really did. But he was totally brilliant tonight. He did not play that way against Auburn. But he is a money ball player, and we'll hear a lot more from him."

With a faintly pained smile on my face, I said, "Baldy, what did you say his name was? I'd like to remember it for next year."

"Bailey Howell," came the reply. "Bailey Howell."

I never forgot that name.

Helen's daily reports on Billie were grim. There were days that Billie's condition slightly improved, but it always seemed that it was merely the calm before the storm. The disease was relentless, and the pain was constant.

Billie had a horror of taking narcotics to ease the pain. She had seen so much drug addiction in her medical work that she had requested the doctors not to give her any until the very last. She was going to tough it out until the pain became overwhelming. I was not enthused about this at all, for I felt that the patient should be kept as pain-free as possible. But Billie had thought that the drugs, if taken too early, would lose their potency when they became absolutely necessary. My trip to her bedside after the Mississippi game found her debating when she would have to make the decision to take stronger drugs. I knew that she would hold out until the very last.

I was reminded of our days in Lexington when she was employed at the Baptist Hospital. She had asked the administration for a transfer to the cancer wing. Billie had always felt fulfilled caring for and comforting the very distressed. She would always seek out the new patients who had recently been told they had cancer. Gloom would hang heavy over them, mixed with shock, anger and depression. But Billie would bounce up to their beds and say, "Why are you so depressed, I'm not." She would then wait for the reaction, which could range from stony silence to biting sarcasm or even a curse. Then she would fasten those penetrating dark eyes on them and say, "I have only two—two years to live, and I'm not depressed."

Most of the time they would respond to this beautiful angel of mercy who, in many cases, was more ill than they. She had opportunities to counsel with patients, offering her views of inner strength and the power of the mind over the body. But she knew that this was an answer only to a certain degree. There would come a point in the battle when even the strongest of the strong could not withstand the relentless onslaught of debilitating pain. It saps one's energy, and one soon becomes so obsessed with the pain that he finds it difficult to deal with anything else.

One evening I received a phone message from Helen that Billie was now taking the strong pain killers. I felt both relief and remorse—relief that she was now finding some release from pain, but remorse because I knew that Billie was now beginning to wear down.

I still believed, however, that something miraculous might yet take place, that she would be healed or that the cancer would go into remission. Ever since that night in July when I had been a part of her unbelievable miracle of healing, though temporary, it had seemed to whet my appetite for the next round. I found myself much more open to the possibility of miraculous healing. But, as much as I thought about it, I remembered all the conversations that Billie and I had had on the subject. Of course, there was her previous decision not to seek out faith healers, since she believed that God could cure her wherever she was.

So, the more I thought about it, the more I realized that I wanted Billie healed for my own selfish reasons. I did not want to be left alone. I did not want to face life without her gifts and graces. I did not want to miss her touch, her smile, her sweet southern voice, her concern and love. Try as I might to not think of myself, I found myself praying urgently for her healing. I always ended with, "Thy will be done," but I never even thought that God's true will might not coincide with mine.

We were approaching the last few weeks of the season. Our conference record was still seven wins and two losses to Tulane and Mississippi State. We faced a big weekend, a Saturday night contest with Georgia Tech and a big return battle with an ever-improving Vanderbilt club. On the Saturday afternoon before I left for the pre-game meal at five o'clock, I received an urgent call from Helen. "Billie's not doing well at all, Ed," she said, her voice trembling.

"I'll fly down right after the game," I said. "I'll be there early tomorrow morning."

I had already discovered that I could drive the 60 miles to

Louisville and catch a night flight to Atlanta that arrived in the early morning. There I would rent a car and arrive in Macon by daybreak.

At our pre-game meal that night, I told the coaching staff that I would leave immediately following the game. John Brewer's parents lived in a suburb of Louisville and they would take me to the airport. I would be back in Lexington on Monday in time for the Vandy game. Though I'm sure that this was disconcerting to my coaches in this crucial home-stretch, I never received anything but support from them.

We beat Tech that night easily. Our SEC record now stood at 8 and 2. The Monday night game was key because if we got Vandy, we would be in the driver's seat for the stretch run to the end. Even so, I was much more concerned about my wife's stretch run in her game of life.

The plane would not leave Louisville that night until 1 a.m., so that gave me time to eat the post-game meal with the team. Word of my impending trip had circulated, and many of the fellows came by to wish me well. More than ever I depended on their steady and strong support.

I arrived at the airport early and bought a newspaper before the departure time. Turning to the sports page, I read about our victory several hours earlier. Then I stared horrified . . . stretching the full width of the next page was the headline: BILLIE BECK DYING. Billie's picture was printed with a long article concerning her condition, how she had been at our game in Atlanta some weeks before and my night flights to be at her bedside. It was not that anything in the article was untrue, but I felt sick in the knowledge that this was *not* the appropriate time for such a story. *Had this gone out across the wire services?* I worried. *Would it be in the Georgia papers and would Billie's family, or worse still, Billie herself, see the headlines?* It was not that we had never discussed her dying. However, it's one thing to discuss the one you love in confidence; and quite another to see it broadcast in glaring newspaper headlines.

I was so upset that I could not sleep on the flight to Atlanta. I drove to Macon as fast as I could, hoping to arrive before any newspaper was delivered. I rushed into the quiet hospital lobby around 6:30 and picked up a Macon paper. Sure enough! A small article on the sports page gave a digest of the much larger article that I had read some six hours earlier.

Stuffing the paper under my coat, I rushed to Billie's room. I was uplifted, however, to find her alert, though still in much pain as she had fought without taking a shot most of the night. Helen and I urged her to accept the comfort of a hypo so that she could rest. She finally agreed. Dear Helen, hollow-eyed with face drawn, had been there all night and the day before, so I asked her to go home for a break. She said that Billie's mother would be up later that day, so I took over until she arrived.

I walked out with Helen, down the hallway a bit, and showed her the article in the Macon newspaper. She sadly shook her head but said she realized that eventually something like that would be written. We promised each other to keep it from Billie, and I returned to her room.

After a few hours with Billie that morning, I could understand why Helen had called. Billie's condition had deteriorated even more. She was violently ill, continually regurgitating blood and body tissue. Unable to eat any kind of food, she was being fed intravenously. At times they had to put the feeding tubes through her nose into her stomach, but on that Sunday she was clear of them. She demanded more pain shots. After the nurse had just given her one, she looked up at me through tear-filled eyes: "Oh, Ed, darling, I have turned into such a weakling. I just can't bear the pain anymore."

I leaned down and kissed her moist forehead. "Honey, please, you're the strongest person I know."

She slowly shook her head, and I turned away so she wouldn't see the tears in my eyes.

When Billie's mother arrived, she told me out in the hall that she had seen the newspaper article and that she was upset about it. I explained I could not prevent it, that the reporters had held off as long as we could expect them to. Now, there was nothing to do but live with it.

"But it's Billie I'm concerned about," she said, "and what her seeing an article like that would do to her."

"I know," I sighed, "we'll just have to keep the papers away from her."

I left the hospital that afternoon to shower, eat and sleep for a few hours at Helen's house. I returned to the hospital in the evening. Billie was calm now and very lucid. She placed her hand on mine and said, "Ed, I'm so concerned about your leaving the team at their crucial time."

I looked down at her hand, still lovely in form, but now much thinner. "It's no problem, darling," I assured her. "I'm going back in the morning to play tomorrow night against Vandy."

A glimmer sparkled in her eyes when she heard we were leading the SEC race with a good chance to get into the NCAA. "I know how much the championship would mean to everyone," she said, smiling, and then added, "and to me." She looked up at me, and I could see a ghost of her old humor in her eyes, "You know I'm a part of the team, too."

"Forget the championship, darling," I urged, leaning down and kissing her lips, so hot and dry. "You're my concern, sweetheart."

She sighed, "I know exactly what's taking place within me, Ed. Remember, I've seen it in other patients." She shifted her body a little, her voice more intent. "But I'm still making tape recordings explaining my reactions to some new medicines they've been giving me."

She seemed to fade into her pillow as, eyes closing, she added softly, "But all the therapy and medicines haven't done very much for me, I have to admit."

"Darling," I cried softly, "I love you so much, I cannot think of losing you."

Her eyes remained closed, but the corners of her mouth worked, as if she were trying to tell me she understood.

Weeping, I knelt by the side of her bed. It was now past 11 o'clock. The hallways were dark, and Billie's room was in shadows except for a small light glowing over her bed.

"Oh God," I prayed, "I thank you for her inner strength and total commitment to your kingdom."

And then, as I continued pleading for Billie, I did something I had never done before in her presence, "Oh Father, I pray for Billie's healing. Heal her physically, cure her of this disease. . . ."

At that, a hot little hand was place over my mouth and Billie gasped weakly, "Oh, Ed, please, please do not pray for my healing.

Just pray for my understanding. Ask God to use this disease for his honor and glory."

I leaned my head on her thin arm as she continued to gasp for breath after exerting so much energy to talk, and I could only plead aloud, "Oh God, help us both to understand. Help us both to understand."

Soon she was quiet, and I looked at her closely. She was asleep. I sat back in my chair and just looked at my wife, my love, feeling closer to her than at any other time in our relationship.

What a lovely person she was. What faith she had. Even though a lump of sorrow filled my throat, a deep sense of peace slowly came over me. I knew that if I could take her place in any way, I would gladly do so. But I also knew this was impossible. My heart and mind were now beginning to accept the finality of what was happening to Billie.

I combed her chestnut hair for a long time. Somehow it was therapy for me. After a while an early gray light touched the sky outside her window. I hated to see the night end, as it meant I would have to leave my love. How I wanted to stay, to not ever leave. But I knew what Billie would want more than anything else. I had to honor our covenant. Leaning down, I kissed her forehead. "Good-bye, darling," I choked as my tears fell on her cheeks. Steeling myself, I straightened and started out of the room.

Suddenly, I stopped. Had she said something? I turned and looked at Billie. Her lips were slowly moving: "Play well tonight . . . darling. I'll . . . I'll be praying for the team and you . . . play well."

"I love you, darling," I whispered, fighting back sobs that threatened to rack my entire being, "I love you, and will see you soon."

27

'Life Magazine Is Calling!'

I had slept on the plane back to Lexington and rushed to the noon meal. I received the scouting report for Vandy, but since we had played them before, there was nothing new. I went back to my room to rest. There is nothing that can fatigue a person more quickly than the presence in a hospital room with the suffering. I had been there for only about 40 hours, and I was exhausted. I thought of dear Helen who had been there day and night for weeks.

Brewer showed me the newspaper back in the room. There was a big article concerning the tightening of the SEC race. We were still in the driver's seat, but the next few games would make the difference. Coach Lowry of Tennessee was quoted about the Vandy-Kentucky game. He picked Vandy to beat us but commented that he was unsure how the illness of Ed Beck's wife might affect the Kentucky team effort. I painfully realized that Billie's illness was now being used as a psychological ploy by all sides.

I was awakened from a deep sleep by Brewer. It was time to go for our pre-game meal at 5 o'clock; I felt lifeless and heavy. I realized it was just fatigue, but I began to worry about whether or not I would snap out of it before game time. At the table the team was somber and silent. The importance of this contest was etched deeply on our minds.

That night we executed our warm-ups, then returned to the court for the pre-game foul shots and loosening-up exercises. The game announcer introduced, the Vandy team and Bob Polk, their head coach. Then the Kentucky line-up was introduced and the Lexington crowd roared at each name. Since I played center, I was always the third name called. That night, however, my four teammate's names were announced first, and then I heard, "And playing center tonight for Kentucky—Number 33, Ed Beck." The crowd's reaction was spontaneous and electrifying. The audience of nearly 12,000 people stood up with deafening applause. They would not let up. Embarrassed, I continued to shoot the basketball as if they were not there, but there was no escape. They were not honoring me as much as a brave woman fighting for her life in a hospital in Macon. I wished Billie could have heard it. I knew that she would not be listening since she was now struggling for every breath, but I prayed that somehow she could feel the energy of love sweeping out across the miles from these people, most of whom had never met her but who now felt they knew her as a member of their school's family.

They continued to cheer. I looked toward the Vandy side of the court and the whole team, along with Coach Polk, were standing and applauding. The Vandy center trotted down the court and shook my hand, and the roar was even more deafening. My whole team had stopped, and I was the only one bouncing a basketball. I saw Coach Lancaster and Coach Rupp standing and applauding. The mood was contagious. It must have been that for so long the emotion had been pent up, no one really knew how to handle it. No one really knew what to say. But now it had all broken loose as they cheered and clapped for more than two minutes. The entire press row and all the radio announcers even got into the act. Tears welled in my eyes, and I blinked to hold them back. But they cascaded down my face, and unashamedly I wiped them away and walked toward the bench. It was not until I arrived at the bench that the noise began to quiet. Adolph, Harry and my teammates all shook my hand and patted me on the back.

The game was a very close and, with two minutes to go, it was still in the balance. Then, as if inspired, I did something out of character for my personal style of play. I was primarily a defensive specialist and a rebounder. But, within less than a minute, I took three passes from my guards and shot three straight times. Any other time I would have passed off or fed breaking guards as I blocked their men going by. But this time I knew the moment I got the ball it was going up on the boards. Miracle of miracles, all three times the shots went through. We won by five points. Now we were in the driver's seat on the way to the SEC title.

Within a few days letters began pouring into the UK athletic department about Billie. All announced that the writer was praying for her. Some were very touching. I wanted to answer all of them, but that was impossible, so the athletic department sent back a form letter of appreciation.

I began receiving telephone calls from television game shows and interview talk shows. It was wearing me down. Finally after a discussion with Coach Rupp, we decided the switchboard would transfer all calls to his office for clearance. I never heard from any of them again, although at times Adolph would give me a list of those he had heard from. There was one call from *Life* magazine, however, that got through to my room. They wanted to do a pictorial story on Billie and me. At first I shrank from the idea because I did not want any pictures published of Billie as she now appeared. But then, I had second thoughts. I knew how much the athletic departments at all schools need national publicity. Perhaps I should look into it to see if there would be any benefit for my school. My other thought was for the marvelous team of doctors and nurses working in the Macon Hospital clinic and how valiantly they worked in Billie's behalf. I had gotten very close to the medical staff and knew how much they cared for all cancer patients and the research that was going on. I had also been asked by the American Cancer Society to be the honorary chairman of the Cancer Crusade in Kentucky for the coming year. Perhaps, I thought, the *Life* magazine article might be a good start.

I was also influenced either by my ego or a hope that the article might be a means of sharing with others Billie's faith and our commitment to the teachings of Jesus Christ. This was confusing because at the time I was unable to separate my desire for the article from my faith or worldly acclaim. Because I did not want to do anything for the wrong reasons, I told *Life* I just wasn't sure. They said they would contact me later.

We were scheduled to play DePaul in Chicago and were going to be on *The Tonight Show*, which was then originating from that city. It would be televised nationwide with excerpts from the game and interviews with the players and the coaching staff. Since the game was non-conference match, the team looked forward to having a pleasant stay in Chicago without the usual pressure.

However, the news from Macon was still not good, and I wanted to see Billie before our last push to the SEC title, including the vital practice week before the NCAA tourney. Of course, I knew how very difficult it would be for me to get away during that time. But finally it was all resolved by my coaches. On Thursday afternoon after practice Rupp and Lancaster suggested, since the Chicago game was not crucial to our NCAA tourney bid, that I go instead to Georgia right after our Saturday game. That way I could be with Billie on Sunday and Monday and rejoin the team in Lexington on Tuesday.

I was elated. Once again I took the night flight to Atlanta and drove down to Macon.

I detected almost immediately that Billie's mind was being affected by pain-killing drugs as well as by the disease. At times she was extremely lucid and articulate, and the next moment she might be a little girl on the farm, walking with her father through the peach orchards. On almost every nostalgic imaginary journey she was on that farm with a member of her family talking about things that happened so very long ago.

After one such scene, when she was telling of a walk with her father one summer day, she suddenly awakened and saw me bending over her. She said with frightened eyes, "It's the medicine, Ed. It's the medicine. It makes you say and do things that you don't realize or remember."

"I know, Billie, but you were talking about some wonderful and happy experiences. So don't worry about what you are saying . . . it's all right." She seemed to be more calm after that.

I also realized that the measurement of time was slipping from her. She knew that I had been there less than a week before but could not put it within a time perspective. In fact, there were times I felt she did not even know I had been gone. There was only one brief moment when she asked me about our basketball season, and I shared momentarily that we were still leading in the SEC race.

Later that Sunday afternoon word came that two men wanted to see me in the hospital lobby. They were *Life* magazine photographers from the Atlanta office; their New York headquarters had asked them to contact me in Macon about the article they had proposed earlier.

For a "little 'ole country boy" this was heady stuff, a magazine that covered the nation with a circulation in the millions. But still, something bothered me about it. The two men were very cordial, and as we talked I told them that since I didn't want Billie hurt in any way I was totally against having any pictures taken of her.

"Well," said one, "that's easily handled. We could photograph you standing by her bed and not focus on her."

However, I still had mixed feelings and asked them to wait until I talked with her family and doctors.

"Fine," said one of them. "We'll spend the night here in Macon and check with you Monday noon."

My mind raced, comparing pros and cons of it all. "Could I see the story before it was printed to O.K. it?" I asked.

No, that was impossible since *Life* was a weekly magazine, they replied, but they would check with New York the next day.

After they left I met with Billie's family. Everyone seemed fairly cool about it. Mrs. Ray slowly shook her head. "You know, some dear soul from the Valley had already shown Billie that awful newspaper article, and she had wryly remarked, 'So they think I'm going to die.'

"Really," continued Billie's mother, "I just don't know how she'd react to any article now."

The next morning I discussed it with Billie's three doctors. I could sense their mixed feelings. They, too, I'm sure, were tempted by the nationwide coverage of their work and the Macon hospital. But they put it squarely in my hands.

"Look, Ed," said one, "we don't think the article would affect the eventual outcome in Billie's case in any way at all." I was certain they felt that she was beyond noticing printed material. "And we would be willing to be interviewed if you wanted the story. Frankly, if you're asking us, we're not endorsing it at all. However, it's your decision."

At noon I sat down with the two *Life* photographers over lunch. I still had mixed feelings but was willing to hear what they had to say.

"Here's how we see it," said one. "We'll take all the hospital pictures today and then fly with you to Lexington for pictures there. We'd have the article into New York by Thursday to make the next issue."

"Could I see it before it's printed?" I asked.

They shook their heads, "Impossible," said one. "The New York editors do the final editing."

"Well, could New York read it to me over the phone?"

"No," one answered, leaning back in his chair. "It just isn't *Life's* policy to do that."

That clinched it for me. "Well, I'm sorry," I said, "but I just can't go through with it."

"Well," said one, slowly moving a spoon around on the table, "I must tell you that one of our top editors in New York feels this story has the possibility of becoming a three or four-page layout . . . " he looked up at me for emphasis, "could mean a cover as well."

He waited for the words to sink in. "We're talking about a split cover with you standing by the hospital bed," he continued, "and another shot showing you outside Kentucky's Memorial Coliseum in your basketball uniform."

My mind reeled at the prospect. The cover of *Life*! Usually only famous people appeared on it. Excitement filled me.

Yet, something didn't seem right about it. Perhaps it was because I had silently prayed for direction because I felt it would be trading on Billie's illness.

"I'm sorry, fellows," I found myself saying. "I just can't do it."

The two men left rather dejected, but more than ever I felt I had done the right thing. Billie's family and the doctors seemed relieved. I did find myself wondering, however, how Coaches Rupp and Lancaster would react when they heard about it. I knew that college athletic departments need all the publicity they can get because of the constant need for financial backing. What would they say when they heard I had turned down a *Life* cover, part of which would have featured the school?

I put it out of my mind and didn't watch our team play their Chicago opponents on television in favor of sitting by Billie's side that night. People came into the room off and on to give periodic reports on how the Wildcats were demolishing the Blue Demons. Then, when one of the doctors rushed in to announce that Coach Rupp had wished Billie well "right on the television cameras!" a faint smile crossed Billie's face. She still knew what was going on.

I combed her hair early the next morning for a long time. It seemed to make her feel so much better and allowed me to feel as if I were doing something for her. I hugged her goodbye, so aware of her thin body, and said, "I'll see you, darling, after the NCAA tournament."

She looked up and smiled, "It will be the end of the season, won't it?"

"Yes, the season will finally be over, and I will come to you."

Her eyes moistened. "Please play well, and tell the team I'm praying for them to win."

I leaned down and kissed her again. "I love you and I'll see you soon."

After my arrival in Lexington early that afternoon, I went immediately to see Coaches Rupp and Lancaster. They were both in Adolph's office. I thanked them again for allowing me to go to Macon and told Coach Rupp how much I appreciated his mentioning Billie on the TV program.

I then told them about *Life* magazine, how I had vacillated and my reasons for finally declining. They both sat silently for a moment, studying the top of Rupp's desk. Then Coach Lancaster looked up and said, "Ed, you did the right thing. We don't need that kind of publicity. We'll get enough from the court. Let's go to practice."

We clinched the SEC championship the last week of the regular season, which allowed us to qualify for the NCAA tourney. We received a first-round bye and were scheduled to play in the quarter-finals. Our section of the tournament was scheduled to be held in Lexington, and we felt fortunate to be playing on our home court. Our first opponent would be the University of Pittsburgh.

The practice sessions leading up to that tournament were the most basic I had ever experienced. The coaching staff believed that the major tournament games were won or lost by the little things. The good passes, the good rebounding positions and the lack of mental errors. So, for a week leading up to our first game, we went back to the elementary level of basketball.

We beat Pittsburgh without too much trouble. The score was fairly close, but it was one of those games you know you have under control. The next night we were scheduled to play Michigan State. They had some sensational players and one who came in with All-American honors named "Jumping" Johnny Green. I was scheduled to guard him.

I had kept in constant contact with the hospital. Billie was unable to talk very much except to say weakly, "I love you, Ed." There had been one exception to her abbreviated phone conversations, however, and that was to someone else. I didn't learn about it until later.

After we had won the SEC title, I called to give Billie the good news and found her awake and quite alert. In fact, she even sounded excited and wanted to know all about the NCAA tourney coming up. I told her that our UK basketball season would be over in a week if we lost the first round, and win or lose in the second round, the whole tourney would be completed within two weeks.

"The season will be over, and I'll come to you as I promised," I said. "I do miss you and love you so, Billie."

Her response had been light and loving, "Oh, don't worry about me. Helen and everyone are taking such very good care of me. I just want you to play well. Win the championship and then come to me."

Immediately after our conversation she had put in a long distance call to our dear church friend, Helen Hunt, I found out later. In her soft, southern voice she had said, "Hel-leen, I want to ask a favor of you. All of you have been praying for me, but I want you to tell

Clancy (Rev. Yates) to pray for Ed instead of me. You know, Hel-leen, we have everything all worked out—but somehow as my time of departure gets nearer, I realize that it is more difficult for Ed than me. Hel-leen, it's like when someone you love leaves you to go somewhere and you're the one left. The one going will see new people, new places and have new experiences. The one left has just the same people and same places, and misses the one that is gone." Then she continued, "Hel-leen, you know what I mean, don't you? I'm sure you do. I'll be talking to you soon, and please look after my Ed."

When Helen Hunt told me about that call later, I hung on to its message as a drowning man hangs on to a rope thrown to him in the water.

Our second NCAA game against the Big Ten champion, Michigan State, was a bruising contest from the opening tip. We played very well and were ahead by 10 points at the half. We felt very confident in the dressing room. We knew that we only had 20 minutes left and, with a 10-point lead, we could win. Then in seven days it would be on to Kansas City and playing for all the marbles. Call it over-confidence, call it let-down, call it fate—but we led in that game until the last two minutes. Jumping Johnny had fouled out with about five minutes to go in the game, and that's when we started to celebrate the victory. But it was not to be. In a bizarre two minutes of basketball, a substitute from the Spartan's bench came into the game and ignited the team by shooting long bombs that hit nothing but net. We lost the game. It was a nightmare! We stood on the court stunned.

I grabbed my warm-up jacket from the bench and walked up the ramp to the dressing room. I was the last player to turn the corner heading toward the doorway. Harry Lancaster was leaning up against the wall looking down at the floor. I stopped in front of him, and he extended his hand.

"Coach," I asked, "what in the world happened out there? I don't believe it. We had that game won all the way. What happened?"

"I don't know, Ed, but someday we will know. Someday we will know," he said quietly.

That seemed like a strange statement, but everything was strange that night.

The dressing room was a disaster scene. My teammates were rooted to the benches, refusing to get out of their sweat-stained uniforms. In shock and disbelief, some of them were crying. I felt like crying too but had no tears left. Coach Rupp pushed through the swinging doors and said, "Gentlemen, the game is over, and I want you to forget about it. You'll never be able to play it again, so just forget it. But there is one thing I do not want you to forget. At the start of this season you were not ranked in the top 10, and some people did not even rank you in the top 20. But tonight you are the Number Three team in America, and you are there for only one reason. You gave me more than you actually had, you gave me your very best. And I want to thank you."

We sat somewhat stunned, for he had every right to let us have it for not winning a game that we should have won. Instead, we went into the showers still feeling dejected but realizing there was going to be another year and we were going to be back.

After showering and dressing, I walked out of the locker room and headed down the corridor of champions. Coaches Rupp and Lancaster were sitting in the basketball office. I started to apologize once again, but before I could get a word out, Coach Rupp said, "Ed, tell Billie hello for all of us. We'll be pulling for you."

I had been so down about our loss of the game that I had forgotten our season was now over.

"I'll be leaving tomorrow for Georgia. I don't know when I'll be back," I said.

Lancaster said, "If you need anything—anything at all—just call me. Adolph will be at the tourney in Kansas City, but I'll be here."

I went to my room and called for airline reservations for the next morning. Then I called the hospital. It was late, but they were allowing my calls to go through to Billie at any hour. Helen answered and said that Billie was resting—she had had a terrible day with lots of pain. I asked her to have one of Billie's brothers pick me up at the airport the following day, I would not be renting a car. I was coming to stay.

I was just about to hang up when I heard Billie's voice. "Helen, who is on the phone?" Helen gave her the phone, and she said, "Darling, why are you calling me so late?"

I decided I would just get the bad news behind us right away, and

I said quickly, "Billie, we lost tonight. Michigan State beat us in the last two minutes."

She replied, "Oh, my dear, I'm so sorry."

"I'll see you tomorrow afternoon, darling," I said optimistically. "The season is over. I'm coming to you as I promised." Despite our loss, I was elated. I would soon see the most important person in my life.

"I'll try to look my prettiest for you," she laughed, "so I had better get my beauty sleep."

I said, "Sleep well, my darling, sleep well. I'll see you tomorrow."

When I arrived the next afternoon, she was radiantly beautiful to me, but she was already in a semi-coma. She had slipped into it early in the morning as her brother sped me to her side.

28

A Question
Answered

The signs were unmistakable now—her quick shallow breathing, the pale yellow skin, the skeletal body. Cancer was winning the battle, and yet the valiant young girl continued to fight.

It was the longest week of my life. I longed for those few moments when Billie seemed to relax. For some reason this happened only in the early morning just as the sun was rising. All through the night she would struggle to breathe and moan in pain. The doctors said that she had probably passed the threshold of pain and was moaning from reflex, but I could not be totally convinced of that. She had been in a semi-coma when I arrived on that Sunday, but later that day she had been in a fairly clearheaded state for almost an hour. Probably it was because of the drugs—the doctors had left orders to keep Billie as free from pain as possible.

Her body had been punctured so often by the shots it had become a veritable pin cushion. When she was lucid the shots were excruciating. As she shifted in bed from one side to the other, tears of pain filled her eyes. When she did sleep her eyes did not close entirely. Perhaps her subconscious longing to stay alive would not allow her eyes to close entirely, believing that they might never open again.

As much as I loved those few moments when Billie was clear in her perceptions and reactions, I also was grateful for her semi-comatose state in which she was not suffering the intense discomfort of a tired, worn-out body. She was so thin, and though her stomach had been drained of fluids via a long needle, her abdomen still appeared greatly swollen. She was fed entirely intravenously since food could not be retained. I had to be extremely careful combing her hair because that was beginning to be painful rather than comforting.

Helen, who had been at her sister's bedside most of the previous 42 days, had become a walking zombie. There was not much any person could do now except to try to fill the room with a presence of love. I urged Helen to stay home and try to rest, but she insisted on coming each day. We finally compromised and worked out an agreement where she and/or her mother would be there during the day, and I would come at night. However, as the week progressed and we wondered when her next breath might be the last, we began to overlap each other.

It was mid-morning Wednesday and Billie's mother was to arrive shortly. Billie's early morning calmness had disintegrated into the restless thrashing of a pain-inflicted body. As Thelma Ray came into the room, seeing her daughter in agony, she reached out as only a mother could do. "Billie," she said, "I do wish you did not have to suffer so, I do wish there was something we could do."

Billie quickly responded clearly and lovingly, "Just remember, Mom, my Lord and Savior Jesus Christ had to suffer and die for me, and he will not ask me to suffer any more than he had to that day."

My chest was racked by deep sobs as I heard Billie say, "Mother, please read the Twenty-third Psalm—I know it by heart, but I love to hear it read."

"The Lord is my shepherd," her mother began, "I shall not want. . . ."

But as I walked out of the room, I *wanted*, and what I wanted was peace for Billie.

Early Friday morning, long before sunrise, Billie began to stir.

She had been in a coma for more than 24 hours. I went to her bedside and leaned over her. "Ice . . ." she murmured, "please . . . ice for my lips. . . ." As I gently placed an ice-filled cloth to her lips, she asked who was there. By this time the disease had affected her eyesight.

"Billie, it's me, Ed, your husband."

"Oh, Ed, you did come, and you are here."

"Yes, I'm here, right here. Is there anything that I can get for you?"

"My lips are so dry," she said. I took the Vaseline from the drawer and gently rubbed a thin layer over her lips.

"Thank you, my darling."

I reached down and very softly kissed her.

"Please kiss me again," she murmured.

I kissed her on the side of her cheek near her lips. She moved her head slightly, and I moved to her lips again. I kissed her again and again with momentary pauses in between.

"Billie, I love you—oh, how I love you." My tears glistened on her face.

"I know you do, and darling, I love you. Thank you for being here with me."

"Billie, I don't want you to suffer any more. I don't want you to struggle any more. I want you to be free." Now her eyes closed. She lay so still.

I was holding her hand. "Do you know what I'm trying to say?"

In answer, she squeezed my hand in one long-pressured clasp. There was no mistaking our signal. She understood. I leaned over and kissed her again, and then I whispered in her ear, "Darling, I release you. I give you to God. I give you to the Christ whom you love and who loves you. You are free to go. Don't hold back because of me or for anyone. You are free to go. Do you understand?"

Again, that unmistakable squeeze of my hand. I sobbed, "Oh, Billie, I love you so, but I must let you go. I love you so."

She opened her lips slightly and sighed, "I love you, my Ed."

Those were her last words to me.

I waited with Helen all day on Friday. Billie was now in a deep coma. Helen went home on Friday night, and early in the morning I again whispered in Billie's ear. I held her hand and said over and over again, "Do you understand what I'm saying to you?" But there was no answering squeeze.

Saturday morning I read in the paper about the NCAA championship game to be played that afternoon in Kansas City between Michigan State and the University of North Carolina. Our team should have been there playing North Carolina, and we would have been if we hadn't lost to Michigan State! How much I had wanted to win that game for Billie!

But now it didn't matter quite so much. The real meaning of my life lay on the bed before me. It was then that Helen came into the room and urged me to go home for a shower, shave and breakfast. I did. That was the afternoon I awakened from my nap with the inner feeling that I must hurry back to the hospital. That was when I experienced the terrible moment in the parking lot when I *knew*, knew in my heart that I had failed to keep my promise. I was too late. Billie, my love, had slipped into the next world without me. I had not been at her side to hold her hand.

Tears burned my eyes as I fought this terrible realization. But the certainty of what had taken place did not waiver. I knew Billie had died. I was too late.

I pushed open the car door, crawled out and hurried blindly toward the hospital entrance. But there was no need to run. Billie was gone.

"Ed!"

I spun around. It was Dr. Moody, one of the hospital physicians. He was a basketball fan and we had often discussed the current collegiate season over lunch in the hospital cafeteria.

"How's Billie?" he asked, as he caught up with me.

It was a question that had become almost a ritual this past year. I was about to give the usual feeble response of "Oh, she's fine" or "Doing a little better today," when I found myself blurting, "Doc, Billie is dead."

Moody's mouth dropped open in astonishment, and my mind reeled under the impact of what I had just said. Why had I done it? I wondered. The last word I had received from Helen was that Billie was all right. Yet, again, that deep-down feeling within spoke so much more authoritatively than anything of this earth.

"When did she die?" gasped Dr. Moody.

"When?" I stopped walking, my hand on the hospital door. "A few minutes ago."

"But how do you know?" he stared at me quizzically. I knew I looked tired and drawn, and I wondered if he thought I'd become irrational under the strain.

I took a deep breath and looked at him squarely. "I'm not sure, Doc, but I know she's gone, and I'm going to her room right now." I wheeled, pushed open the door and strode into the hall. Dr. Moody silently walked with me.

We stepped into the lobby—the lobby which I had entered so many times with so many different feelings; hope, sorrow, relief, fear. But today was different. The elevator was empty and I punched the fifth floor button. The two of us stood silently as the floor lights flashed. The cage halted, the door slid open, and we stepped out. I turned to the right and headed toward Billie's room at the end of the hall. The hospital had placed Billie there to seclude her from newspaper and radio reporters, over-eager well-wishers and the curious.

As I passed the nurse's station, a white-uniformed woman looked up at me. Her stricken look confirmed my feelings.

Dr. Moody continued walking with me, stride for stride. As we approached Billie's room, her doctor came out of the door. It was Dr. Bill Somers, the head cancer specialist, a stethoscope dangling from his neck. He reached out and took my hand, tears in his eyes. "I'm sorry, Ed," he choked, "but Billie's gone."

I stared at him for a moment, my mouth quivering. "When . . . when did she die, how long ago?"

He glanced at his watch, "About seven to ten minutes ago . . . not long at all."

I stood shaken. Just as I thought, while I was on my way to the hospital.

I mumbled something to Dr. Somers and Dr. Moody, turned and walked into Billie's room. Helen was standing in front of the bed. She looked up and came toward me without a word, tears streaming down her cheeks. We held each other for a long moment as if confirming that our lives were very precious and important. Helen was the closest person to Billie that I knew, and I was sure she felt the same about me. As we clung to one another, we were reaching out to Billie who had meant so much to both of us.

Words were unimportant. Then, as if moving in slow motion, Helen went over to the bed, leaned down and kissed Billie goodbye. Then she came toward the door, stopped, kissed my cheek, whispered that she would wait outside, and left the room.

I walked to the side of the bed and looked down at Billie's physical form that I had loved and held so often. She appeared to be in a quiet peace. Oh, how we both had longed and prayed for peace. And yet, in her dead presence, I found it so unacceptable. I knelt by the bed and took her hand as I had promised I would during her passing. I began to pray silently, and then I was overwhelmed with a strong impression—*I'm not too late. True, there is no breath, no vital signs whatsoever, but I am not too late.*

I am aware that emotions can play terrible tricks on grief-stricken minds, but I was very much in control of myself, in fact I felt a sense of peace. I knew that Billie was finally healed and that she had been truly liberated. But now I seemed to be sensing a unique nuance in that room, not in the bed or even near it. I felt as if I were being pulled toward the window, to the right of it in the corner. As I approached the area I could see nothing there, but I had the impulse to look slightly up. I still could not see anything but had the strange feeling that I was finally in the right place.

Billie was there. Her presence was so very near I could almost hear the swish of her nurse's shoes in the corridor. I could hear her musical laughter. I could see her faint glowing smile and those sparkling dark brown eyes. I could feel her slender fingers as she lovingly stroked my cheek. I could sense her delicate body as I had so often done before.

No, I was not too late. God had given us this final moment together.

For a long time, I stood looking up into that corner where I had sensed her presence. The body on the bed was not Billie . . . I knew that. And I knew that she was now with her Lord and Savior whom she loved so dearly.

But whatever it was, I felt a sensing in my spirit that Billie and I were still in close communion for a fleeting moment, as if God had allowed us that final time of togetherness just before she joined him eternally.

I left the room and walked down the corridor to the room where Billie's family waited. I told them. They all came into her room to give their hushed, sad farewells.

Shortly afterward I went out to the telephone booth and called Harry Lancaster. It was approximately 2 p.m. I knew that he would be getting ready to listen to the NCAA game on the radio.

"Coach," I said, "Billie just died, about an hour ago."

"Ed, I'm sorry." There was a long pause and then he said, "Ed, now we know, don't we?"

"What do you mean?"

"We know why we lost last Saturday night. If we had won we would be in Kansas City today. It was best that you were in Macon."

I said nothing, moved by his perception. He continued, "Adolph and Bernie Shively are in Kansas City. I'll call them. Do you have any idea when the funeral will be?"

"It's uncertain, Coach, but I think it will probably be tomorrow afternoon. I'm sure the family will not want to delay it," I replied. After telling where he could contact me, I hung up.

I went back to Billie's room. The family had left except for Helen. She was beginning to pack Billie's things. The bed was empty.

We walked out of the hospital after saying goodbye and thanking that marvelous staff of workers who had loved Billie and taken such good care of her.

I followed Helen home. We were still in shock. We had expected Billie's death for months, but now that it had happened, it was overwhelming. It hit me even harder later in the afternoon—I would never hear Billie's musical voice again. I would never feel her reaching out to touch me. I would never feel her embrace. Driving out to the Ray farm, following Helen in her car, these thoughts kept rushing through my mind. I would never feel her warm and tender lips on mine. I would never see her sparkling eyes radiantly alive. I would never feel her hand on the back of my neck; or hear her whisper in me ear; or hear her laugh. "Oh, God," I cried out loudly, "I miss her so . . . so very, very much!"

The loneliness of separation was coming over me in waves. I

noticed Helen slowing down. She pulled off to the side of the road and got out of the car. The sun was on its western slope and a late spring breeze whispered through the trees and grass. I got out of my car too and moved toward Helen who was now heading in my direction. We were both crying. We just embraced and held each other for a long moment, trying to accept the reality of death's loss by filling life's needs of closeness. Then Helen turned and walked back to her car.

Later we went to the funeral home and made the arrangements. I selected a cemetery plot in the late evening hours just at twilight. I knew tomorrow I would be saying my farewell at this same place.

I returned to the farm for a late meal with all the family. My mother and father had arrived from Jacksonville, Florida, and we had an emotion-filled visit. I followed Helen back to Macon because I feared for her safety. It was late when we arrived at her home.

Helen and I had agreed to drive to the Valley in the morning. I had called Clarence Yates in Lexington. Strangely, though Billie had a relative who was a preacher, one of the communications I felt I had received from her in that last moment of togetherness in the hospital room just after her death was to ask Clarence to preach at the service. We both had grown so close to him during our short time together in Lexington. Clarence said he would be honored.

I prepared for bed, but could not sleep. I was restless, so I got up and walked out of my bedroom to say goodnight to Helen. Helen stood and came toward me. She reminded me more of Billie than any other person I knew. Again, I held her close and thanked her for loving Billie. I returned to my bedroom and laid down. It was a long and restless night. I kept feeling my hand being squeezed and hearing the words, "I love you, my Ed." And all I could answer was "My darling, I love you, too."

If there was a smile on any of our faces, it was because we knew she was dressed in red. I was with Helen at the mortuary just before we closed the casket for the last time. Helen had told me of how Billie had said to her, "Helen, when I die I want to be buried in a red dress."

Helen had incredulously exclaimed, "What in heaven's sake for?"

Billie had laughed, "Because when the bugle of the Lord is blown, I want to come out dancing."

I touched her hair, said goodbye and smiled at her red dress as I closed the casket.

My Methodist Church in Fort Valley was crowded with blacks as well as whites. They had come from all walks of life to say goodbye. Some who had groaned inwardly at our wedding vow "til death do us part," now cried openly. Coach Rupp and the athletic director, Bernie Shively, sat nearby. Clarence Yates, our Lexington pastor, shared his most intimate memories concerning Billie's life and loves. The casket remained closed. She did not want to be remembered in that way, and we who loved her already had our vivid memories of her before her illness. Through tear-dimmed eyes, I looked up at the stained glass window I had come to know so well. Yes, the lamb still looked secure within the arms of Jesus. And I knew Billie was, too.

The funeral was at four o'clock and internment immediately after. We left the cemetery and drove back to the farm. A large crowd had arrived to express their love. After greeting them, I noticed the sun sinking into the west. Twilight was near, and I had an appointment to keep. I climbed into the Black Tank and drove down the meandering gravel road to the cemetery. I purposely lowered the car windows, and as the wind ruffled my hair I could almost feel Billie sitting close to me, smiling as she did when she enjoyed our evening rides.

When I pulled up to the cemetery and walked over to Billie's grave, there were about 15 minutes of light left; the sun had just set and a mauve light filled the western sky. A large mound of multi-colored flowers covered the grave. I stood for a moment, looking down at them; then for some reason I looked back at her car . . . it seemed as if I could see her sitting there behind the steering wheel, laughing and waving for me to hurry back. I knelt on the damp grass, trying to listen, to what I did not know. But I continued to kneel there for a few minutes and, as the evening breeze wafted my cheek, the old words took on new meaning: "The wind blows where it will, and you hear the sound of it, but you do not know where it comes from or where it goes; so it is with everyone who is born of the Spirit."

The little girl who was with him now was certainly born of the Spirit. I knew that and it comforted me.

The next day I went up to Billie's simply furnished bedroom, our only "home" in the Valley. For a moment it was so quiet, as if time was holding its breath. And then, somewhere below, a screen door slammed, a woman's voice called to a kitten, and out in the field a tractor engine coughed and settled into a distant drone. Life was returning to normal on the Ray farm; yet, it would never again be the same.

Pulling out the top drawer of the old dresser, I began to sort through the things that had belonged to Billie. Under some carefully folded sweaters, I found her diary. I did not even know she had kept one.

Sitting on the edge of the bed, I opened it reverently and the first words on the beginning page filled me with the warmth of her presence.

"My name is Billie Ray Beck. I'm 23 years of age and I'm suffering from a fatal disease. All that I have been able to read and study about this disease leads me to believe that I will die within two years."

For a moment I could not continue; tears flooded my cheeks. Then I read on: "I am not afraid, for I thank God for the greatest blessing that he has ever allowed me to experience, because through Hodgkin's disease I have come to know my Lord and Savior in a greater and more wonderful way than ever before. . . ."

I could not read any longer; the lump in my throat was too painful. But as I carefully put the diary into my suitcase, I silently thanked my wife for answering one of the most demanding questions I had about why she had to suffer so.

29

The Assignment

It was almost as if I were hearing her whisper in my ear. "Remember our covenant, darling, no matter what happens, you must finish school."

School was the last thing I was thinking of then. Everything of this world seemed so mundane, so useless. Why was anything worth striving for when the reason for one's life was extinguished?

Still it was as if Billie were reminding me that she was fine where she was and that I had a promise to keep.

So, on Thursday night, I phoned Woodie Ballard in Lexington and asked if she could pick me up at the airport there late Friday.

"Of course."

"I just don't want anyone to know when I'm arriving," I said.

"I understand."

At 9 p.m. my plane touched down in Lexington. I slipped off, and with my bag, walked directly to Woodie's car in the parking lot. I opened the door, threw my bag in the back and slumped onto the front seat.

She reached over and took my hand.

"It's rougher than you thought it would be, isn't it?"

"Yes, a lot rougher."

"I knew it would be," she said softly. I knew she was remembering her own loss. "You won't get over it," she added, "but you *will* get used to it."

Starting the engine, she glanced at me. "That's the one great thing about time, Ed. It allows you to become accustomed to the pain."

I thanked her for coming on such short notice as she dropped me off at my dorm. From her I learned that the night following Billie's funeral my team and a number of fans had gathered for the annual basketball banquet. Adolph Rupp's speech was about a "little southern belle who showed us all what strength, determination and commitment are all about." He then dedicated the Big Blue's 1957-58 season to her memory.

That was like Adolph, I thought, iron on the outside, butter in his heart.

As Woodie drove away I stepped into a quiet dorm—all my roommates had gone for the weekend. I was glad; I needed to be alone for those two days.

Tired, I quickly went to bed. However, I could not sleep. Billie's face kept appearing before me, and all the past week's events rolled by as if on an endless film. Finally I slipped into slumber. I was awakened by the phone ringing. Glancing at my clock, I noticed it was nearly 10 o'clock in the morning.

Groggily, I picked up the phone. It was the pastor of the First Methodist Church in Richmond, Kentucky. "I'm calling to confirm your speaking engagement," he said. Trying to think through my sleepy haze, I vaguely began to remember talking with this man about it some six months ago.

"I'm sorry," I said, "I had really forgotten about it, but I'll try to make it. When is it?"

He seemed surprised at my question. "It's tomorrow, Ed. The Religious Emphasis Week begins at Eastern Kentucky University tomorrow, and you are the keynote speaker at 11 a.m."

I almost fell out of bed. "Tomorrow? Are you sure?"

"Oh yes," he replied, "all the publicity is out and people are coming from all over to hear you." He was beginning to speak very rapidly, a note of hysteria creeping into his voice. "I realize it's a bad time for you, Ed, but when we did not hear from you to the contrary, we felt that you were going to be with us." His last words were a plea.

I slumped on the bed, stunned. I had wanted nothing more than seclusion these next few days. But then, I knew what Billie would want me to do. "All right," I said, "but I can be there only for my talk. I will have to leave after it."

He sighed with relief. "Fine! Fine! You are slated for 11:20, and you'll need no introduction." He hung up quickly. I presumed it was so I wouldn't have a chance to change my mind.

I showered and began to unpack my things. At the bottom of the bag I found Billie's diary. I opened it and sat reading. It was like having her with me in a way.

The next morning I arrived in Richmond at almost 11 o'clock and was surprised at not being able to find a parking place near the auditorium. Finally I parked several blocks away and trotted toward the place. As I neared the building I saw crowds of people standing outside under opened windows. I heard someone say that the place was filled to capacity, and I was dumbfounded.

Who attended Religious Emphasis Week on college campuses any more? I worked my way to the back of the building and found an open entrance. Inside, I asked directions to the door leading to the podium. It was exactly 11:20 as I stepped through it and made my way to the one unoccupied chair on the stage. A murmur rippled through the audience. Then there was a hush as I was introduced.

Approaching the lectern, I said a little prayer and looked out across a wide sea of expectant faces.

"For my text today, I am reading from the gospel of John," I said, turning to my Bible. "I am the resurrection and the life—any person that believes in Me, though he or she shall die, yet shall he or she live, whosoever liveth and believeth in Me shall never die."

I closed the Bible. "I want to tell you a story. I want to tell you about my wife, Billie. How she taught me two great truths of human existence—how to live and how to die." I opened the diary and held it up. "I discovered her diary just a few days ago, after she died. I want to read a small portion of her writings that are very special to me." My throat caught as I began to read, but then I felt a special strength.

"My name is Billie Ray Beck . . ." I began reading. When finished, I added, "Billie said to me once, when she heard me pray for her healing, 'Don't pray for my healing, pray for my understanding.' She believed God had a purpose for her. She had always wanted to go across the sea as a medical missionary. Then God allowed her to see that her mission field was here. She had a strong faith in Jesus, and she realized her work was to live out her faith here so that the rest of us could know the certainty of the gospel of love that she knew and wanted so much to share. . . ."

After I concluded my remarks and prepared to sit down, I was dumbfounded for a second time that morning. The entire audience seemed to be streaming to the altar, and most of them knelt in prayer.

With emotion-filled voices and tears in their eyes, many of those people told me they had decided to become Christians or were rededicating their lives to Jesus Christ through hearing Billie's testimony and story.

Now I could see how Billie's message, and, in a very special way, her spirit, was living on. Yes, it is true that the power of the resurrection can turn defeat into glorious victory.

On my drive back to the university that afternoon I felt liberated by sharing Billie's insights of love, life and victory over death. However, I found myself still struggling with questions. *What actually had taken place in that auditorium?* I asked myself. I did realize that my perceptions were subjective since I was still working through grief. Yet with so many unanswered questions, I was not able to draw any logical conclusions.

Why did Billie's simple story of victory over pain grip so many? Why did her death, which had appeared to be defeat, give them hope? Why had so many people even come to hear me speak? Was it just sympathy for a young woman and a young athlete? Was it mere identification with someone they had read about? Curiosity? Was it even a subtle form of entertainment where, in a macabre way, certain persons find satisfaction in others' pain and heartache? A thousand thoughts, and, though all may have held some truth, I clung to the ultimate truth which could only be found in the gospel of Christ's life itself.

I began to understand something about Calvary's scene that I had not seen before. It was a brief insight, but I realized that those who watched the crucifixion could see no victory whatsoever. I knew that in the ancient world the earth was considered sacred, and if a person who deserved to die was executed in contact with the ground, the earth would be defiled. To protect their earth god, the people devised a cross that would lift the victim off the ground to die agonizingly in the air. Thus the very act of raising a cross upright with the victim impaled on it was to show the watching world that death could never be viewed as a victory. No hope of any kind could be seen in it.

On the day Jesus died on his cross, no one could see the slightest potential for good, even though Jesus had tried to tell his disciples this would be God's victory. They could not comprehend it.

Even now, 2,000 years later, when Christians supposedly affirm their faith in the resurrection, most of us are still like the ancients who see only defeat in the greatest sign of victory for humanity.

I realized there *is* victory in dying. I believe that hidden within the deepest recesses of every person is a glint of hope, an awareness that no matter what happens to us there is something within us that can never be destroyed—some entity, some reality that will be strengthened rather than shattered. That innate conviction can never be damaged by any circumstances unless we first allow it to be touched by our own defeatism.

Some may call it instinct; I call it soul. Call it what you will—it is the awareness that you control your attitude in accepting whatever takes place. As I drove back down the sunlit highway to Lexington that Sunday afternoon, the reality of Billie's victorious attitude toward death rolled over me like waves of assurance again and again.

I did not know what went through the minds of the people who heard me speak that morning at Eastern Kentucky University, but I knew that Billie's victory had profoundly touched my life with the presence of God.

I could not fathom all these thoughts then; I cannot fathom their depths even now, for as the Bible says, "We see through a glass darkly." But I did know that day that the words of the Scripture, "Though she be dead yet she speaketh," were coming truer each moment. For the first time in my life, I began to understand that wonderfully descriptive phrase, "the communion of saints." I felt I was in communion with Billie and, though I was still uncertain of exactly what I should do with this new insight, I strongly felt a major need to communicate it to others.

In some way God would have me share his simple story of victory over seeming defeat and the healing that comes out of hurt.

30

An Inner Sanctum

On an early Tuesday morning, with trees casting long shadows on the well-manicured lawn, I found myself walking toward a big, white mansion. It was the home of the governor of Kentucky. Why, I wondered had he asked to see me?

A phone call had come from a state official late the Sunday night after my talk at Eastern Kentucky University. He said that the governor had tried to contact me earlier while I was in Georgia but had failed. He was now out of town but would it be convenient for me to see him at the mansion Tuesday morning?

It really wasn't convenient because I needed every minute to catch up on my school work. But I saw it as an opportunity to catch two birds with one swipe of the net. As I had just been asked to serve as honorary chairman for the Kentucky State Cancer Crusade, I asked the official if a photographer could take a photo of the governor giving me a donation to be used in the crusade's promotional campaign. He saw no problem and a short time later called back to report that an official state photographer would be in the governor's office at 10 a.m. for the photograph.

"But can you still be there at 7:30?" he asked.

"Certainly," I answered, wondering why the early hour.

Now, as I neared the mansion, I thought about the man I would soon meet.

A. B. "Happy" Chandler was Governor of Kentucky all of the years I played basketball at the University. He was probably our team's greatest fan. He followed us avidly, and after every home game his hearty voice would resound through the dressing room as he patted us all on the back. If we had done extremely well, he would hug our sweaty necks as he continued to pound our backs saying "God love you, son!"

I particularly remembered the previous December at the Sugar Bowl basketball tournament. After we had just won the championship, and I was trotting off the court, the loud speaker suddenly boomed: "And now, the most valuable player in the 1956 Sugar Bowl Tournament—from the University of Kentucky—Number 34, Ed Beck!"

Stunned, I froze in my tracks, then returned to the court to accept the greatest basketball honor that I had thus far received. As I left the floor in a daze carrying the trophy, Happy Chandler greeted me with a hug and a shouting whisper, "Congratulations, Ed. God love you!"

"God love you!" was almost a trademark of this big bear of a man, but I guess I had never felt its true impact. However, I was to experience it this morning in a deeply unusual way, much of it because of Billie.

As I walked up the steps leading to the mansion door, a Kentucky state trooper greeted me and escorted me into the dining room where I was to join the governor for breakfast.

He was already seated at the table, drinking a cup of coffee and reading a newspaper. Hearing our approach, he raised his curly gray head, stood and came toward me, again greeting me in that inimitable way.

As we enjoyed breakfast together, I sensed the genuine warmth of the man. It was not affectation for the benefit of the public but a real expression of his heart. He thanked me for coming and apologized for not getting in touch with me sooner. Despite my earlier apprehension, I soon found myself comfortably chatting with him.

I began to worry about his time. I knew he followed a hectic schedule, but he quickly let me know that his morning had been cleared until 10:15 when he would be meeting with some legislators.

After breakfast we walked to the capitol, flanked by the ever-present security officers. Inside the capitol we went straight to his office, where I found myself overwhelmed not only by its stately elegance but also by the obvious importance Governor Chandler had placed on our meeting. After introducing me to his office staff, he asked his secretary to hold all calls while we talked. I knew that our photograph wasn't scheduled until 10 o'clock, so I wondered what would take place within his inner sanctum during the next 45 minutes.

He closed his office door, invited me to sit down and sank into the big leather chair behind his massive desk.

"Ed, I'd like to share something with you that not too many people know," he began, hands folded on his desk. "You have to realize that in the political arena certain things can be cheapened by both your supporters and opponents if they are misunderstood. Thus, there are some things that take place in this office that only a few people know about. And I wanted to tell you this so that you'll know that you were not forgotten throughout your ordeal with Billie."

He leaned back for a moment, in deep thought.

"You know, Ed," he said, pointing to his office entrance, "most people who come through that door are in need of something. It's true that some come without the best intentions. But most people who come in here are in real need. I don't have too many coming in, saying, 'Governor, everything's going great with me or my company, and I just want to give $50,000 or $100,000 to the state so you can use it to help others.'"

He smiled wryly and shook his head. "Oh no, Ed, they come in here with their hands out and their hearts open. Mind you, they are not beggars or rip-off artists but people in need, and they know that this office can help them. They elected me to serve them, and that's what I want to be—their servant."

He rose from his chair and walked to the side of his desk.

"Every morning when I come in here, I close the door behind

me, no matter who's out there waiting, and spend a few minutes right here on my knees." He pointed to the carpeted floor at his feet. "I seek divine guidance in the decisions that I must make that affect the lives of so many people."

He looked at me earnestly and continued, "Some people wouldn't understand that or might even ridicule it, saying that I'm playing politics with God. But, as I know my heart, I'm not. I realize just how much I need his help in this job, so every morning I pray for God's help."

His eyes misted, and my heart was moved. Placing his hand on my shoulder, he continued, "And Ed, over the past weeks you have been a part of those moments here. I've prayed for the comfort of God to be with you. I know you have a strong faith, but I also know how much extra help you must have needed."

Now, my eyes moistened as I looked at this big man who had just poured out his heart to me. I really did not know how to respond. I was deeply touched and believed that he was sharing an intimacy so close to him that until now I have never felt free to let anyone else know about it.

Moved by his concern, I rose from my chair and asked if we could pray together then.

"I sure would like that," he responded. Together we knelt, and I felt his arm around my shoulders and across the back of my neck. I prayed for Happy Chandler and his leadership responsibilities. I asked that he be given divine guidance in all decisions and that they would be for the good of all and not for the benefit of the few.

The governor then thanked God for my life and asked that a "healing balm" be put upon my heart. When he was through, he hugged my neck again and with tears in his gray eyes, said huskily, "Ed, God love you."

That morning in the governor's mansion I learned that there are "big" people in this country who still look up to God as their guide and leader. The "size" of this man is indicated by the fact that he had already been named our nation's Commissioner of Baseball and went on to be inducted into the Baseball Hall of Fame.

Thanks to this man, big in stature and heart, who took time from his busy schedule for a bereaved young student who could be of no practical use to him politically, the healing within me started.

31

A New Dawning

I spent the spring of 1957 buried in my studies to make up for the time lost during the winter months. But from time to time, sometimes even at midnight, I would leave my books, jump into the car and drive to that apartment on Limestone. I would park there for a few minutes, looking up at the dark windows and remember the laughter and love Billie and I shared there.

I found myself walking across certain sections of the campus she particularly loved, sensing her presence beside me. And often I would drive from Lexington to Paris in the late afternoon and almost hear her exclaiming at the brilliant blue grass and the snow-white fences rushing by.

That summer I returned to the Valley for the last time. I worked again at the Blue Bird bus factory and almost compulsively drove to the hospital at noontime when I used to meet Billie. Then I would drive fast down that six-mile stretch of undulating road toward the Ray farm. At certain moments it seemed I could see her Black Tank gaining on me and then flying past just before I would reach the dangerous curve she had always warned me about.

At sunset I walked by the quiet-flowing stream where I first told her I loved her, and she had responded in warmth. On our wedding anniversary I found myself making my way to our restaurant in Macon. I parked in the lot but couldn't go inside. I returned slowly on the back roads to the Ray farm, parked in the orchard and watched the stars. Billie was very near to me. I could almost sense her warm breath on my cheek, her slender hand on mine, the scent of her chestnut hair.

Why did she have to die? And why so soon? Why did we have such a short time together? Questions screamed from my heart. As I sat there looking up at the stars, God seemed to answer gently.

Billie could have died alone without the happiness of our blissful interlude together. *Would that have been better?* he seemed to ask.

And what has happened to you? I began to see beyond my aching heart. Not only had I experienced indescribable joy during our time together that would remain with me forever, but I had also learned something fine and wonderful from Billie's uncomplaining sacrifice. Her concern for others during her excruciating ordeal had taught me so much.

I had grown in ways that I never would have experienced otherwise. My loss had broken my heart open with a new sensitivity to the pain and suffering of others. Billie's life and her death had made me a new person, one far better suited for the work to which God had called me than the callow youth who first knew her an eternity ago.

One year later, on the anniversary of Billie's death, we again found ourselves in the NCAA finals. How we came this far was a puzzle to everyone, especially the sports writers. We were not loaded with individual talent, and the team had managed only a so-so record. That 1958 basketball season was one of the most unusual ever for the University of Kentucky. Pre-season rankings listed us as only fourth in our conference, the lowest opinion of a Wildcat team in many years, and we struggled throughout the season. We lost six games, and in several of those we did win, we barely squeaked through. To say that we were not an overpowering team is an understatement.

We seemed bent on fulfilling the sports expert's predictions that we wouldn't get close to winning even the conference title. Not since 1951, seven years before when it chalked up the school's third trophy, had UK been in a championship game. In 1948 the "Fabulous Five" had won the school's second title with probably the most talented team UK ever had. This season Adolph Rupp had said all along that we weren't concert violinists ready for Carnegie Hall, but we were good fiddlers. So now the sports writers were calling us the "Fiddling Five."

But there was one element they had not taken into consideration. Coach Rupp had talked about it a year earlier at the 1957 UK basketball banquet when he paid tribute to us as "the closest knit team of any I have ever coached."

"The help we got from a little girl down in Georgia did an awful lot to help this team click," he said, adding, "This team had great fight and great hearts, if not great ability."

Billie had drawn us all close together in our junior year. We 10 senior players had dedicated the 1958 season to her. I believe we all felt that in some way her spirit was with us. Though none of us were legitimate All-Americans, we did defeat Temple University to win the SEC, and then fought our way to the final NCAA tourney to face Seattle University and its formidable All-American center, Elgin Baylor.

Some 19,000 Kentucky fans jammed Louisville's Freedom Hall that wind-whipped March night to see their underdogs play the nation's number-one-rated team.

The atmosphere in that gigantic stadium was electric, and the pre-game excitement in the locker room was no less intense. Coach Rupp came in and gave us our last-minute instructions. He ended by saying, "We are going all the way tonight."

The we jogged out onto the court. The excitement that I felt was everything I had ever dreamed it would be.

Seattle gained an early 10-point lead and it seemed as if the sports experts were right. At the end of the first half Seattle was still well out in front of us.

In the locker room at half time The Baron laid it on the line. "We're gonna win!" he promised "You've been missing too many easy shots and free throws. From now on I want you men to direct everything at Elgin Baylor. Run right at him. Get him in foul trouble."

That's what we did in the second half. Maybe we were the

"Fiddling Five," but working in harmony we began catching up on the score.

The fans exploded into an uproar as we got nipped at Seattle's heels. We were playing for the title. We were playing for Billie. And we were going to make good on our promise to her.

However, with less than eight minutes of play remaining in the game, we were still behind by 11 points. Now there was a real danger of Seattle putting on a freeze to keep us from scoring. But the Wildcats managed to stay close enough to the Seattle Chieftains so they weren't able to get into position to stall.

By now the stadium was rocking to the din of screaming fans.

Working closely together our players fought furiously, edging the points closer and closer until the score was even. In the final stretch drive we sank five baskets with the closing whistle shrilly celebrating our victory.

The stadium exploded into a deafening roar.

Bill Surface, of the Lexington newspaper, wrote,

> Basketball's ugly ducklings, who weren't supposed to swim, really took to water in more ways than one last night. Celebrating vigorously in Dressing Room B after winning an unprecedented fourth NCAA championship, the valiant Wildcats of Kentucky immediately hustled Assistant Coach Harry Lancaster, Trainer Rusty Payne and Manager Jay Atkerson into the Freedom Hall showers—clothes and all.

By the time a police-escorted Coach Adolph Rupp arrived, the crowded steamy dressing room erupted into unbridled hysteria again.

It was the gratified Rupp who had told 18,803 fans earlier that the experts had regarded his team "as the ugly ducklings who weren't supposed to swim."

"I just sincerely don't know how we did it," he said. "We never had a boy on the All-SEC team—much less All-American. I never got a vote for 'Coach of the Year' so I know the boys were not over-coached."

The thousands of fans and students who stormed the dressing room door to praise the new national college basketball champions will swear that the unflinching Wildcats used sheer courage to overpower Seattle.

The crowd pressed hard against the dressing-room door but it was closed to the press and would-be congratulators. It was an intimate gathering of the team members, coaches, trainer, manager and the governor of Kentucky.

Adolph Rupp turned to his perspiring, tired basketball team and said, "Gentlemen, this is a high point in the history of the University of Kentucky and this Commonwealth. We will never be this close to each other again. How do you want to remember this moment?"

The room was silent for a moment. Then Adolph turned to me and said, "Ed, why don't you pray."

Everyone in the room bowed his head, some knelt by the benches, and I began, "Dear God, we thank you for the victory that you have allowed us to experience tonight as a team. We thank you far more for the victory which each one of us can know through your Son, our Lord, Jesus Christ. And thank you, dear God, for the memory of Billie, and what she has meant to us all. Amen."

An hour later I walked out alone onto the empty playing court where three hours earlier I had jumped against Elgin Baylor to ignite the title contest. The stadium had been filled with the screaming and shouting of thousands of fans.

Now the stands were empty, most of the lights had been turned off, and a deep quietness filled the stadium. I knew that I would never play another game for the university. As I reached the middle of the court, I knelt down on the maple boards and began to pray, "Thank you, God, for life and memories. Thank you for allowing me to give more than I actually had within me at times, and thank you for allowing me to be a part of a team that went all the way. Help me never to forget these truths that you have inscribed on my mind and sealed in my heart. And dear Lord, bless Billie and hug her for me. Amen."

That summer I played 83 basketball games in Japan, Korea, Formosa, Hong Kong, Viet Nam, Malaysia and the Philippines. Our special team, called "Venture for Victory," consisted of Christian athletes. During half times, instead of going to the dressing rooms, we stood in the middle of the court and shared our faith with the crowds. I spoke in colleges, universities and town squares for Jesus.

Our last game was at Razal Stadium in Manila where we played before 25,000 people in a three-overtime game. We finally won the contest against the finest national team of that country. We journeyed later that night to a large group meeting consisting of government officials, teams that we had previously played and Christian missionaries. I was asked to express our thanks to representatives of the Orient for all their hospitality. I did, and then closed by saying, "If you will bear with me for a few moments, I would like to say something that is rather personal. Most of you have heard me speak here and in other countries about my Billie who died nearly 18 months ago. I've shared with you some things about her faith, her courage and how she taught me how to live and how to die. There is one thing I have not shared, and that is what I want to do now before I leave tomorrow for my home in the United States."

For a moment I almost faltered as a lump rose in my throat. Then, as if God gave me the strength, I continued.

"Billie's one great wish was to be a medical missionary on some soil across the sea. Though she was a great missionary in her own country, she still felt somewhat a failure by not being able to work in other countries for her Lord, Jesus Christ. I just want to thank all for you for allowing me to be here in the Orient these last seven weeks. I feel Billie has been with me in this missionary work and that she finally has fulfilled one of her deepest desires."

Tears streamed down my cheeks, and I could go no further. I concluded by saying, "Thank you all." Then, still standing there, not able to say it out loud, I whispered within, "Billie, I love your memory and the meaning that you gave to my life. I hope you know just how much you will always mean to me."

A few hours later I boarded a jet for Tokyo. As it roared off the runway and climbed over the deep blue Pacific, I could see the rosy blush of first light on the eastern horizon. Daybreak would soon illuminate our world. I smiled, remembering the last morning of first light that I shared with Billie when she could still speak. She had murmured, "I love you, my Ed."

It seemed I felt a soft squeeze of my hand and I settled back in my seat in deep peace. Morning had broken and all was indeed well with the world.